Arts Centre LRC

D1355645

ITV: THE PEOPLE'S CHANNEL

ITV: THE PEOPLE'S CHANNEL

Simon Cherry

Reynolds & Hearn Ltd
London

Photo page 2: John Steed (Patrick Macnee) rescues Mrs Emma Peel (Diana Rigg) in a scene from *The Gravediggers*, a 1965 episode of ABC's *The Avengers*.

First published in 2005 by
Reynolds & Hearn Ltd
61a Priory Road
Kew Gardens
Richmond
Surrey TW9 3DH

Editor: Marcus Hearn
Picture Editor: David Pratt
Index: Jo Ware
Designer (main text): Chris Bentley
Designer (jacket and picture sections): James King
Managing Editor: Richard Reynolds

A CIP catalogue record for this book is available from the British Library.

ISBN 1 903111 98 6

Printed and bound in Great Britain by Biddles Ltd.

CONTENTS

ACKNOWLEDGMENTS

This book could not have been written without the work of all the people involved in the making of the television series *The Story of ITV: The People's Channel*. The series itself was conceived by Melvyn Bragg, who was responsible for my presence among the production team, and whose robust opinions and editorial decisions permeate this volume. The archive researchers Ann Hummel and Tim Morrison worked their way through miles of film and videotape to come up with the many clips which appeared in the series, and many more which only decorated the edit suite's virtual floor, but which greatly increased our knowledge and appreciation of ITV's programme history. The directors Bob Bee, Matt Cain, Aurora Gunn and Dan Wiles, and the video editors Mark Manning, Tim Pearce and Julian Caidan all shaped their raw material in ways which have influenced my thoughts and provided me with particular comments and scenes which have become part of this narrative. Assistant Producer Suzannah Wander and Researcher Antonia Bolingbroke-Kent resourcefully and reliably hunted down and sifted essential facts, ephemera and trivia, and Fiona Sanson and Kirsty Jamieson in the Information and Research office responded unflaggingly to our many requests. I am grateful to all of them. I would also like to thank my friends and colleagues Bryan Izzard, Jenny King, and Trevor Popple, for sharing their immense collective experience of the ways of the ITV companies, Rob Turnock and John Ellis for access to current academic research into the early days of the network, and finally Dick Fiddy of the BFI.

The author and publishers would like to thank the following for permission to reproduce illustrations: Advertising Archives for pages 11, 145, 146, 147, 148 and 149; British Film Institute for pages 81 and 84; Canal+ Image UK Limited for pages 2, 91 (top), 100, 101, 102, 103, 104 and 178 (bottom); Corbis for page 14 (top); Getty Images for pages 8, 10, 12, 13, 14 (bottom), 15, 17, 18, 21, 25, 27, 152, 153, 154, 160 and 174; ITN Stills for pages 248, 249, 250, 251, 252, 254, 255, 256, 257 and 258; Joel Finler for pages 163 and 164; Fremantle Media for pages 60, 87, 113, 114, 115, 119 (bottom), 173 and 271; Mark One Productions Limited for page 105; Rex Features for pages 31, 35, 36, 52, 53, 54, 55, 56, 57, 58, 59, 61, 62, 64, 66, 67, 68, 71, 75, 82, 83, 85, 86, 91, 92, 93, 94, 97, 110, 111, 116, 117, 120, 121, 122, 123, 126 (bottom) 133 (bottom), 140, 158, 159, 160, 168, 178 (bottom), 171, 172, 175, 193, 194, 195, 196, 199, 201, 205, 208, 209 (bottom), 210 (bottom), 216, 217, 219, 220, 221, 222, 223, 225, 226, 227 (top), 228, 230, 231, 232 (bottom), 233, 234, 236, 237, 238, 242 (bottom), 243, 244, 262, 265, 266, 269, 274, 283, 287 (top), 288, 289, 290 and 291; Shed Productions: 76, 77, 78 and 301 (top). All other images courtesy of ITV. Special thanks to Majella Lavelle and Kathryn de Belle (Granada), John Curtis (Rex Features), and Katrina Finch (ITN). ITV company idents on pages 19, 22, 27, 151, 155, 156, 157 created by David Jeffery with aditional research by Richard Elen/ Transdiffusion.org.

FOREWORD

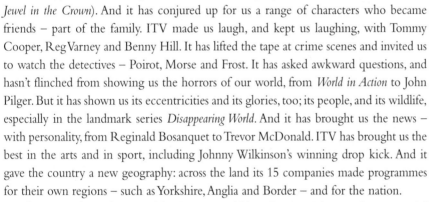

THE IDEA FOR a series of programmes about the story of ITV came to me in a rather unlikely place, in the House of Lords, when we were debating the future of broadcasting in this country. I thought then and I think now, that the contribution of ITV was unjustly underrated and not very well understood. In its own way, ITV is as unique and as British as the great BBC.

ITV has created the country's most popular drama series ever (*Coronation Street*), and the most lavish (*The Jewel in the Crown*). And it has conjured up for us a range of characters who became friends – part of the family. ITV made us laugh, and kept us laughing, with Tommy Cooper, Reg Varney and Benny Hill. It has lifted the tape at crime scenes and invited us to watch the detectives – Poirot, Morse and Frost. It has asked awkward questions, and hasn't flinched from showing us the horrors of our world, from *World in Action* to John Pilger. But it has shown us its eccentricities and its glories, too; its people, and its wildlife, especially in the landmark series *Disappearing World*. And it has brought us the news – with personality, from Reginald Bosanquet to Trevor McDonald. ITV has brought us the best in the arts and in sport, including Johnny Wilkinson's winning drop kick. And it gave the country a new geography: across the land its 15 companies made programmes for their own regions – such as Yorkshire, Anglia and Border – and for the nation.

There is nothing else quite like ITV in world broadcasting. It's a tough commercial channel that has also delivered 33% of its production as public service broadcasting; programmes often of the highest quality: in the regions, in current affairs, in the arts, right across the board.

From the beginning, its greatest ally was not the Opus Dei of the establishment, but the viewers. And from the beginning, ITV reached out to its viewers, brought them into its studios, sought them out in the streets, shared jokes with them and sometimes played jokes on them. And in Bruce Forsyth, Cilla Black and others ITV found presenters the viewers loved.

Millions over these 50 years have been entertained by it, enthralled by it, elated by it, confronted by it, affronted by it, and often glued to its window on worlds galore.

ITV was and is the people's channel – at its best, democratically elitist.

Melvyn Bragg
July 2005

1

'THE FREEDOM OF THE KNOB'

Television is at last given the real freedom of the air. The event is comparable with the abolition of the law that kept motor-cars chugging sedately behind a man carrying a red flag.

Now it's the 'go' signal, the green light for TV, too — with no brake on enterprise and imagination.

So far, television in this country has been a monopoly restricted by limited finance, and often, or so it has seemed, restricted by a lofty attitude towards the wishes of viewers by those in control.

That situation now undergoes a great and dramatic change. Viewers will no longer have to accept what has been deemed best for them. They will be able to pick and choose.

And the new Independent TV programme planners aim at giving viewers what viewers want — at the time viewers want it.

(from the first edition of *TV Times*, September 1955)

ITV SPRANG TO LIFE at 7.15 pm on Thursday 22 September 1955. It was not the most predictable opening for a channel that would depend on popular appeal for its commercial life. Not a game show, or a drama, or a song and dance spectacular, not one of the programmes with which ITV would later top the ratings, but a grand ceremony at the Guildhall in the City of London. Formal dress. A seven course banquet (nine had originally been planned, but the sorbet and the beef were dropped to spare the budget). And along with the clear turtle soup, the lobster chablis, and the roast grouse, the 1947 Krug, and the 1934 Fonseca, there were speeches by the Lord Mayor and the Postmaster General, a performance of Elgar's *Cockaigne Suite* by the Halle Orchestra, and the National Anthem.

Above: In America, where commercial television had been established in 1941, the NBC series *The Price Is Right* was one of the most popular game shows for nine years.

Opposite page: Former BBC Controller of Programmes Norman Collins became the leading spokesman for the introduction of a new television service.

Above: 22 September 1955 – ITV's first programme featured live coverage of a grand opening night ceremony at the Guildhall in the City of London.

The pictures were beamed on Channel 9, from the single operational transmitter at Croydon. They reached an area bounded by Luton in the north, Reading in the West, Horsham in the South and Maidstone in the East – where some 180,000 homes had sets which were capable of receiving the signal, and an estimated 100,000 chose to tune in.

Later in the evening this television audience would be treated to a variety bill featuring some of the future stars of the new channel, from Hughie Green to Harry Secombe. Robert Morley would introduce Sir John Gielgud and Dame Edith Evans in extracts from *The Importance of Being Earnest,* Terence Murphy and Lew Lazar would square up in the boxing ring at Shoreditch in a 12-round contest for the Southern Area Middleweight Championship, and Lady Pamela Berry would be on hand at the Mayfair Hotel to present the latest creations from London's leading fashion houses.

But from 7.15 to 8.00 p.m., the first 45 minutes of ITV's airtime, it was the great and good at the Guildhall who occupied the screen. The next morning, the *Daily Mirror* complained that it was bad showmanship to waste so much time instead of getting on with the job that ITV has been

Opposite page:
'It's Gibbs SR toothpaste, the tingling fresh toothpaste that does your gums good too.' The first advert on British commercial television was broadcast at 8.12pm on 22 September 1955.

brought in to do – entertain.' But those 45 minutes were more like a state occasion than bread and circuses. ITV desperately wanted to please the establishment, many of whose members had done their damnedest to try to make sure that the channel was never even born.

In the aftermath of the Second World War, British broadcasting meant the BBC – and the BBC meant radio. There was a television service, but it existed as a minor extension of sound broadcasting. It resumed operations in the London region on 1 June 1946. There was soon a plan in place to build new transmitters which would bring nine out of ten British homes within reach of the signal by 1954. The BBC had adopted the motto 'Nation shall speak peace unto nation', but the few television programmes from the early Fifties which survive show the middle-classes of the Home Counties speaking to themselves. It was all terribly nice and awfully polite, all deference and decorum, guided by the principle laid down by the Corporation's first Director General, Lord Reith. Reith believed not in giving the public what they wanted, but what the BBC – blessed with infinite wisdom and impeccable taste – decided would be good for them; a kind of cod liver oil of the airwaves. Within the BBC itself, television was regarded as a rather vulgar medium, which would never be anything but radio's junior. The BBC's programme schedules barely sneaked onto the back pages of the fittingly-named *Radio Times*.

This conservative attitude was too much for the BBC's Controller of Television, Norman Collins. Collins had been sent to America to see television in action – and had come back convinced that it represented the future. In 1949, he had made his prediction in the *BBC Quarterly* magazine: '...once TV is truly national it will become the most important medium that exists. Everything that it does or does not do will be important. The very fact that it is in the home is vital. Its only rival will be the wireless, and the rivalry will not be strong. The wireless set will remain silent, except for music where the contribution that vision has to make is, to say the least of it, still unexplored. Indeed, the first casualty of television, possibly the only casualty, is not the local cinema or the county theatre, it is sound radio.'

This prophecy was at odds with the BBC mainstream. When Collins found a radio man appointed above his head to the new post of Director of Television – an appointment which kept television firmly within the control of the Corporation's radio mandarins – he walked out. This was 1950, when resignation from the BBC was regarded as professional suicide. There was nowhere else to go. But Collins had other ideas. He

Sir William Beveridge (left), the author of the Beveridge Report and founder of the modern Welfare State, recommended a continuation of the BBC's broadcasting monopoly in 1951.

set up shop as High Definition Films, and became the leading spokesman for the introduction of a new television service. The BBC's then Chairman, Lord Simon, later declared that, 'If we hadn't fired Collins there would be no commercial television' – ignoring the fact that Collins was not pushed, but jumped ship.

After its sterling efforts in the war, the BBC might reasonably have assumed that its position as the nation's broadcaster was impregnable. In Britain and abroad, it had come to represent the voice of the free world in the fight against tyranny. But as the 1940s ended the values of the free world – freedom of speech, the free market, free choice – were turned against the BBC's monopoly of the airwaves. There was a rising tide of opinion that the BBC's exclusive rights should come to an end. Collins had plenty of allies in the parliamentary Conservative party – ranging from Winston Churchill to the back benches.

The Labour government had set up an enquiry into broadcasting, the Beveridge Committee, in 1949. Arguments which would rumble on over the next five years were rehearsed for the first time. Reith told the committee that it was only the 'brute force of monopoly that had enabled the BBC to become what it did and to do what it did' – open the gates of competition and the barbarians would flood through. The Bernstein brothers, Sidney and Cecil, proprietors of the Granada cinema chain, also argued against private ownership of the means of broadcasting, telling Beveridge that 'the right of access to the domestic sound and television receivers of millions of people carries with it such great propaganda power that it cannot be entrusted to any persons or bodies other than a public corporation or a number of public corporations.'

The Beveridge Report was published in 1951, and recommended the continuation of the BBC monopoly. But the case for a second channel had only just begun to be heard. Within months, the 1951 General Election had brought the Conservatives to power, and the proponents of a shake-up of broadcasting into prominence. They were a ragtag alliance: politicians who were opposed on principle to monopoly; dyed-in-the-wool Tories who thought the BBC was a hotbed of left-wing propaganda and wanted to see its power checked; manufacturers of television sets who wanted to expand the market; advertisers who wanted a new platform at a time when newsprint was still rationed.

But what were they arguing for? Should the new channel be a second broadcaster funded from the Licence fee – an Uncle to the BBC's Auntie? Should it be commercially backed, and – if so – should the advertisers put their money into commercials or into sponsored programmes? The latter option raised the spectre of advertisers determining editorial policy.

Interested parties joined the fray, often loudly and shrilly. Most of the newspapers were forcefully against commercial television, seeing in it a threat to their own cosy hold on advertising revenue. One correspondent to *The Times* pointed out that 'we do not allow salesmen to walk at will into our homes nor to paste display advertisements upon our walls.' Labour's Herbert Morrison told the Commons that 'This proposed development is totally against the British temperament, the British way of life and the best or even reasonably good British traditions.' A Labour party pamphlet attacked the 'Conservative TV (too vulgar) policy', and Labour leader Clement Attlee promised a miners' rally that when Labour was returned to power it would abolish any commercial television station that had been set up by the Tories.

Lord Reith thundered on. 'Somebody introduced Christianity into England, and somebody introduced smallpox, bubonic plague and the Black Death. Somebody is minded now to introduce sponsored broadcasting ... Need we be ashamed of moral values, or of intellectual and ethical objectives? It is these that are here and now at stake.'

What Reith and his fellow objectors feared was an invasion. An invasion in its way as dangerous, they believed, as the one the country had just withstood, but this time from the commercial culture of those wartime allies, the Americans. Before the days of cheap transatlantic travel, few had shared Collins' first-hand experience of American commercial television. But many had heard second or third-hand travellers' tales, and were convinced that it was a land of media monsters.

The opponents of commercial television drew ammunition from the way the 1953 coronation was screened in America. One of the advertising breaks featured NBC's celebrity chimpanzee, J Fred Muggs.

Lord Reith, the first director-general of the BBC, objected to the introduction of commercial television on moral grounds.

Above: NBC's celebrity chimp J Fred Muggs was refused entry to Britain after he appeared in an advertising break during American television coverage of the coronation of Queen Elizabeth II.

This juxtaposition of monarch and monkey was viewed as an unprecedented and terrible affront to royal dignity. Exactly what we could expect, they argued, if such values were imported to Britain.

It took the British Establishment a year to exact their revenge, by refusing to allow Muggs to enter the country when NBC hurriedly dispatched him on a world tour after he bit a fellow presenter. But it took the opponents only days to begin to make public appearances with an ape to reinforce their dire warnings.

Less than three weeks after Muggs ran roughshod over royal protocol, Lady Violet Bonham Carter hosted the inaugural meeting of the National Television Council. The resistance to commercial television was getting organised. Its ranks included EM Forster and Bertrand Russell, and several MPs, including Labour's Christopher Mayhew. His pamphlet *Dear Viewer* sold over 60,000 copies, and was the spearhead of a public relations campaign. 'I ask you', Mayhew concluded, 'to exercise all the influence you have, as a free citizen of the most democratic country in the world, to prevent this barbarous idea being realised.'

But anything the opponents could do, the supporters could match. A month later Rex Harrison, Somerset Maugham and AJP Taylor were among the founders of the Popular Television Association, its aim to being to 'awaken the national conscience to the dangers, social, political and artistic, of monopoly in the rapidly developing field of television.' Another prime mover, the cricketer Alec Bedser, fronted a 12-minute film which was sent around the country to drum up popular enthusiasm

Below: Bertrand Russell (left) and EM Forster (middle) opposed commercial television while Somerset Maugham (right) was a keen advocate.

for a new channel, as the debate took to the road.

The argument reached Westminster in November 1953. With the grandees of government in favour of breaking the BBC's monopoly, a White Paper had been drafted, and was up for scrutiny. The Mother of all Parliaments hosted the mother of all arguments. It seemed that the very soul of the nation was at stake. It was the biggest turn-out since the war. Peers previously unknown at Westminster rode in from the shires. Herbert Morrison told the Commons that on this debate depended 'the future thinking of our people and our standards of culture.'

Herbert Morrison, former Labour foreign secretary, foresaw commercial television as a significant influence on standards of British culture. He later became president of the British Board of Film Censors.

With not a programme proposal or draft broadcasting schedule in sight, the participants were free to conjure up miracles or monsters from their own imaginations. Some were vivid. Lord Hailsham waxed biblical in favour of the BBC's monopoly.

In my sleepless hours the other night… I thought I found myself in the camp of Israel, when their Assembly was debating the suitability of erecting a golden calf in addition to the established church of the time. The Government of the day was in favour of the proposal on the ground that the calf was only a little one. They said: 'Of course, we all admire Jehovah and think Jehovah did a very good job of work in getting us out of the land of Egypt; but a little golden calf will provide just that element of healthy competition.'

Beverley Baxter MP came up with a more prosaic defence. The great threat of television was that it would be addictive. So for the good of the nation, television should be dull. And the best safeguard of dullness was to ensure that the BBC remained in sole charge.

One member argued that if British broadcasting were associated with advertising, national prestige would suffer, and foreigners would lose respect for us. Another railed that by allowing advertising 'propaganda' for beer, pills, pools and patent medicines, we were preparing 'a paradise for the cheapjack'.

Lord Esher described it as a 'planned and premeditated orgy of vulgarity', and the Earl of Listowel warned that it would soon reduce the standards to 'the lowest common denominator of taste', dishing up 'crude and trivial entertainment'.

Earl de la Warr countered that 'there are many theatres left in London and in the provinces. They are not all specializing in strip-tease – although to hear some noble lords speak one would think they were... Are we seriously going to say from now onwards that our entertainment has to be limited to what is approved by elderly and superior persons?' The British were allowed to vote for themselves, surely they could be trusted to choose between one television programme and another.

In the same vein, Viscount Hudson called for the 'freedom of the knob' – a motto which inexplicably failed to catch on. Viscount Samuel sounded the trumpets. 'This movement comes forward under the banner of a great crusade for liberty, with the battle cry, "Set the people free"'. The rhetoric banged back and forth, from chamber to chamber. The two parties seemed irreconcilably at odds.

But the debate did make progress. It became apparent that the proponents had two sticking points: the BBC's monopoly was to end, and the new broadcaster would be funded by advertising – short commercials in 'natural breaks' in the programmes, not the sponsored programming which raised the possibility of editorial interference. They were prepared to be practical about everything else; indeed, on both sides of the debate there was a clear acknowledgement that the potential influence of a new broadcaster was so great that safeguards must be put in place. It would operate under a new regulatory body. Its programmes would have to meet strict standards of impartiality, must not offend against good taste or decency, or incite crime or disorder. They must be predominantly British in tone and style. There must be a variety of programmes to balance the more commercial entertainments – news, religion, local programmes, for which (if other forms of revenue were not sufficient) there would be a contingency production fund of up to three quarters of a million pounds. The restrictions were then and are still more exacting than those which govern the BBC, and would lead to many future battles.

The following March, as the White Paper became a Bill, Collins won an important PR victory. Nobody had seriously considered what this new regulator should be called. Collins suggested the BBC's 'Corporation' could be matched for clout by an 'Authority', and that it should be named the Independent Television Authority. It sounded suitably grand and official. Its detractors hated it: in parliament, opponents mounted a failed attempt to force an Amendment to the Bill to call it not 'Independent' but the far less impressive 'Commercial'. For

Family viewing in the early 1950s. At this time there was only one channel to watch and a television set would typically cost around £50.

years, many in the BBC continued to refer to 'commercial television' to sneer at it. And so did the Beaverbrook newspapers (under orders from their proprietor), until he belatedly invested in it and became a supporter.

It took four months for the Bill to pass through Parliament (with breaks for debates on less important matters such as the budget, the NHS, and atomic power). More words were spoken on the subject than are contained in the Old Testament. It was passed in the Commons by the narrow majority of 291 to 265. On 30 July 1954, the first Television Act became law.

The Act contained a clause stipulating that no programme featuring members of the Royal Family should be interrupted by adverts. (Not even, in the fullness of time, the much-loved PG Tips chimps). One American commentator scanned the regulations and told his commercial television watching compatriots that 'The British have decided to paint the gaudy thing a sombre grey to blend with the general fog.'

But British viewers were to disagree in their millions.

2

GOOD TASTE AND BIG BUSINESS

IT WAS A small advertisement, on the front page of *The Times* on Wednesday 25 August 1954, in the days when the front page of *The Times* was all advertisements. Twelve lines over a single column: total cost four pounds and ten shillings. Below the Henley Polo Club's announcement that Capt. Balding and Col. Guiness would be appearing in the weekend's Remenham Cup Tournament, below Miss Gem Mouflet's '2 Friends 1 fee' offer on dancing classes in Knightsbridge, was an invitation that would change British broadcasting and British life.

> *The Independent Television Authority invites applications from those interested in becoming PROGRAMME CONTRACTORS in accordance with the provisions of the Television Act. Applicants should give a broad picture of the types of programme they would provide, their proposals for network or local broadcasting of their programmes, some indication of their financial resources, and the length of contract they would desire. All applications will be treated in the strictest confidence.*

The news reached the office of the largest theatrical agency in Europe, run by the Grade brothers Lew and Leslie. According to Leslie's son Michael Grade (himself a major ITV player of the future) 'Lew walked into my father's adjoining office in Regent Street, and said, "Leslie, have you seen *The Times* this morning?" My father went, "*Times*, I haven't got time to read *The Times*, what's *The Times*?" "No, no, no have a look at this," and he pushed in front of my father that small advert. He said "Leslie, we're going into the television business."'

But they weren't – not immediately, anyway. The ITA would turn their application down.

Opposite page:
Talent agency manager
Lew Grade established ITC
(Incorporated Television
Production Company) in
1954 in order to bid for one
of the ITV franchises.

Faced with the prospect of an unknown new television channel, Parliament resorted to a very British solution: it set up a committee. The Independent Television Authority had the job of interpreting legislation which, also in typically British style, founded its instructions to the future broadcasters on terms such as 'taste', 'decency' and 'due impartiality', and bequeathed the necessary job of defining them to others. As far as the broadcasters were concerned, the ITA was God – and like God it would fully exercise its right to move in mysterious ways, accountable to no-one. But in its first year, it also had to move very quickly indeed.

The ITA met for the first time on 4 August 1954, and immediately set about deciding the shape of the network. Its nine great and good members had impressive and no doubt very useful connections with big business, manufacturing, banking, the Armed Forces, newspapers, educational establishments and the National Association of Boys' Clubs. A senior Post Office civil servant was Secretary. The nearest it came to someone with actual experience of broadcasting or programme making was the film critic Dilys Powell. Its Director General was Australian Robert Fraser, a former failed Labour parliamentary candidate, whose appointment was instant ammunition for the already hostile Tory press.

The Chairman was Sir Kenneth (the future Lord) Clark, Chair of the Arts Council and former Director of the National Gallery. To many commentators, the appointment of this patrician figure seemed bizarrely inappropriate. Was he going to attempt to placate the cultural doom-mongers by trying to steer ITV towards his own highbrow tastes? In fact, Clark did an excellent job of striking a balance. He later wrote that 'I saw a number of ways in which the Authority could intervene and prevent the vulgarity of commercialism from having things all its own way.' But that was a long way from trying to extirpate vulgarity altogether, and Clark recognised that some 'vital vulgarity' was 'not without value'.

Clark's attitude is most vividly seen in a programme he made in 1958 for ATV, in which he asked, 'What is good taste?' while wandering through studio room sets decorated in a variety of styles. First, there is simple modernist design, restraint reified in pale colours and thin-legged furniture. This, says Clark, is many people's idea of good taste, but he abhors its absence of vitality. As he poses the question 'What is bad taste?' he leads the viewer into a working-class front parlour which might have been used as a template for the Ogdens' home in *Coronation Street*, complete with flying ducks. Here, Clark tells us, is a clash of ornament and patterns, most of them in what are known as 'cheerful' colours (he chews the adjective as if it were a piece of gristle). Bad taste?

Opposite page: ITA chairman Sir Kenneth Clark asked 'What is good taste?' in a programme for ATV in 1958.

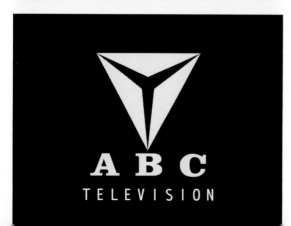

'I must honestly say,' Sir Kenneth continues, 'that in some ways I find it rather cosier than the other room. I can relax in it. I could open a bottle of stout in it without trepidation. And as a matter of fact, more people I like live in a room like this than in the other room.'

Clark leaves the viewer in no doubt that he detests many of the objects in the room and the lack of discernment with which they were assembled. But he recognises that this uncoordinated cosiness made millions feel comfortable. And to ITV's great benefit, he would reflect that insight in his attitude to programming, never trying to force the 'ghastly good taste' of restraint on the new channel.

Where the new channel's programmes would come from was a question that required the ITA's urgent attention. The first wave of ITV was intended to use the BBC's transmission equipment to cover the three broadcasting areas of London, the Midlands, and across the Pennines (though it soon became apparent that this was technically impossible and that the ITA would have to build its own transmitters). The system must include competition between programme providers. They discussed a plan to have one company provide morning programmes, another women's, another children's, a fourth news and topical programmes in the early evening, and a fifth the later evening entertainment. Another scheme was to give different days of the week to different companies. Either of these proposals might have produced a dramatically different set of programming ideas from the plan that was eventually adopted. The country would be divided geographically. The first of the familiar and long-standing ITV regions were born.

But the division was complicated. Equal

competition was the brief. Each contractor was supposed to have – as nearly as possible – a market of equal value in which to operate. The geographical areas would have to be divided up piecemeal to make this happen. Complicated budgetary sums were worked out, and the advert in *The Times* was booked.

There were 25 replies, many of them containing very limited proposals. One promised three hours a week of high culture; another to provide off-peak programmes about local news and local shops to viewers in Birmingham. Five serious contenders emerged.

The Bernstein brothers had decided, in spite of their evidence to Beveridge, that if commercial television was coming they wanted a slice, and their Granada company was awarded the northern station from Monday to Friday. London Monday to Friday went to Associated-Rediffusion, a group with experience in commercial radio and electronics, and with backing from Associated Newspapers. London on Saturday and Sunday, and the Midlands from Monday to Friday, was given to the Associated Broadcasting Development Corporation (or ABDC for short). This company was led by Norman Collins and others who – unlike the other contract winners – had been consistently in favour of commercial television.

Weekends in the Midlands and in the North would be in the hands of the Kemsley-Winnick group, which combined finance from Lord Kemsley's newspaper empire, and the experience of impresario Maurice Winnick, who had already brought the hit panel game *What's My Line?* from America to the BBC.

The Grade brothers' application was the fifth and last to be given serious consideration. The Incorporated Television Co. Ltd had assembled a list of names that was virtually a *Who's Who* of British showbiz, including impresarios Prince Littler and Val Parnell, and associations with the Moss Empires and Howard and Wyndham theatre chains. With financial backing from Warburg's merchant bank, it was an impressive application. Too impressive for the ITA, who feared that with their contacts and clout they would immediately dominate what was meant to be a delicate commercial balancing act between the first four contractors. To the group's amazement, they were turned down, though the ITA made it clear that they hoped they would still make programmes for the other four to broadcast.

The four contractors were in place. But by the time ITV hit the air, the line-up would change dramatically. It was a bold step to consider taking a stake in the new ITV. Set-up expenditure would be high. Studios

Opposite: The on-screen idents of the four initial contractors for the ITV regions — (top to bottom) Associated-Rediffusion, Granada, ATV and ABC.

had to be built. Rental had to be paid to the ITA to use its transmission equipment. The financial predictions were for heavy losses in the first two years. And no-one knew how British viewers would respond to television advertising – if they shunned it, income would simply dry up. Under the provisions of the Television Act, the first contracts would only run for ten years – would that be long enough to recover costs? And what if Labour were re-elected and stuck to its promise to abolish ITV?

Moreover, the system was designed to make it even more difficult for the companies, by requiring competition between them. The ITA's vision was for a cut-throat market in which each contractor put together its own broadcast schedule by buying and selling the best programmes from and to the others. The market would drive up quality, and less good programmes would potentially become unsaleable and costly mistakes. Robert Fraser spelt out the situation in a memorandum to Kenneth Clark in September 1954:

> *I want a network connection technically capable of giving an unlimited introduction of programmes from any one region into either of the others. I want London to be in full competition with the Midlands in selling programmes to Northern, Midlands and Northern in selling to London, Northern with London selling to the Midlands. Each will be eager to sell, each eager to buy. This will be competition with a vengeance, and with all its fruits. The network must be optional or it is not competition but cartel or market-sharing.*

'Competition with a vengeance.' And it was supposed to get even more uncomfortable. The expectation in Parliament, at the ITA, and among everyone who had been involved in the conception of ITV, was that within a few years there would be at least two ITV stations broadcasting in each region, battling it out head to head. It was just a matter of time before more transmission frequencies could be used.

In these circumstances, Collins' ABDC were finding it difficult to raise enough backing for their successful application. They wanted to bring in the *Daily Express* and the *News of the World*. But the ITA were already under attack from the Labour Party for allowing the pro-Conservative Kemsley and Associated Newspapers to take a stake in two of the contracts. A third apparently Tory-leaning company could, they feared, cause an outcry that would derail the whole plan. Unfortunately for all of them, none of the left-wing press that ABDC approached wanted to go in with them. The solution was a merger with Grade's ITC, bringing

their financial backing on board. The price for Collins was that he never had the chance to run a company in the ITV system he had done so much to create. Collins became Deputy Chairman of the new company, ATV. But the day-to-day control would be in the hands of the Managing Director Val Parnell, and his successor Lew Grade.

Financial problems were also dogging the fourth contractor. Kemsley and another major backer got cold feet. The ITA decided their company had collapsed, and the deal was off. They resurrected a previously rejected application from the Associated British Picture Corporation, and with assurances that the plan carried the will and the bank-balance to make a success of it, the new ABC company became the replacement fourth contractor. The deal was signed just one day before ITV's first transmission. Kemsley had unwittingly turned his back on a future gold-mine. In the Sixties, he would see his newspaper empire bought up by Roy Thomson, using profits made from a braver decision to invest in Scottish Television. Winnick left the country to avoid the pain of seeing ITV open without his involvement.

Representatives of the ITV programme contractors signing an agreement with the Variety Artistes' Federation in December 1955 setting out terms and conditions for television appearances. (Left to right) Captain T.M. Browning (General Manager of Associated-Rediffusion), Harry Alan Towers, Val Parnell and Lew Grade (ATV). In front, signing for the Federation, is their chairman George Wood (Wee Georgie Wood).

Bruce Forsyth hosts
'Beat The Clock' on ATV's
*Sunday Night at the London
Palladium* in 1959.

3

'I'M IN CHARGE'

ASSOCIATED TELEVISION LTD.

'All my shows are great. Some of them are bad. But they're all great.'

Lew Grade

THE GRADES WERE steeped in showbusiness. Their grandfather had run one of the first silent movie houses in the Ukraine. Their father had been an actor, their mother a semi-professional singer. In 1911, the Winogradski parents decided they had had enough of living with the atmosphere of anti-Semitism that pervaded their homeland, and brought their young sons Louis and Boris to London's East End. Louis Winogradski became Lew Grade, and as a young man took to the boards as a highly successful professional Charleston dancer. Boris − by then Bernie − followed, changing his name to Delfont to avoid confusion on the circuit. When they hung up their shoes (though throughout his life Lew never seemed to need much persuading to twinkle his toes) Lew joined the third brother Leslie in building up their theatrical agency,

Above (top to bottom):
The ATV on-screen logo;
the Tiller Girls perform on
ATV's *Sunday Night at the
London Palladium* in 1962;
Lew Grade (1906-1998).

27

Above: Life at Oxbridge General Hospital in *Emergency – Ward 10*: (left to right) Harriet Harper, Majni Biro and Sheila Fearn in 1962.

Below: Television's first interracial kiss – John White (as Mr Giles Farmer) and Joan Hooley (as Dr Louise Mahler) in a 1964 instalment of *Emergency – Ward 10*.

while Bernard became a major impresario.

While Leslie ran the London office, Lew scoured the globe looking for talent. In America, he saw commercial television in action, and recognized the future. With the formation of ATV, they became part of it. But though they knew their own business inside out, the television industry took them into the unknown, as Michael Grade remembered:

The ATV consortium was put together and they were advised by the great merchant bank, Warburg's. There was a lot of documentation and negotiating between the shareholders and the banks, who were providing the money and so on – quite a complex deal. And it was all finally agreed and there was a big meeting in the boardroom of Warburg's, which was hallowed walls as far as Lew and Leslie were concerned. I'm not sure they even dared to go near their banks in those days because of the overdraft. And there was a big meeting at Warburg's with all the banks, the financiers, the lawyers and the shareholders and they sat around a huge table groaning with documents to be signed and Lew and Leslie sat there and these documents were passed around, sign here, sign, everybody signing and heads down and the documents were going round, and it took an hour to get all the papers all the way round the table with all the signatures on. And then Henry Grunfeld, who was Sigmund Warburg's partner, who was leading it, said, 'Well gentlemen, we have completed the business,' and the flunky came in with a silver tray and some champagne and everybody had a glass, you know, they were all cheers, here's to the venture, good luck everyone, cheers, cheers. Lew and my father, who didn't drink, put the glass down and they went back to Regent Street to book a few more acts around the music halls. Henry Grunfeld told me the story that at about three o'clock he got a telephone call from Lew saying, 'Could my brother and I come and see you?' Henry said, 'Well, of course, Mr Grade, I'd be delighted to see you and your brother', so they got a taxi and they rushed across to the city and they came in, they shut the door and there was just the three of them – Henry Grunfeld, partner in Warburg's, Lew and Leslie Grade, variety agents. And he says, 'What can I do for you, you look very distressed?' and Henry told me that Lew said, 'My brother and I want to ask you a question.' He said, 'Of course, what is the question?' He said, 'What did we sign this morning?' So, they had no idea what they were doing, but they were visionaries, they could see the potential and Lew was the driving force.

Noele Gordon (centre), as motel owner Meg Richardson, celebrates with Roger Tonge (centre left, as Meg's son Sandy) and other members of the late Sixties cast of *Crossroads*.

Lew's vision made him one of the great architects of ITV, one of the creators of its distinct personality. He always said that he had the taste of the ordinary person, but no ordinary person had his ability to turn taste into programmes. Through ATV and the production company ITC he made popular drama, set in Sherwood Forest with *The Adventures of Robin Hood*, in Oxbridge hospital with *Emergency – Ward 10*, in the boardrooms of *The Power Game*, and in television's most notoriously rickety motel – *Crossroads*. He topped the ratings with sometimes curious game shows –

from the join-the-dots quiz *Dotto* (the most popular show of 1958) to Bernie and his bolt in *The Golden Shot*. He bankrolled Gerry Anderson's puppet adventures, and with an eye to the export market dug into his pockets in 1964 to make *Stingray* the first British TV series to be filmed entirely in colour. He even funded the Muppets.

When once asked, 'What's two and two?' he replied, 'Buying or selling?' He was wheeler-dealer of the old school, who backed his own judgement with hard cash.

According to Nicholas Parsons:

Above: Super-submarine *Stingray*, the eponymous star of Britain's first television series to be filmed entirely in colour.

Lew was first and foremost a showman. And if a show worked, he had a great instinct for that. I remember my agent telling me once, you don't go to Lew with a long written synopsis and detailed market research and so forth. You go in with an idea sketched out on the back of an envelope. Lew would look at it and say, 'That sounds good, I think we'll go for it,' and you're in.

Above all, Lew knew variety. And he and ATV changed the way television entertained us all with song and dance spectaculars. The BBC's idea of television variety was *Café Continental*, an imitation Parisian night-club where a doorman whisked the viewer inside before, in Michael Grade's words:

…the turns would come on, you know, the odd ventriloquist and juggler and occasionally a singer was allowed on and that was the BBC's idea of mass entertainment, which was absolutely hopeless.

Opposite page:
Eric Morecambe and Ernie Wise meet and perform with The Beatles on a December 1963 edition of ATV's *The Morecambe and Wise Show*.

The BBC was stymied by its restrictions and practices. Why would top-of-the-bill performers come to the studio for a live show, when they could be earning several times the BBC's highest fee with a theatrical engagement? And the Corporation felt that it was far too taxing to mount variety shows once a week – with new scripts to be written and learned, new sets to be built, new musical numbers rehearsed, once a fortnight was as much as they felt they could manage. BBC viewers couldn't get into the habit of tuning in 'same time, next week'.

The Tiller Girls perform on the 250th edition of ATV's *Sunday Night at the London Palladium* in 1962.

When ATV came along, its connections with Grade's roster of talent and the clout of the Stoll Moss empire meant they could offer the top stars a package of theatrical dates and a TV booking at the biggest stage in London – the Palladium. And there was no question of their television show taking two weeks to mount. From its debut in 1955 *Sunday Night at the London Palladium* became a weekly fixture for millions of viewers. They had never seen anything like it – stars they queued to see at the cinema were in their front room. Producer Val Parnell could offer Johnny Ray, Bob Hope, Gracie Fields and the rest – the cream of international variety.

Michael Grade recalls the era clearly:

I remember going to the dress rehearsal the Sunday before the first live transmission of Sunday Night at the London Palladium with Tommy Trinder and they ran the show for an audience just to rehearse it. And I remember even at that age, I was 12 years old, saying to my dad, 'Is this really going to be on television, this is unbelievable' – it was just so different to anything we'd ever seen.

While the BBC was losing the battle for talent onscreen, its complacency was also costing it on the other side of the cameras. Brian Tesler was one of the BBC's brightest young entertainment producers at the time.

I think as an example of the way that the BBC as a whole was complacent, my contract came up for renewal a year after ITV began and so when I went to see the personnel manager for my interview he said, 'Well, Tesler, you've done quite well. We'd like to offer you another two-year contract. How do you feel about that?' And I said, 'Thank you very much, I'd like it.' And he said, 'Is there anything else you want to say?' and I said, 'Well I'm earning £1,700 a year at the moment. Could I have another £100, could I go up to £1,800 a year for the next two years?' And he said, 'Oh no, working for the BBC is reward in itself.' And that was absolutely characteristic of the BBC in those days from top to bottom. I went back to the studio where I'd been rehearsing with Eamonn Andrews on a show, and his manager said, 'You're looking very glum, what's up?' And I told him, and he said, 'Would you be prepared to work for ITV?' And I said in the heat of that moment, 'Dammit, yes I would.' So he said, 'Well give me five minutes, I just want to make a phone call.' And he came back five minutes later and said, 'I've been talking to Lew Grade and he's offering you a three-year contract at £3,500 a year with two weeks every summer to study American television in New York. Are you interested?' I bit off his hand.

In 1958, Tesler was at ATV directing a showcase for rising talent called *New Look*. The series included Roy Castle, Lionel and Joyce Blair, and Des O'Connor. And there was a young entertainer who had been spotted in seaside summer season by Bernard Delfont's right-hand man Billy Marsh. He was Bruce Forsyth, and the wide-reaching Grade family empire was about to create ITV's first great home-grown star.

First there was a guest spot on *Sunday Night at the London Palladium*, where his ad-lib treatment of host Tommy Trinder was noted. Shortly afterwards in September 1958, Forsyth was offered the job of taking over as the new host. Within weeks of his first TV appearance, he was singing, 'Welcome to *Sunday Night at the London Palladium*.'

I was working in a concert party in Eastbourne at a dreadful old theatre. I think they've renovated it now – [it was] called the Hippodrome, it was an awful place. And the business was really bad, because I wasn't a name of any sort. Just appearing in the show. We had a cast of 13: that included the two pianos and the drummer. And to go from there, after working there all the week, sometimes there might be 50, 60 people in the audience – Saturday night you'd get maybe 100 people – to go from that to the Palladium with 2,500 people, a 30-piece orchestra and this huge stage, you can imagine my feelings, walking into the theatre that day. So it's something I'll never forget. The opening bill, I can remember three of the acts. There was Jewel and Warriss, who were the biggest double act of the time, just as big as Morecambe and Wise came to be. Anne Shelton, who was a wonderful,

Members of the audience play against the clock in the 'Beat the Clock' segment of a 1959 edition *Sunday Night at the London Palladium*, hosted by Bruce Forsyth (standing, right).

wonderful singer. The interesting one was Peter Sellers. Peter Sellers used to do a variety act in the old days. This was before his film career. They all wished me good luck and it was a wonderful night, a night I will never ever forget.

Where Trinder had been a joke-teller, Forsyth was a song and dance man. But he adapted quickly to playing to the cameras, throwing asides in words and looks. And he had a knack for what the profession calls 'business'.

I did outrageous things. I remember that I had the audacity to get two stage hands off stage with a clothes line just hanging across the middle of the stage, with a tin bath underneath and a drip dry shirt on a hanger – because they'd just come out and I used them all the time when I was touring. And I said, 'I want to show you ladies, you don't need to iron these shirts,' and I put it on the hanger all dripping wet and put out the collar, did the sides and the cuffs with my thumbs, and it dried as though you'd actually ironed it. It was something different. I was a different type of personality.

Where he really shone was in dealing with the members of the audience who became contestants in the central section of the programme. *Beat the Clock* set them challenges involving odd tests of dexterity, balloons to be kept in the air, footballs on lengths of elastic, and ping-pong balls to be bounced into wastepaper bins. Bruce would cheat, blatantly, to help contestants to a prize, all the while commenting wryly on their performances, a mixture of mock-sharpness and friendliness that was an instant winner.

One week the challenge was to throw plates onto a board without upsetting its balance. The couple involved were doing so badly that Bruce ordered the clock to be stopped while he explained the idea to them. As he turned round he saw they had started again. 'Wait a minute', he said. 'I'm in charge.'

By the next day, this was his new catch phrase, shouted after him in the street by some of the show's vast audience. The programme was a phenomenon. Twenty-eight million viewers. An audience share of 84 per cent. Pubs emptied as people went home to watch. A vicar in Woking moved his Sunday evening service half an hour earlier to allow his congregation home in time to catch it.

Not everyone understood what this sort of unprecedented exposure meant. One audience member who blithely stepped onstage to take part

Opposite:
Bob Monkhouse and 'Golden Girl' Anne Aston, co-presenters of *The Golden Shot* in which contestants fired crossbows at moving targets to win cash prizes. One of ATV's most successful game shows, *The Golden Shot* ran for eight years from 1967, initially hosted by Jackie Rae, later by Norman Vaughn and then Charlie Williams.

ATV's *The Muppet Show* made an international star of the porcine diva Miss Piggy, (voiced and operated by Frank Oz) and the show's amphibian MC Kermit the Frog (voiced and operated by Jim Henson). From 1976 to 1981, the series clocked up 120 instalments with guest appearances by Roger Moore, Peter Sellers, Elton John, Rudolf Nureyev, Raquel Welch, Diana Ross, Sylvester Stallone and Peter Ustinov among many others.

in *Beat the Clock* had been on the run for three years. It clearly never occurred to him that he would be arrested when a police superintendent spotted him onscreen and picked up the phone to Scotland Yard.

But Forsyth understood the fame that the show brought him. In 1959, a year after his big break, he was named the first Variety Club Personality of the Year for ITA. The winner for the BBC was the considerable figure of Richard Dimbleby, who used the occasion as a platform to lecture the audience about the threat that a commercial television station, chasing viewers and income, might feel compelled to be the master of the public instead of its servant. When Bruce stepped up he looked at the pair of film cameras recording the event. 'Which one's ours?' he asked, with a thumbs-up to the ITV viewers. 'Hello! Nice to see you!'

The contrast between the two is a small example of how the Grades' showbiz mentality had refreshed British television. But they weren't the only founders to have a profound influence on ITV's personality.

4

GRANADALAND

from the North

GRANADA

The rooftops of Weatherfield
– the iconic image of
Coronation Street.

'What's good enough for London will be good enough for the north.
But they'll want something in addition. And I think we'll provide it.'
Sidney Bernstein, Granada's opening night broadcast

S IDNEY AND CECIL Bernstein came, like the Grade brothers, from immigrant stock. The family had emigrated from Latvia in the nineteenth century. The brothers had built up a chain of opulent cinemas in the south of England, two of which can still be found in Tooting and Woolwich. The latter opened in 1937 with a promise of 'Two acres of splendour – the most romantic cinema ever built.' The Bernsteins turned

the simple act of going to the pictures into a luxurious night out. This was the Granada chain, which took its name from the Spanish city that had impressed Sidney during a walking holiday.

In spite of their statement to the Beveridge committee, opposing private ownership of television, when it became clear that independent television would become a reality, the Bernsteins decided to pitch for a slice. All their cinemas were in the south, but they turned their attention to the northern region, covering Lancashire and Yorkshire.

They would give the region a new name – Granadaland.

Rainfall has often been cited as the reason behind their choice. The Bernsteins are supposed to have reckoned that, because it was wetter in the north, people would stay in more, and watch more television. Denis Forman, who was Sidney Bernstein's right-hand man for years and filled several senior roles at Granada, can set the record straight. The story was pure PR spin. In reality, says Forman, the Bernsteins thought that Norman Collins was certain to get the five-day London contract. And they didn't want the weekends, because they thought religious programmes would be 'a lot of bother'.

Above: Sidney Bernstein (second from left) discusses progress on the site of the new Granada studio centre in 1955.

Opposite: Pat Phoenix as Elsie Tanner on the set of *Coronation Street* in 1961.

Below: Cecil Bernstein pictured at a function in 1975.

So it was a choice between the Midlands five days, and the north five days. And if you looked at the north you saw two great counties, Lancashire and Yorkshire, probably providing 80, 85 per cent of the audience. If you looked at the Midlands, it was a much more mixed community, much more difficult to operate from the point of view of identity. We thought the north had an identity, as it always has, Yorkshiremen, Lancashiremen, the northern person, whereas the Midlands didn't, it was pretty faceless. So we went for the north.

Like the Grades, the Bernsteins were an effective business double-act. Cecil was a shrewd buyer and negotiator. Sidney was the driving creative force, a mixture of high mindedness and chutzpah, and he fashioned Granada in his image.

Sidney was a socialist and art lover, who numbered George Bernard Shaw and the Russian film director Sergei Eisenstein among his friends. He hired the Russian theatre director Theodore Komisarjevsky to design

extravagant Gothic cinema interiors. He had been a production partner of Alfred Hitchcock, but the excesses of Hollywood life and business weren't to his taste. And Sidney was also a showman, who put portraits of the American circus owner P T Barnum – he of the 'greatest show on earth' – in every office, to remind his television staff of the nature of the business they were in. (Mr Pook, the Granada office manager, doggedly replaced them when, as frequently happened, the staff defaced them or consigned them to wastepaper bins.) And when Granada built their state-of-the-art complex in Manchester, the studios were given only even numbers, to make it appear to impressed visitors that there were twice as many of them.

The company's birth was far from plain sailing. It was soon clear that they would need two transmitters, one to serve each side of the Pennines.

Ena Sharples (Violet Carson, left) and Elsie Tanner (Pat Pheonix) exchange words in a 1961 episode of *Coronation Street*.

Lancashire would be ready in time for the first night, on Thursday 3 May 1956. But the Yorkshire side was delayed by several months. Sidney threatened to sue the ITA, who were responsible for providing the transmission equipment, before they had even gone on air.

On the opening night Sidney hired his old friend, the American anchorman Quentin Reynolds, to lend expertise to the first live transmission. Ironically, for a programme that included an item called pub corner, Reynolds is said to have warmed up for the cameras by getting blind drunk, and had to be put under a cold shower and frogmarched around the building while black coffee was poured down his neck.

Above: Sidney Bernstein (far left) on Granada's opening night in 1956.

The opening night included *Meet the People,* a live introduction to the individuals who had made the new station possible, in which Reynolds slurred his way from Kenneth Clark to the studio carpenters. There was variety from London, and boxing from Liverpool. Sidney cheekily concluded with a 'Tribute to the BBC', not so much an act of deference as a warning that the opposition was coming down from the Pennines.

'I've watched their television service since it started,' Sidney told the audience, 'I only hope we can do as well.' But Granada wasn't the BBC – far from it. Denis Forman:

We felt great respect for the BBC and we thought their broadcasting record was terrific but much too posh. We thought they were all great and good people who talked Oxford English, and had no contact whatsoever with the Mirror *readers or the* Sun *readers. And it was our feeling that what we could do was to bring television within the reach and intelligibility of the mass readers of the tabloids. And in that way we felt we were quite different from the BBC and we felt we didn't want to have any middle-class people around. In fact, if you'd been to a public school you had a hard job to get into Granada. Eton, no – absolutely no chance.*

The impeccably spoken Forman (Loretto School, Musselburgh and Pembroke College, Cambridge) became one of the gatekeepers of Granada's employment policy. Former BBC staff, who were regarded as contaminated by establishment views, also stood little chance. They

An ordinary terrace in the Manchester suburb of Weatherfield, recognised around the world as the fictional setting for *Coronation Street*.

scouted Canada to recruit experience. And they cast around for fresh voices. One recruit during the early years was Michael Parkinson.

I could never have got a job on the BBC with my accent. I might have got a job as a doorman, but I would not have got a job as a newscaster or a presenter of a talk show, whatever it might have been. Sidney had a notion, an instinct for what a thing should be and he had the great capacity to hire people to fulfil that, and to give them the capacity and the courage to actually work, to enjoy it. And that was the nice thing about being at Granada at that time. Everybody shared a notion of what we were doing. The fundamental characteristic of Granada was its attitude. And its attitude was North Country. It was arrogant, it was blunt, it wore clogs, it was salty; it was all those things. We must have been regarded as a pain in the arse by a lot of people and we probably were. But the fact of the matter was, he encouraged a distinctive approach that had never been seen on television before. It gave a voice to a lot of people. You have to imagine Britain at that time. Now it's much more fused than it was then. Then it was two or three separate countries, and there was a distinct demarcation line between those who lived in London and those who lived above Watford, and particularly those tribes who lived in Lancashire and Yorkshire. And they didn't quite feel dispossessed but they felt that they weren't getting a fair crack at the whip in many, many ways.

Above: Stan and Hilda Ogden (Bernard Youens and Jean Alexander), residents of number 13 Coronation Street from 1964.

'From the North Granada Presents.' The onscreen production ident left viewers in no doubt where the programmes were coming from. Granada gave voice to northern writers, commentators and comedians. It rolled up its sleeves for a scrap and led the way in changing how television dealt with politics and current affairs. It was a counterpart to Lew Grade's showbiz sparkle, often gritty, even grumpy, a maker of inquisitive and sometimes confrontational programmes. Grade acknowledged Sidney Bernstein as 'the architect of cultural television'. But Sidney Bernstein and Granada nearly passed on what most people will tell you is ITV's greatest programme, a clarion Mancunian voice that has travelled the world – *Coronation Street.*

Below: Minnie Caldwell (Margot Bryant, left), Ena Sharples (Violet Carson, centre) and Martha Longhurst (Lynne Carol, right) gossip over a milk stout in a 1961 episode of *Coronation Street.*

Tony Warren was a young scriptwriter who modelled his image on Noel Coward but found himself working on Granada's 'no expense spent' series based on Captain W.E. Johns' *Boy's Own* adventures about his pilot hero Biggles.

I knew absolutely nothing about aeroplanes and I hated it. And I climbed on top of a green tin filing cabinet and started yelling at the man who got me into television, a Canadian called Harry Elton. I said, 'I'm not coming down, I'm not coming down till you let me write what I know about.' And he said, 'Well calm down, now what do you know about?' and I

said, 'I know about show business,' because I'd been in the theatre since I was 12. 'That's the kiss of death', he said. I said, 'And I know about the north of England,' and he looked out of the window and said, 'What about the story of the street out there?' And I burst out with, 'That's no good. I've tried it twice, the BBC have turned it down twice,' and he said, 'You're supposed to be under contract to us,' and I said, 'Well that was before.' He said, 'Go away and write it again, come back tomorrow with a script that will take Britain by storm,' and I swear he said it to get me down off the filing cabinet, because his next meeting was due in. Of course I'd junked the old scripts so I had to stay up all night and dream up another. The versions that were offered to the BBC were much broader, much more situation comedy, but it had helped me enormously because I knew what I wanted to write and it just came, it was magic, it was one of those times when the pen writes for itself.

Above: Ena Sharples (Violet Carson) and Elsie Tanner (Pat Pheonix) exchange words in a 1977 episode of *Coronation Street*.

What Elton had seen from the Granada office window was the back-to-back streets of Salford, where Warren had found his original inspiration.

I've invented so many stories about what did and didn't happen but I'm pretty sure of a moment that probably inspired the whole thing. I was at stage school and my cousin Roy was at the Junior Arts School and we always used to go to Cross Lane Market in Salford on a Saturday afternoon. We were coming home and the lights were just going up on the stalls, there were naphtha flares and kerosene lamps. And outside Salford Hippodrome it said 'Strip Strip Hooray, we've nothing on tonight' and Parker's fish and chip shop, you could smell the fat wafting over, and there was wrestling on the telly on the shop on the corner. And I said, 'Oh I love it, oh I love it, and I'd like to preserve it all like flies in amber. It's going to change, it's going to alter.'

Warren also drew on his own family for characters and dialogue.

Opposite: Pat Pheonix on the *Coronation Street* set in 1964.

If you go back to the very first scene of Elsie Tanner's when she's looking in the mirror, she says, 'Elsie, you're about ready for the knacker yard.' Well, my auntie Lily used to say, because she originally said that line, 'Watch what

you say or that bugger will write it down and you'll be on television a fortnight later.' I was always worried about what my grandmother would say when she saw Ena Sharples, and she sat and she watched it and I watched her very closely and she said, 'What's that when it's at home?' She said, 'I wouldn't like to meet that face on a dark night,' and then she said, 'I'm trying to think what that face reminds me of.' Violet Carson *[who played Ena Sharples] once said to my mother, 'Let's face it, Ena is based on Tony's grandma, isn't she?' And my mother looked her up and down rather coldly and said, 'Well my mother was certainly a very large woman'. But then there was quite a lot of Annie Walker out of my mother.*

Above: Elsie (Pat Phoenix) tied the knot with American Steve Tanner (Paul Maxwell) in 1967.

Below: Elsie (Pat Phoenix) chats with Rita Fairclough (Barbara Knox) in a Christmas 1972 episode.

Warren wrote two sample scripts under the title 'Florizel Street'. They hugely impressed producer Elton and drama director Stuart Latham, who pushed them forward to the management.

With hindsight, we know that Tony Warren struck gold. But to many eyes, the first scripts looked outlandish. Television had seen nothing like them before: a gallery of working-class grotesques swapping music-hall dialogue in a regional accent. Granada's senior Television Committee discussed whether to give the production the green light at a lunchtime meeting in their offices in Golden Square in London – two hundred miles and a whole world away from Salford's terraces. Denis Forman:

It went before the board and two of the members of the board were deadly opposed to it – they thought no-one would understand the argot, they thought it was low life, down market, disagreeable and Sidney Bernstein himself said it wasn't his cup of tea and he wasn't going to vote. But his brother Cecil and I both thought it was well worth a try. I

suppose it took 20 minutes, half an hour, we won the others round, and it was given a limited licence of six episodes provided the name was changed.

Elton, Latham and Harry Kershaw – who would be the programme's first script editor – locked themselves in an office with a bottle of whisky to sort out a new title. They narrowed the field to two, each suggesting a connection to events at the time the street would have been built: *Coronation Street* or 'Jubilee Street'. Bottle exhausted, they voted and went home. The next morning, *Coronation Street* it was – though on sobering up two of the three were convinced they had cast their vote for 'Jubilee Street'.

Even with a pilot episode made, the management were not convinced. Tony Warren:

Above: Bet Lynch (Julie Goodyear) and Mike Baldwin (Johnny Briggs) in 1976.

They took one look and said 'no way, no way.' 'If this goes out,' one said, 'the advertisers will withdraw their advertising, the viewers will switch off. No.'

Below: Stan (Bernard Youens) and Hilda Ogden (Jean Alexander) in 1977.

Elton rigged monitors around one of Granada's Manchester studios, and invited the staff to a lunchtime screening, where they were given questionnaires to fill in. Only then did Granada realise that they might have a hit on their hands. The staff either loved it or loathed it – but far more of them loved it. It took the people to get the first episode of *Coronation Street* onto the screens.

On 9 December 1960, Granada viewers saw the formidable Ena Sharples buttonhole shop owner Florrie Lindley on the question of where she had come from. 'Esmeralda Street, eh? Very bay window down there, aren't they? Oh, well you'll find it very different up here. There are some very funny people in this street.'

The next day, the *Daily Mirror*'s TV review

Above and opposite page: *Coronation Street* stalwart Ken Barlow, portrayed by William Roache since 1960, as seen in the series (left to right) in 1961, 1969, 1973, 1976, 1980 and 1987.

Below: As Ken Barlow's son Peter, 11-year-old Linus Roache appeared alongside his father in *Coronation Street* in 1975.

greeted the new arrival. 'The programme is doomed from the outset – with its gloomy tune and grim scene of a row of terraced houses and smoking chimneys.' But the viewers liked the 'funny people' – Elsie Tanner the siren of the ginnel, Annie Walker the affected landlady of the Rover's Return, Ken Barlow the university boy uncomfortably back among his roots.

The series of course, ran on. By May 1961 it was fully networked. Lew Grade took it to the Midlands either because – depending on which source you believe – he was surprised and impressed by how well it performed in London, or he capitulated to his wife's demands to be able to watch it. It topped the charts that September. An institution had been born.

Pat Phoenix became the first queen of the soaps, opening supermarkets in white fur, champagne to hand, giving the public the glamour that she believed they wanted, but never losing the quality that made the audience recognise Elsie Tanner as one of their own.

Corrie has continued to make stars out of previously unknown actors. And it has presented a rich gallery of human types: battleaxes, from Ena Sharples to Blanche Hunt; bruisers, from Len Fairclough to Tommy Harris; skivers like Stan Ogden and Jack

Duckworth; schemers like Terry Duckworth and Cilla Brown; the downtrodden, from Jerry Booth to Roy Cropper; and the dreamers, like star-crossed couple Curly Watts and Raquel Wolstenholme; the brassy women – Bet Lynch, Karen McDonald, and in her days as a nightclub chanteuse Rita Sullivan – all heirs to Pat Phoenix's lipstick. And one immortal: the most successful lady-killer in television history – Ken Barlow. A librarian, an exotic dancer, a chiropodist, a yoga instructor, a trade union official, a headmistress and a headmaster's daughter (played by Joanna Lumley) – Ken has ploughed the field, but repeatedly comes back to Deirdre. Their on, off , and on again relationship has made them the Burton and Taylor of Weatherfield. When they remarried in April 2005, nearly 13 million viewers tuned in. Charles and Camilla's nuptials attracted only seven million the following day.

Below: 13 million viewers tuned in when Ken Barlow (William Roache) and Dierdre Hunt (Anne Kirkbride) remarried in April 2005.

Many of the Street's most enduring creations have begun as near-caricatures, but over time writers and actors have given them depth. Often, it appears that viewers treat them as though they were flesh and blood. Twenty thousand letters a year arrive in the *Coronation Street* office, written to the characters as well as to the actors who play them. Their plots invade the real world. In 1983 when Ken, Deirdre and Mike Baldwin were locked in a love triangle,

the crowd at a Wednesday-night Manchester United match saw flashed on the electronic scoreboard, hot from Weatherfield and a screen near them, the news that Deirdre was staying with Ken. When Deirdre was wrongly imprisoned in 1998, she made the front pages of the tabloids as 'The Weatherfield One', and the Prime Minister promised to intervene.

Coronation Street's immense popularity can be a poisoned chalice. Many actors have left the series believing they were huge stars, but found the show was bigger. In the public eye, the fictional self wholly consumed the real one. Some have found it difficult to work again.

Coronation Street has always embodied the sense of nostalgia that Warren felt in Cross Lane market. As the real back-to-backs of Salford were cleared, it kept its cobbles. But it never kept pace with demographic changes, particularly ethnicity. It has only recently admitted a sympathetic gay character. Perhaps most potently, it is a place where everyone still knows everyone else's name and their business, and where the pub and the shop are still the hubs of a community – which seems ever more attractive in an increasingly impersonal world (though in reality the level of gossip, and the density of past and present entanglements between characters, would surely be intolerable).

At its best, it is as good as anything on television, though it has had its ups and downs over the years, and sometimes within the episodes of a single week. It has been a proving ground for many of television's best writers, from Jack Rosenthal to Paul Abbott. It is a vast, sprawling, human comedy. And with its focus on the lives and loves of working and lower-middle class characters, its ripe regional turns of phrase, and its willingness to embrace and celebrate life, it could not have come from any other broadcaster. It was through *Coronation Street*, more than any other programme, that ITV embedded itself in people's lives.

But ITV didn't just make contact with the audience at home. It found new ways to bring them into the studio, to make them part of the show.

Opposite: Jack and Vera Duckworth (William Tarmey and Elizabeth Dawn) behind the bar of the Rover's Return in 1995.

Above: Bet Lynch (Julie Goodyear) has a laugh with Percy Sugden (Bill Waddington) in 1985.

PUTTING PEOPLE ON THE BOX

5

Above: Judith Keppel becomes the first contestant to win the top prize on *Who Wants to Be a Millionaire?*

'They are not punters. They are stars.'
Jeremy Beadle

FROM THE START, people liked ITV, and ITV liked people. It broke open the closed shop of broadcasting, and put members of the public on the screen. Its news programmes asked people's opinions on the stories that affected them. Its current affairs shows put them face-to-face with politicians – often explosively so. Above all, it made them part of its entertainments. It still does.

Above: Leslie Crowther (with microphone) hosted Central's *The Price Is Right* during its initial run between 1984 and 1988.

Opposite page: Lenny Henry gets his big break on *New Faces* in 1975.

Above: Quizmaster Michael Miles (right) questions a contestant in the 'Yes/No Interlude' on *Take Your Pick*. Alec Dane (left) is ready to bang his gong if the contestant responds with either a 'yes' or 'no' answer.

Below: Hughie Green (right) gives a young contestant the opportunity to win £1,000 on *Double Your Money.*

The current kings of the studio are Ant McPartlin and Declan Donnelly, with their *Saturday Night Takeaway*, which pulls people from its audience to compete for prizes.

DEC: *Any one of those people believe that it could be them and you see their faces flicking on our big master computer, and there's a real anticipation and an excitement and it gives a real energy to the studio. Hopefully some of that comes across on screen as well. But they're vitally important to that show. They're the life blood of that show. We get up there and we do our bit.*

ANT: *But the energy comes from them.*

DEC: *We buzz off them… and it's them that gives us that impetus really.*

This love affair with the audience goes back to some of ITV's first hits. Associated-Rediffusion shows *Take Your Pick* and *Double Your Money* made their first appearances in 1955, and were both fixtures in the top ten television programmes for a dozen years.

Take Your Pick was the first on air, and the first quiz on British television to offer cash prizes. It was also the first to use the audience as part of the show. Contestants would first be challenged to get through a minute of fast-paced questions from quizmaster Michael Miles – 'And I believe you're from Sheffield?'… 'Your husband's a lorry driver?' – not so simple when an answer using 'yes' or 'no' was met by the dreaded gong. A general knowledge quiz gave contestants a chance to choose the key to one of 12 numbered boxes. Three contained dud prizes – a box of spent matches, or a previously squeezed lemon, perhaps. Miles would try to buy the key back off the contestant, and as his cash offers increased the audiences cries of 'Take the money!' and 'Open the box!' racked up the excitement.

Double Your Money, presented by Hughie Green, had a hook familiar to viewers of *Who Wants to Be a Millionaire?* Each correct answer doubled the prize, to a maximum of £1000. On reaching £32, the contestant was taken into a soundproof box for the 'Treasure Trail' – a gimmick which was intended to increase the tension, but which also ruled out the possibility of audience members shouting out an answer (this being before the days of multiple choice questions, when a cough is enough to cheat with). 'The Trail' created television's first celebrity winner.

Plantagenet Somerset Fry was an Oxford student notable for an encyclopaedic knowledge of historical facts and a red beard. When he

won £512, not wishing to risk it all for the £1000 jackpot, he became so well known that he employed another student as his press officer. A book deal, appearances on other quizzes, and an invitation to Associated-Rediffusion's current affairs programme *This Week* soon followed.

Television presenters had never treated contestants like this before. Miles trying to trip them up in the quickfire chat, or pressurising keyholders by waving money at them. Green schmoozing them while always looking for a gag – often at their expense – to throw to the studio audience and the camera.

Michael Miles (centre) and Alec Dane (left) were the presenters of Associated-Rediffusion's *Take Your Pick*, a quiz show which ran on ITV for 13 years from 1955. It was revived in 1992 with Des O'Connor as quizmaster and ran for a further five years.

Nicholas Parsons, genial quizmaster of Anglia's *Sale of the Century* from 1971 to 1983. The chairman of BBC Radio's *Just a Minute* since 1967, Parsons had earlier provided the voice for Sheriff Tex Tucker in Granada's 1960 puppet series *Four Feather Falls*.

But if ITV loved the public, the presenters who sparred and joked with them were not necessarily so enthusiastic. There was skill, certainly, in handling them. Miles was avuncular, Green – as he would come to say in his catchphrase – meant everything 'most sincerely, friends'. But, as Sam Goldwyn once said, the secret of success is sincerity – if you can fake that, you've got it made.

Miles was interviewed on the BBC's *Late Night Line-Up* in 1967, as his series neared the end of its life. With a show of evidently false good humour as he was put on the spot, Miles defended himself against charges of feeding clues to contestants who weren't up to what interviewer Noel Picarda called 'even the reasonably low standard of your questions.' 'Even the simplest question can be very difficult if you don't know the answer,' Miles replied. 'And you would be surprised at the number of people, really and truly, who come on the show who have no idea of a simple answer to a particular question.' The bonhomie that he habitually turned on in his quizmaster role wears even thinner when he is asked if he would like to take part in the rival hit show. 'Knowing Hughie Green, I would loathe to be on *Double Your Money*.'

One current host was never convinced by Green, Miles, and other pioneer presenters. Chris Tarrant:

There was no attempt really at in any way relaxing the contestant and putting them at their ease. They were very much cannon fodder. And I think only Bruce Forsyth really had that ability to relax little old ladies, and genuinely care whether they won a prize or not.

One highly successful quiz show host of a later generation was Nicholas Parsons. He fronted *Sale of the Century* – 'From Norwich – it's the quiz of the week' – which ran for over a decade, at first locally on Anglia and later on the network. It topped the ratings in 1978 – a BBC strike boosted its audience to over 21 million, the highest ever for a quiz show. Parsons took care to chat to the contestants beforehand to relax them. But it was not only for their benefit. It helped Parsons to remember key facts.

I didn't have any autocueing in Anglia. It started as a modest show, so I memorised the names of the contestants, their jobs, where they came from, the towns they lived in, the names of their families and everything. And I used to talk to them also to get to know them. They were simply at ease with it.

But it didn't always pay off:

On one particular occasion, which is absolutely stuck in my memory because it was unbelievable, I spoke to the three of them and the first one turned out to be a school teacher. I chatted to her for a bit. I turned to the second contestant, and I said, 'It says on my card that you're a pawn broker.' He said, 'Well, Nicholas, I'm not really a pawn broker. I'm a street trader and

Nicholas Parsons, Carole Ashby (far left) and Karen Loughlin (second from left) present a contestant with a prize Mini on Anglia's *Sale of the Century* in 1981.

Above: Central's *Family Fortunes* invited competing families to guess the findings of public surveys. Original host Bob Monkhouse was succeeded by Max Bygraves in 1983.

Below: Central's darts quiz *Bullseye* acquired a cult following and ran for 16 years from 1981. The show was hosted throughout by comic Jim Bowen (second from right).

I've got my barrow down the East End, all cash business, you know, money in the back of me hand. What the eye don't see the heart don't grieve over, that's what I say you know! But it's a family business, we've all got these barrows, all cash business, nothing declared you see, and I thought I can't come on television saying I've got a cash business, don't declare nothing. I'd be in real trouble wouldn't I, so I thought I know, I'll call me self a pawn broker – covers a multitude of sins, doesn't it?' And then he said, 'I'm going on a bit, aren't I?' And he turned to the third contestant and said, 'Oh, er, what do you do for a living?' and the man said, 'I'm an income tax inspector.' Collapse of stout party, as they say. I've never seen anybody go white on the spot. He didn't do very well.

Even when they were at their ease, Parsons increased the tension as the quiz progressed.

You need a sense of drama. Now I am an actor, and I've done stand-up comedy and all that, and I knew that one had to instil a sense of theatre into it. I suggested to the producer when I took on the job: 'Let's start quite easily with very simple questions to put them at their ease, get their adrenalin going, get their confidence, and then move forward.' And I wrote all the questions for a number of years, and in the last sequence I wrote very quick snappy questions which were very concise, and actually some of them were very easy, so it didn't require so much knowledge as quickness of the call, so I could go very fast. And I think I was one of the first people to do this very pacey thing at the end which builds up a mix for tremendous excitement.

The inheritor of the title of top quizmaster is Chris Tarrant, who in recent years has led *Who Wants to Be a Millionaire?* to great

popularity. With a single competitor sitting in the hot seat, a screen displaying multiple choice answers to the questions, and up to £1 million at stake, the programme creates a unique relationship between contestant and host. Chris Tarrant:

> *It's a very strange kind of very public, and yet also very intimate, adventure between me and them. Because, in the end, they will forget all the noise of the audience around them and the millions watching at home, and the TV cameras. They will only really be aware, they all say that, they will only be aware of that screen and my voice.*

Tarrant's voice often presses them – are they sure that is their final answer? They still have lifelines left, do they want to use them? Are they certain they want to play, not just walk away with a cheque? It sometimes seems that he knows whether the answer they have picked is right or wrong, and is deliberately making them sweat. But, he says, he has no more knowledge than they do. And he is on their side – up to a point.

> *I just want them to win. I really genuinely want them to win. I may stretch them over the coals during the course of it, and they know I'll do that, but I want them to win. I don't necessarily want them to all win a million, and I certainly don't want them to lose.*
>
> *And I mean quite often, you will do it at home going, no, no, no, it's not that – whatever the guy's saying, you know, I know the capital of Poland is Paris – and you're thinking, no, not it's not, get out of there.*
>
> *There's nothing worse than the moment where you think, oh my God, you have just lost £218,000, and I'm about to tell you that, and I can tell by your eyes, you still think you've won. It's an awful thing. I may know the answers or may not. Realistically, my general knowledge is pretty good, but there are great blanks in my knowledge, like anybody else. And only when they do finally answer, does something come up on my screen saying whether they're right or wrong.*

This page:
Judith Keppel correctly answers a question about Eleanor of Aquitaine to become the first contestant to win £1,000,000 on *Who Wants to Be a Millionaire?*

But although Tarrant agonises over the answers with the contestants, he has a trick or two to prolong the suspense for both contestant and audience.

> *It's been one of the greatest moments of my career, my life, whatever, when you look down, and you think, oh my God, I'm just about to tell Judith Keppel that she has just won £1 million. I mean it's just the most*

The talent show has a long history on ITV. The daddy of them all was *Opportunity Knocks*, a second long-running show for Hughie Green. He would interview a sponsor who had brought an act along, to find out something about their background, before revealing the

Originally produced by Associated-Rediffusion, *Opportunity Knocks* survived the reallocation of the ITV franchises in 1968 and was subsequently produced by Thames until 1978. Former child actor and Canadian air force pilot Hughie Green hosted the show throughout its 22-year run on ITV.

extraordinary moment in your life… I think I'll take a commercial break before I tell her. Which is an extra dimension and makes them sweat. And it's fantastic telly, you know, and I love all that stuff.*

Who Wants to Be a Millionaire? gives contestants a chance to win the biggest prize pot in British television history. But there is another lure with which television attracts participants, a lure potentially even more lucrative and even more powerful – the chance to go out a nobody, and come back a star.

performer to the television audience. Singers, comedians, acrobats, and novelty acts, child performers and pensioners, amateur, professional and semi-professional, polished, raw and simply dreadful, they all passed through 'make your mind up time' featuring audience applause and the low-tech clapometer, before the viewers and their postcards had their say.

From the first show on Associated-Rediffusion in 1956, to its last ITV outing on Thames in 1978, opportunity really did knock for some of the performers. Les Dawson, Mary Hopkin, the Black Abbotts (with future solo star Russ Abbott on drums), Lena Zavaroni, Freddie 'Parrot Face' Davies, Peters and Lee, Frank Carson, Little and Large, Tom O'Connor, Pam Ayres, Bobby Crush, Freddie Starr and Su Pollard (who was beaten into second place by a singing dog) were among the enduring names who got their first break on the programme. Tony Holland's name is probably less well-known, but few viewers who saw him flexing his musical muscles to the cha cha cha will ever forget the sight. The same viewers may still be struggling to forget the sound of schoolboy Neil Reid's mawkish 'Mother of Mine', which rocketed to number two in the pop charts on the back of his victory on the show. Reid's fame was less durable than those listed above, but still far outlasted the hundreds of performers for whom the few minutes exposure on Green's showcase was in itself the highpoint of their careers. Many more failed to make it

past the auditions – though one rejected singer called Gerry Dorsey overcame the disappointment and achieved success when he adopted the stage name Englebert Humperdinck.

Where *Opportunity Knocks* featured the warm support of the sponsors of the acts, ITV's next major talent show became famous for the often acerbic judgments of its panel of judges. *New Faces*, which ran on ATV from 1973 to 1978, opened the door to Victoria Wood, Lenny Henry, Marti Caine, Jim Davidson (who had failed his *Opportunity Knocks* audition), Gary Wilmot, Roger de Courcey and Nookie Bear, Showaddywaddy and Patti Boulaye. Failure on this show didn't just mean obscurity – it could end in tears.

Tony Hatch – the composer whose most enduring contribution to ITV was the theme tune to *Crossroads* – became known as the hatchet man for his hard line with disappointing turns. He once awarded a comedian two points out of ten 'for nerve'. Pop producer Mickie Most and the other judges were all more than capable of matching him. There can hardly be an act in showbusiness history that has not at some point been improved by the honest straight-talking voice of experience. But to see them taken apart on screen was often like watching raw meat being

Hopeful performers were frankly criticized and awarded marks out of ten for Presentation, Content and Star Quality on ATV's *New Faces*, hosted by Derek Hobson (far left). Arthur Askey (far right) was one of the regular pundits.

Above: *New Faces* showcased talented newcomers who had not previously been seen on television, including comedienne Victoria Wood who appeared on the show in 1974.

thrown to the big cats in the zoo. Over 160 episodes, it was the judges who became the biggest weekly attraction on *New Faces*. That would be remembered when ITV launched a new pop talent show in 2001.

LWT's Head of Light Entertainment Nigel Lythgoe was on holiday in Australia when he saw a series that followed the creation of girl band Bardot – from mass auditions to debut single. The next week – holiday or not – he made sure he stayed in to watch. Like much of Australia, he was hooked. He snapped up the format for the UK.

Popstars would bring new twists to the talent contest. No studio, no sponsors, no host, no star presenters. Instead, there would be a series of increasingly exacting auditions, shot on location, bringing reality television to Saturday night entertainment. Two of the three judges were soon in place: Paul Adam from Polydor and publicist Nicki Chapman. For the third Lythgoe wanted a modern equivalent of Hatch and Most, an experienced voice who wouldn't pull punches: 'someone', as he put it, for the viewers 'to boo'.

Simon Cowell, a major player at music label BMG, turned them down. Pop Svengali Jonathan King was too busy. Lythgoe himself entered the fray. He certainly had the experience – he was a former dancer and choreographer, whose first TV appearance had been in the chorus line at the Palladium (he stood next to the N of Night as the title revolved onstage, so his parents would be able to pick him out on TV). Nigel Lythgoe:

The rest basically was history. They used it as a slogan for the show, 'Pick me, Nigel.' So this name that I have hated all my life – Nigel – was plastered all over the country, everyone going, 'Who's Nigel?' and then the press got hold of Nasty Nigel – the alliteration of it – basically because there was Nasty Nick from Big Brother *and so they just had another: 'Oh, let's go with nasty again shall we?' They wouldn't say, 'Nice Nigel,' would they?*

Opposite page: *Pop Idol* launched winner Will Young (left) and runner-up Gareth Gates to successful chart careers.

They wouldn't – not when they saw the way he laid into the unsuccessful contestants.

Popstars eventually created the boy-girl band Hear'Say, who rocketed

Popstars created boy-girl band Hear'Say who performed their first live show at London's G.A.Y. club at the Astoria nightclub in March 2001.

to number one on the strength of their massive TV exposure and press coverage. Their debut single became the fastest-selling in history. Their career was a bubble – but the show had more mileage in it.

By giving the audience a look behind the scenes at everything from the audition process to the release of the first recording, complete with all the glitches and spats that were fit to be screened, *Popstars* had revolutionised the TV talent show. Variations on its template followed. *Soapstars* turned members of the public into a new family for *Emmerdale* – but the fictitious Calder–Westons hung around no longer than Hear'Say.

With *Pop Idol*, impresario Simon Fuller brought Lythgoe a new format. Simon Cowell finally arrived onscreen in the hard judge role, and with the rest of the panel whittled the field of would-be stars down to 50. But from then on, while they made the comments, it was the public who made the decisions with a phone-in vote. Picking up their mobile was so much simpler and more immediate than sending a postcard to Hughie Green had ever been. Millions of viewers suddenly felt they had the power to be starmaker or starbreaker, without ever leaving their sofas. 'This time, you decide' was the slogan, and in February 2002 the public decided to choose Will Young over Gareth Gates in the final head-to-head showdown. The programme made Simon Cowell a television face, gave Ant and Dec a primetime hit as its presenters, and unleashed Young and Gates on the blameless and unsuspecting Beatles classic 'The Long and Winding Road'.

Other series have followed. *Popstars: The Rivals* looked for two bands – one boys, one girls – and followed the *Pop Idol* innovation of the public vote. *Pop Idol* itself returned. And Cowell devised *The X-Factor,* which looked for acts in different age categories. The show was successful enough to spawn a second series. The talent show is at its highest ebb on ITV since Hughie Green told all his viewers to 'Remember, friends – it's your vote that counts.'

But when it came to putting people on the screen, ITV had another trick up its sleeve right from the start. A woman stands onstage, and is given a hammer and asked to smash whatever is hidden under a cloth in front of her. She sets to. The cloth is pulled back to reveal the shards of what used to be her best china. She bursts into tears. The audience laugh.

In February 2002, viewers voted for Will Young over Gareth Gates in the *Pop Idol* final, propelling Young to the top of the UK chart with his debut single 'Anything is Possible/Evergreen'.

The show was *People Are Funny*, an ATV production hosted by comedian Derek Roy, which began its run on the first Saturday of ITV's life. Volunteer contestants became the butt of practical jokes disguised as party games – and were rewarded with a prize for their co-operation. It invited viewers to revel in their discomfort – and it became ITV's first controversial programme.

'Repulsive' was the verdict of Isabel Quigly in *The Spectator,* reviewing ITV's first week under the headline 'Television: Free and Easy':

Unfortunate (though idiotic) members of an audience are called up on stage and subjected to various indignities and then consoled with a washing machine or a wireless or a bunch of pound notes. Here's 'freedom' indeed! If

People Are Funny ever turns up on my doorstep, at the risk of sounding like a sourpuss, I shall yell.

The programme came from the stage of the New Cross Empire. The constituency MP complained about it to the Postmaster General. But his constituents set about a defence in the local paper. Many viewers liked the show – they had never seen anything like it on the staid BBC – and it shot into the top ten ratings. But it was too much for the ITA. They asked ATV to tone it down. ATV, probably recognising that without the edge of cruelty, they had no show, decided to kill it rather than try to dilute it. It ended its run before the year was out, leaving a waiting list of hundreds who wanted to take part in it.

The *People Are Funny* contestants had at least volunteered for their ordeal. ITV soon had another practical joke show which enjoyed a long run, despite the fact that its tricks were foisted on unsuspecting members of the public. This was *Candid Camera*, the hidden camera show. The format was imported from America, and began its British run in 1960, hosted by Bob Monkhouse.

The jokes were often simple. A talking postbox. A flower on a restaurant table that bent and sucked up a diner's drink. Someone struggling to deal with cakes coming off a factory conveyor belt which, unknown to them, was running at twice its normal speed. Monkhouse dressed up as a policeman and showed his own photograph to passers-by, asking if they had seen this man: not one recognised him under his helmet. They tried to sell 'left-handed' teapots, and to pay taxi drivers with wet notes pulled off a washing line next to a printing press. The comedy was in the reaction to the jokes. But it could take a long time to get a reaction worth broadcasting; for every minute that appeared onscreen, 25 were shot – an unheard-of shooting ratio for its day.

Sometimes the gags backfired. After one presenter dipped his hand into a goldfish tank, palmed a piece of carrot and crunched it down

Bob Monkhouse, the original presenter of ABC's *Candid Camera*, was British television's most prolific game show host with stints on ITV's *The Golden Shot*, *Celebrity Squares*, *Family Fortunes*, *$64,000 Question* and *Bob's Your Uncle* among others.

leaving onlookers aghast, a woman rang in to say her son had just jumped up from the TV and swallowed the family's real goldfish. In another trick, Monkhouse tried to sell five pound notes for four pound ten shillings to holidaymakers in Blackpool. He was confident that they would think them counterfeit, or assume that there was a trick involved, and turn them down. His producer was less confident, and insisted that Monkhouse use his own money, not the programme's. Monkhouse was £50.00 down within half an hour.

Jeremy Beadle (in white suit) stages a memorable prank on a 1983 edition of LWT's *Game for a Laugh*.

One of the most memorable tricks was seen in the first programme. A car was run down a gently inclined road into a garage, where the attendant was asked to change the oil. When he opened the bonnet, there was no engine. He looked under the car, in the boot, in the back seats, utterly bewildered.

It was most memorable, but not necessarily most accurately remembered. Viewers asked for a repeat – but when they saw it again two years later there were complaints. Why had the scene where that

Practical joker Jeremy Beadle was one of the four original presenters of LWT's *Game for a Laugh*. He went on to host *Beadle's About*, *Beadle's Box of Tricks*, *People Do the Funniest Things*, *It's Beadle* (above) and *You've Been Framed*.

attendant lost his temper been cut? Where was the moment when he was told the engine had seemed a bit quiet for the last 20 miles? The item had been elaborated and improved in people's memories. It's an example worth remembering when the idea gets aired that 'television was much better in the old days'. The memory on which that judgment is based may be less than reliable.

The practical joke show was revived, with spectacular success, by Jeremy Beadle in the 1980s, with *Game for a Laugh* and *Beadle's About*. These shows were developed not from the model of *Candid Camera* but from another vintage American format to which Beadle bought the rights, *Truth or Consequences*. This was a game show in which married couples were party to tricks being played on their partner. Jeremy Beadle:

> *Candid Camera, in essence, was a basic prop gag show where you caught members of the public completely unaware and you were unaware of that member of the public as well – you knew nothing at all about them. Whereas what we tried to do was to customise, tailor make a joke for a particular person and then create a nightmare for them. But the nightmare had to be dressed up as a mini soap opera with a beginning, a middle, and an end.*

The jokes were only as good, he says, as the people who they were played on. It's common in television to refer to members of the public as 'punters'. Beadle disagrees.

The word punter is a very ugly term and for years I said, 'They're not punters, they're stars. They are the star of the show.'

Beadle's programmes received up to 40,000 letters a year from members of the public who were keen to turn their loved ones into stars. The team would whittle them down, looking for people whose profile fitted the outline of the stunts they were devising. The real skill, he says, was in the casting carried out by the show's researchers, as they tried to find people who would react strongly to the unfolding nightmare, but see the funny side when it ended. Possible stars would be met and vetted under some pretence. Doctors were contacted to check – without breaking rules of confidentiality – whether there were any reasons not to subject them to the stress involved.

With the stars in place, the situations were planned. Jeremy Beadle:

No matter how much thinking goes into it, you are still left with that one impossible ingredient, the star. We don't know how he's going to react. But, over the years, we did learn a few psychological tricks, we learned how to handle people. We learned how to write the comedy, it was all written.

Some of our actors came out with some of the greatest lines. I remember Tony McHale – who went on to become one of the chief writers of EastEnders – we gave him a situation whereby we had a Grade Two listed house on the south coast, on which we painted really stupid smiley faces. The husband came home to his wife enthusiastically asking if he liked it. His jaw dropped open, looking up and he was speechless. Eventually he said, 'Well, my wife's obviously gone mad,' to which Tony said, 'What, is it the colour you don't like?'

And Glenn Mills, another one of our actors who's a football referee and is used to eyeballing people and has got one of those sort of faces that really winds you up. He came out with a great line where he's a workman doing a ditch and he's really created havoc in someone's garden. He's been really rude and uptight and unnecessary to our star, whereupon he turns round to them and says, 'No chance of a cup of tea, then?'

One of the great pleasures of filming a stunt is hearing everybody talking about it on Monday. One which got a fantastic reaction was the van in the dock. A simple idea, this guy's got all his life's work in the back of a van.

He's a market trader, sells greeting cards and we're just going to dunk it in the canal. He loses the lot. It was a wonderful piece of producing, it was a wonderful storyline… the researchers involved who cast it, how the story developed. The actual build of that van was a real technical nightmare – we had to drill holes, we had to put extra weight in, loosen the windows, grease the edge so it would go in, because normally if you try to do that to a truck, it would get stuck.

As their star looked on from across the dock, with the friend who had helped to set him up, a wayward crane pushed his van over the edge. He responded with a look of horror, and disbelieving shouts of 'No!' as he raced towards the scene.

This chap's reaction was undoubtedly one of the finest performances of any star. He had been put through hell and even so in the midst of all this absolute horror, he wanted to be reasonable. He was saying, 'Now listen, let's sort this, let's be calm about this.' And of course we became more belligerent, and the more kind and generous he was, the more unkind and brutal we were to him.

The scene ended as Beadle, in frogman gear, emerged from the dock. This was 'the reveal', the moment when the star realises he has been had.

And so I came out of the water and then he pulled off the diver's hat and the relief, the absolute utter relief. People always said to me, 'Have people ever wanted to hit you?' and I said, 'No, no, no, I'm far too sensible for that. I send in the actors for that. They just want to make love to me because they are so relieved it's a joke.'

The reveal on site was always followed up by another important element. The star would be present in the television studio as his or her story was replayed to the viewers. It gave them a chance to show more calmly that they really were game for a laugh at their expense.

It was very important that we restore them to their dignity because we would catch people undressed, or not looking great, at a short ebb or whatever, and so we would bring them back to the studio with an opportunity to be dressed and smart and looking glam, then to watch themselves and to enjoy it.

Beadle became a key player in developing and presenting another show that put members of the public onscreen in undignified situations. This was *You've Been Framed!*, which first screened in 1990. It made a top ten programme out of home video clips of assorted mishaps sent in by members of the public. Twenty thousand tapes were worked through to find material for the first series. And the production was far more complicated than it appeared:

> *I wish it was a nice simple show — give us your videos and we'll plonk them on air. Nothing like that. It was one of the most expensive shows. We spent all our money on sound because, as cameramen will tell you, the pictures are great with camcorders, but the sound is lousy and so we stripped that off and put on new sound. Often, if I was using foreign clips, the person would say 'Gunter, licht.' When it was transmitted you'd say, 'Henry, turn on lights.' Now, am I cheating? Am I writing comedy? As far as I'm concerned, I'm writing comedy and I have complete* carte blanche *to do anything I like to make you laugh.*

Jeremy Beadle was awarded the MBE in 2001 – but not for playing pranks on members of the public in his television shows. He received the honour in recognition of his charity work with the Foundation for Children with Leukaemia in Barnet, north London.

But laughter was never intended to be an excuse for showing scenes of real distress.

> *I used to go to great effort to make sure that nobody was actually hurt in a* You've Been Framed *stunt. I remember half way through a recording we stopped and I was talking to the audience and people said to me, 'Do any people ever get hurt?' and I said, 'No, and we ring the people up just to make sure they weren't actually hurt. For example, is anybody in the audience, who we've seen in one of the clips?' And a chap went, 'Yes, there was me. I was on the bicycle, I went over the hedge.' And I said, 'And were you injured?' He said, 'No,' and the guy sitting next to him said, 'Yes, you were.' I said, 'Pardon?' and he said, 'Well, yes, actually, I broke my arm.' I said, 'What do you mean you broke your arm? Didn't our researchers ask you whether you'd been hurt?' 'Oh yes, yes, yes,' he said, 'but I said I wasn't hurt because I didn't think you'd use it.' I said, 'You're right, we wouldn't use it.'*

The game plan was very simple. At the start, I said to the production team, 'I don't want to see any clip with a baby with its head underwater.' Think about it. It's a shot that makes the hair stand up at the back of the neck and it's horrible.

When you understand what I'm saying there, then you understand what You've Been Framed *should be.*

Beadle's shows made stars out of ordinary people. The latest fashion in entertainment shows are those that reverse the process and show stars – or at least celebrities – stripped down to ordinariness. We have seen them struggle through the heat of *Hell's Kitchen*, get oiled up on *Celebrity Love Island*, and face challenges – like eating grubs in the 'Bush Tucker Trial' – on *I'm a Celebrity, Get Me Out of Here!*

Audiences like watching people behave in extreme situations: on the receiving end of the verdict of the panel of judges, reacting to a practical joke, or under pressure to complete a task. But since the days of *People Are Funny*, the programmes in which they star have raised questions about whether they are being exploited – victims of their desire to appear on the small screen. Simon Cowell:

Granada's *I'm a Celebrity, Get Me Out of Here!* presents a group of celebrities with the opportunity to raise money for charity by living rough in the Australian bush and allowing themselves to be subjected to a variety of physical tasks in the daily 'Bushtucker Trial'. Homegrown versions of the series have also been seen in Germany and the US.

The first hour of recording Pop Idol *was terrible, because we were all just sitting there, fairly polite. And after an hour I turned to Pete Waterman and said, 'This is ridiculous. I mean, I can't sit there and tell these kids who are absolutely useless that they're quite good, I just can't do it, so we might as well tell them what we think.' But it wasn't planned in advance, it just happened that way.*

You've got to look at things sensibly, you know. I mean this is not life or death, we're not drowning kittens, we're just telling people who are hopeless singers, 'You're hopeless singers.' Sometimes you get someone in who's 17, 18, and they've just left school and this is what they think they're going to do for the rest of their lives, and obviously people around them have lied to them or patronised them. At least with this show, somebody's saying, 'You know what, do something you're good at.' Every so often somebody walks in and they're so unstable you just know instinctively, just don't say anything, but in the main I just deal with people as I was dealt with when I was trying to make a career in the music industry. It's a tough business.

Ant and Dec hosted both *Pop Idol* and *I'm a Celebrity, Get Me Out of Here!*

ANT: *If you take* Pop Idol, *I think our job is to be a friend of the contestants, because they go through such a hard time in the audition room. And the judges say what they think, they say honest things. Sometimes we agree with them 100 per cent, other times we think they go far too far.*

DEC: *And also, as performers we've done auditions before. We know how*

nerve-wracking that can be. When you're doing an audition in a room with four very famous faces and with cameras on you and you know it could be edited and shown to nigh on ten million people, that's even more nerve-wracking. It's very easy to forget that it means such a lot to these people. When it's on TV it's great for the public's entertainment and for our entertainment to watch these people struggling in an audition, but it's real for them and it's difficult for them and it's always nice to have someone to go 'Look, you know, you didn't do too badly and, alright you haven't got

Former Royal butler Paul Burrell receives details of a 'Bushtucker Trial' from hosts Ant and Dec in the autumn 2004 season of *I'm a Celebrity, Get Me Out of Here!*

Ant and Dec pull people from the audience to compete for prizes on their popular Saturday evening show *Ant & Dec's Saturday Night Takeaway.*

through but it's not the end of the world.' So I think we're very much on their side.

ANT: *You've got to make sure that it's words of comfort but not words of...*

DEC: *...false hope...*

ANT: *...because there's no point us saying 'you were absolutely brilliant'. We want to be honest, but I'm not going to be as honest as the people in there because they just went through a traumatic experience. I'm just going to look after you and I don't want you going away in bits.*

DEC: *And similarly on* I'm a Celebrity, Get Me Out of Here!*, you've got these celebrities facing the bush tucker trials and they genuinely are quite unpleasant. So unpleasant that I do feel sorry for them and I wouldn't put myself through it. I think if I was faced with any of them, I'd say let them starve back in camp, because I can't do that. So I've got the utmost respect for them when they actually do it. And again they're having a tough enough time out there and the cameras are on them and maybe they don't feel too good that day, and it's just nice to see a friendly face every now and then, just somebody just to say hey, you know, keep your chin up you're doing really well, and hats off to you for doing it.*

ANT: *But if it is a particularly funny challenge, you know, then you can't help but have a giggle at it. But it's best you try not to be two-faced about it... It's slightly different as well on* I'm a Celebrity. *Because they are* celebrities, I think you do get a little bit of the public going, 'Ah well, they can cope with it, they're really rich and who cares. Go on, take the mick out of them.' But you've just got to sort of rein yourself in a little and think 'no'.

DEC: *Nobody's forced anybody to go into the jungle, nobody forced anybody to come and sing in front of the judges, they've done it of their own free will.*

ANT: *And there are consequences to what you're doing, whether you're going in the jungle or whether you're auditioning for* Pop Idol.

DEC: *There's a big win at the end of both of those competitions. There's a big, big win for somebody, but they have to go through that process just like everybody does.*

Jeremy Beadle:

I really did care very, very much about the people we turned into stars. Yes, we did put them through it. All comedy is cruel at some point, there's always a butt to a joke, whether it be the mother in law or the vicar or whatever… And one of the basic tenets of comedy is that everything is funny so long as it doesn't happen to me. And when it does happen to you, you have to learn to laugh — and the one really wonderful thing about the British is their ability to laugh at themselves. It's a really endearing quality. Was it humiliation? No, because the restoration was there. I worked very hard to make sure that people knew this was a joke.

For all the concern about the members of the public who take part in the programmes, it may, ironically, be the presenters who risk suffering most as a consequence. Press attention has made Nigel Lythgoe 'Nasty', and christened Simon Cowell 'Judge Dread'. The labels and the images will stick. And Jeremy Beadle — in person charming and generous — became the object of a million insults, the winner of a poll to find the person Britons would least like as their neighbour. Beadle is philosophical about the role he has played:

The interesting thing is that, from a long history of presenters — of people that dealt with people — many of them didn't actually like the people that they were working with. Hughie Green didn't like the punters and Michael Miles didn't like the punters and the list does go on, believe me. And yet I really did care, and so I found it very odd when I was suddenly cast as being the bogeyman, the most hated man. All I will tell you is: I never got it in public. But I became the kicking boy for the press, no two ways about that.

Above: Ant and Dec are ITV's current kings of the studio, the hosts of *Pop Idol*, *I'm a Celebrity, Get Me Out of Here!* and *Ant & Dec's Saturday Night Takeaway*.

Below: Jeremy Beadle hosted *People Do the Funniest Things* in 1987. More recently he won a poll to find the person Britons would least like as their neighbour.

6

DRAMA'S REALITY CHECK

Above: An edition of ABC's *Armchair Theatre* is broadcast live.

Opposite page: Zöe Lucker plays ruthless widow Tanya Turner in Shed Productions' *Footballers' Wives*.

The working man is a fit subject for drama, and not just a comic foil for middle-class manners.

Sydney Newman

I**N SPRING** 2005, the fourth series of ITV drama *Footballers' Wives* began its run, with a typically ripe episode. The players of Earl's Park F.C. took a sunshine break in Spain, where sea, sun and sangria led to rape, arrest, and bribery to cover the whole thing up. Meanwhile, at home, two of the leading ladies (both shacked up with the same footballer, but that's back-story) gave birth – an event followed by baby-switching, disguise and apparent infanticide by pug-dog.

As if *Hello!* magazine had been edited by Jerry Springer, the programme is an often jaw-dropping mixture of ostentatious vulgarity and toxic passions, where the game of two halves meets all seven deadly sins. Some viewers regard it as a sharp satire on the country's collective obsession with celebrity, sex and bling. Some look for styling tips. Others simply wait to enjoy the next outrageous storyline. For whatever reason, it has become one of the most talked-about dramas of this or any other season.

Like many programmes on television today, *Footballers' Wives* is made by an independent company – that is, one that has no business

Above: The 2000/2001 cast of *Bad Girls* – (standing, left to right) Debra Stephenson, Jack Ellis, Simone Lahbib, Claire King, Mandana Jones and (sitting) Alicya Eyo.

connections with a broadcaster. In this case it is Shed Productions, who are also responsible for the equally torrid prison drama *Bad Girls* (did even Jerry ever dare to tackle a 'My husband turned out to be gay and won't sleep with me but I want a child so I'm planning to impregnate myself after getting his male lover to sell me a condom they used to have sex' theme?).

The man at ITV who was responsible for giving the green light to their productions is the controller of Network Drama, Nick Elliott.

Above: Sex and Earls Park – *Footballers' Wives* Lucy Milligan (Helen Latham), Tanya Turner (Zöe Lucker), Amber Gates (Laila Rouass) and Katie Jones (Elaine Glover).

Below: HMP Larkhill partners in crime Julie Johnston (Kilca Mirylees, left) and Julie Saunders (Victoria Alcock, right) in *Bad Girls*.

The public turn on drama to hear incredible stories. They get enough realistic stuff at work everyday or at home with their families. They want stories that go, wow, I must get home because someone in Bad Girls *is doing something extraordinary, or have you seen the* Footballers' Wives *girls lately? So I think it is refreshing, though I wouldn't want all drama to be like that.*

Shed's productions are just part of a broad range of ITV drama, from continuing series like *Coronation Street* and *Emmerdale* to single plays like the award-winning *Dirty Filthy Love*, from police series like *A Touch of Frost* to comedy-dramas like *Doc Martin*. This stable is one of the great strengths of the ITV schedule. Its audiences are often skewed toward the more affluent and upmarket, making them popular with advertisers, as well as with viewers.

Over half a century ago, before a single programme was broadcast, Winston Churchill dismissed commercial television as a 'tuppeny ha'penny Punch and Judy show'. But since its birth, ITV has been able to claim it has been the chief storyteller to the nation. ITV invented popular television drama, and has been at the forefront ever since. Of the twenty top-rated dramas of 2004, fourteen were on ITV.

Nick Elliott has achieved this position by

insisting on presenting stories with situations and characters that have mass appeal.

> *If a drama is about anyone – whether it's a politician, or a supermodel or whoever – that I can't relate to, we don't do it. Because I think of the ITV viewer as being someone who lives in a small town, where they have a police station, they have a hospital, they commit adultery and murder, but they don't have radio stations, and they don't do fancy jobs in journalism, and they don't even think and care much about politics. They care about ordinary life, about relationships, family, and about crime and health and things like that.*
>
> *We've got to find out what ordinary people can relate to and who can they root for. I don't want series about journalists for instance. People at home see journalists as cynical bastards – which by and large is true – and not as hero characters.*

Journalists may not be the heroes, but many current ITV dramas deal with issues that could be the subject of tabloid headlines or with the stuff of real-life stories in magazines. Some are chilling – asylum seekers and war crimes in *Prime Suspect VI*, paedophilia in an episode of *A Touch of Frost*, gang violence in *Wall of Silence*, date rape drugs in *Gifted*. Some are warm – adoption in *My Beautiful Son*, the excesses of Christmas decorations (a seasonal newspaper favourite) in *Christmas Lights*, a massive lottery windfall in *At Home with the Braithwaites*, weight and its loss in *Fat Friends*. All appeal to the aspirations and fears of ordinary people. Kay Mellor is the author of *Gifted* and *Fat Friends*:

Above: Michael Sheen and Shirley Henderson in the award-winning 2004 drama *Dirty Filthy Love*. Directed by Adrian Shergold, the play followed the progress of a man with Obsessive Compulsive Disorder and Tourette's Syndrome.

> *The initial inspiration for* Fat Friends *came because I found everybody I talked to was fixated on their body shape. Their sole topic of conversation would be how much weight they had to lose before they could get into their bikini or before they would ask out this guy. And it started to happen to*

The cast of Kay Mellor's
Fat Friends.

men too, they would be going, 'Oh I can't eat that because I've got to lose this belly'. And you start to think, well do we all have to look the same?

At the same time with all this concern about weight, we're living in a society where you don't have to get up to change the television channel over, we don't hang the washing out, we've become very inactive. So there was an interesting dilemma going on which made me want to research it properly. So I thought, I know what I'll do, I'll go up to my local slimming club and I'll join up. I'm sure I've got few pounds to lose by their standard. So I went there and I stood on the scales and the woman said, 'Right. We'll start half a stone at a time'. And I said 'Sorry?' And I looked down at the scales and they said I was two stone three pounds over weight myself. And I thought, well who says that I should be nine stone three? I know what I look like at that weight and it's too thin. So I got a little bee in my bonnet about it, and I felt that I needed to write about it.

I don't write for six people and a dog upstairs in the Royal Court. I write for ITV, because it has a wide audience and a popular audience and I love that. I don't believe writers when they say I don't care how many people watch it. I think, well you should, because what are you writing for? You want to communicate, so isn't it better that you communicate to a few million than communicate to ten, because you're passing your work on. It's a lovely feeling, is that.

Dramas dealing with everyday life are one of the staples of today's television diet. But it wasn't always like this.

On its opening night, ITV's idea of drama was gobbets of Wilde, Coward, and an adaptation of a short story by Saki. Of course, the first night was meant to look classy and to appeal to the great and good. But ITV's first week also brought the launch of its series *London Playhouse*, drawing on the genteel 'well-made' plays that were standard West End fare. It also promised viewers a season of *International Theatre*, which kicked off with Turgenev's *A Month in the Country*, and had Chekhov, Ibsen and plenty more to come. Under the less than reassuring headline 'Classics Needn't Be Gloomy', director John Clements told the readers of an early edition of the *TV Times* that this was a series for 'a really highly educated public'.

The tradition of presenting stage plays would continue, often strongly cast. In the ITV archives of its first decade you can still find such star turns as Sean Connery and Susannah York in *The Crucible* by Arthur Miller, Vivien Leigh in Thornton Wilder's *The Skin of Our Teeth*, and Michael Caine and Patricia Routledge in Harold Brighouse's *Hobson's Choice*. (There is also an extraordinary recording of Associated-Rediffusion's 1962 production of Sophocles' Electra, which was broadcast in the original Ancient Greek – a first and surely a last for ITV.)

British theatre began to change as ITV was learning to walk. In 1956 John Osborne's *Look Back in Anger* opened at the Royal Court. It played to rather more than six people and a dog. And it influenced countless others. Here was the original angry young man, and his voice sent shockwaves through the British stage and British society.

In the 1960 *Armchair Theatre* production of Alun Owen's *Lena, O My Lena*, Peter McEnery played a Liverpudlian student who became obsessed with factory girl Lena, played by Billie Whitelaw.

Before the year was out, Granada put the play on television, hiring ABC's big studio in Didsbury, in the southern suburbs of Manchester, for the job (sadly, no record of it exists). But it would be ABC's own television series, from the same studio, that would revolutionise television drama.

In 1958, ABC hired Canadian Sydney Newman to produce its series of single plays, *Armchair Theatre*. Newman had seen Osborne's play, and been affected by it. He had also seen much of what in the USA is still regarded as the 'golden age' of TV playwriting, which brought hard-hitting and gritty dramas to their small screens in the Fifties. Sydney Newman later remembered how he took on the job:

When I arrived in England the drama on the air largely was not talking to its audience. The upper classes didn't give a damn about it, and yet here were the plays written by Terence Rattigan, Noel Coward, et cetera, about lovely upper class people and 'anyone for tennis' situations. And here was this massive public buying television sets and not really seeing anything about their own lives. So when I took over Armchair Theatre, *I made up my mind that I would talk to my audiences. My audience were working class people, and the best way to touch them was to dramatise their lives, not the 'anyone for tennis' set, And to do that it required original writing.*

Above: William Sylvester and Jill Bennett in *Other People's Money*.

Newman once said that most people wouldn't go to the theatre if you gave them free tickets and beer at the interval. The mainstream stage had nothing for them. And while *Armchair Theatre* put on plays like those in the West End, it would remain equally out of touch. Newman went out to find writers, who could drag his series away from the safe ground it had previously occupied.

He met Liverpudlian Alun Owen at the London theatre where his latest play was running – a dense and chewy theological drama of impeccable dullness. Alun Owen:

He said, 'Saw your play, Owen. Why don't you write for television? If Shakespeare were alive, that's what he would be doing. What would you like to write, Owen?'

Opposite page:
Joan Plowright and Ronald Lacey in *The Secret Agent*.

Owen became one of the best of *Armchair Theatre*'s writers. At a time when actors – whether stage or screen – were expected to speak in well-modulated tones, he began to write in the voice of his native city. It was a bold step, and it met with some serious opposition.

The day after transmission of Owen's *No Trams to Lime Street* in 1959, Newman was summoned by Howard Thomas, the Managing Director of ABC. Next to him was C.J. Latta, the American executive from Warner Bros. who had secured the finance for ABC. Newman could tell from their faces that they weren't happy. Latta complained that he hadn't understood a word of Owen's play. Newman, the Canadian, tried to see off Latta, the American, by assuring him that while the Liverpudlian accent was tough for them to understand, no British viewer would have had any difficulty. Latta was unimpressed.

> *My chauffeur is English, and he didn't get it either. You tell those actors next time to speak f***ing English.*

Newman and his writers didn't waver. Owen's *Lena, O My Lena*, which was in *Armchair Theatre*'s 1960 season, was perhaps his best play. Some would say it was one of the best of all television plays. Owen based it on his own time in a Salford factory. Peter McEnery played a Liverpudlian student who became romantically obsessed with factory girl Lena, played by Billie Whitelaw.

> *'I think you're lovely and real and beautiful and real and real and...'*
>
> *'What are you going on about, of course I'm real. Here, feel... Don't kiss me so hard love, you'll bang my teeth.'*

Colin Blakely (left) and Peter McEnery in the *Armchair Theatre* presentation of Alun Owen's *Lena, O My Lena*.

Billie Whitelaw later recalled the boldness of her line, so unusual for television at that time in the way the idea of breaking her teeth undercut the romance of the scene. Like Lena, the writing was real – or at least, far closer to reality than anything that had been seen before Newman arrived.

Ted (later Lord) Willis was another television writer who recognised the importance of *Armchair Theatre* under Newman.

This 1959 ITV presentation of Merton Hodge's *The Wind and the Rain* featured (left to right) Barry Foster as John Williams, Alan Bates as Charles Tritton and John Stratton as Gilbert Raymond. The play was directed by Peter Wood.

It had enormous impact on social attitudes. Because you were able with increasing boldness as writers, actors, producers to present problems of human relationships on the screen to millions of people. It made people understand that they weren't alone in having those problems, and that it wasn't really so terrible to talk about them.

Owen was more down to earth.

I suppose it was revolutionary in so far as you had to have a revolution to get freedom. In television it's the accidentalness of daily life that is poetic and

revealing and truthful. That's why I wanted to write for television.

There was no shortage of the accidental in *Armchair Theatre*. Like most early television it went out live.

The great majority of the output of ITV's first years was never recorded – it went straight from camera to control room to transmitter. Television was not expected to have an after-life. And Equity, the actors' union, was suspicious of recording. How would they make sure that their members were paid properly for each transmission? If a repeat of a drama was required, the production team would simply set the whole thing up again and perform it live for a second time.

Much of what was recorded at the time employed the crude technique of pointing another camera at a monitor screen showing the live pictures as they were aired – not exactly hi-tech production, and not high quality either.

And live performance didn't just mean live for the actors. Camera moves, vision mixing, technical work on the floor, lighting, microphone boom operation, special effects and sound cues all had to happen on time. (Or not, as the case may be). No retakes, no edits, no second chances.

Armchair Theatre increased the risks by trying to break the conventions of television direction just as much as it broke the conventions of television writing. The cameras, heavy machines with rotating fixed lenses (these were days before the advent of the zoom) were to move, pushing into the drama, instead of sitting back as though they were stuck in seats in the theatre stalls. This approach to presentation was dynamic, but difficult. In *Lena, O My Lena* there is a bold tracking shot across the studio, in which a studio technician's hand, and the cable he is feeding out as the camera moves, are clearly visible.

In other recordings from the period there are plenty of fluffed lines, and missed cues. In one programme, there is a silence of twenty seconds

Opposite page:
Sir Michael Redgrave starred in the Arden Winch play *The Return to the Regiment* in 1963.

Above: John Hurt as the flamboyant self-proclaimed 'stately homo' Quentin Crisp in Philip Mackie's *The Naked Civil Servant*, an award-winning biographical drama from Thames in 1975.

Tim Roth made a memorable screen debut as articulate skinhead Trevor in David Leland's *Made in England*.

while an actor fumbles for his words.

Quite how common these rough edges were is hard to determine, given how little from the period survives. One benchmark might be ATV's warhorse *Crossroads*, which continued for years to record programmes in two long takes, one each side of the commercial break. Their 'as live' recording became notorious for wobbly sets, emergency ad-libs and botched business. Once, all television may have been like this.

Even the *Crossroads* cast never had to get themselves out of the problem that afflicted one live episode of *Armchair Theatre*. The 1958 play *Underground* was an ensemble piece about a small group of survivors of a nuclear disaster. Their own disaster came when actor Gareth Jones died on camera during the performance. The other members of the cast thought he had only fainted under the lights, and filled in until the director Ted Kotcheff cut away. The commercial break that came conveniently soon after gave Kotcheff two and a half minutes to reallocate the supposedly sick actor's scenes and lines. Only after the play ended did the other actors find out that he was worse than sick. It was television's most extreme example of the show going on.

Whatever the glitches, even tragedies, Newman's *Armchair Theatre* was both influential and popular. Never before – whether on stage, on radio, or on screens big or small – had there been such an outlet for new plays dealing with the experience of ordinary people. Between autumn of 1959 and summer of 1960, *Armchair Theatre* was in the top ten for 32 out of 37 weeks. In April 1960 the series presented Harold Pinter's *A Night Out*. It drew the biggest audience of any programme that week, estimated at nearly six and a half million. (It was greatly helped by sensationalist press coverage and an 'adults only' warning because one scene featured a character who was a prostitute). Pinter's play *The Caretaker* was running in the West End at the Duchess Theatre at the time. It would have had to sell out for thirty years to match that single television audience.

We take it for granted now that television drama should deal in the warp and weft of common experience. But it took *Armchair Theatre* to set the pattern. The series didn't always aim high, and it didn't always achieve what it aimed for. But it made it possible for writers to approach television as a serious medium for serious work.

Sydney Newman was poached by the BBC in 1963, the first senior television figure to make the journey in that direction. He made the BBC's *Wednesday Play* the outlet for the next generation of new dramatists.

But ITV continued to produce single plays that stand in the first division of television drama. Philip Mackie's *The Naked Civil Servant* (1975), dramatising the life of Quentin Crisp, and starring John Hurt as 'one of the stately homos of England'. Jack Rosenthal's *The Knowledge* (1979), featuring the trials and tribulations of aspiring black taxi drivers in London, with an unforgettable performance by Nigel Hawthorne as their examiner and nemesis. And David Leland's *Made in Britain* (1983) with Tim Roth frighteningly intense as an articulate skinhead. All examples from the top drawer.

In the last year ITV has presented 23 single and two-part plays. As in all things, the very best come along rarely – but *Dirty Filthy Love*, the award-winning drama about a sufferer from Tourette's Syndrome written by Jeff Pope and Ian Puleston-Davies, may be up there. There are fewer single plays than in Newman's day, but the writer's voice is not dead.

Above: Michael Sheen with Shirley Henderson in *Dirty Filthy Love.*

Below: His face covered with chocolate powder, Mark (Michael Sheen) meets Stevie (Anastasia Griffith) in *Dirty Filthy Love.*

7

ADVENTURES ON SCREEN AND OFF

Above: Patrick Macnee as John Steed with Honor Blackman as Cathy Gale in *The Avengers* episode *Man with Two Shadows*.

Above: Raymond Francis as Chief Detective Superintendent Lockhart in Associated-Rediffusion's *Murder Bag*.

Anything can happen in the next half hour!
Stingray title sequence

THE SINGLE PLAY was not the only type of drama with which ITV attracted audiences in its first years.

Its first continuing serial opened the second day of transmission, at 10.45am. *Sixpenny Corner* was about the lives of newlyweds Bill and Sally Norton, and the garage Bill managed in the town of Springwood. Patricia Dainton, who played Sally, shared the cover of the first *TV Times* with American comedienne Lucille Ball.

In 1957, ITV broadcast its first evening soap, set among the staff and patients of Oxbridge hospital. After a six-week trial as *Calling Nurse Roberts*, it became *Emergency – Ward 10*, and ran twice weekly for a decade. To modern eyes, the extant early scraps of ATV's serial look slow-paced, and could charitably be called inconsistent in their standards of acting and writing. The emergencies are banal compared to today's taste for prosthetic body parts and technicolor gore. Oxbridge's medical standards must have been excellent, though, as it boasted an unfeasibly low fatality rate. And someone must have been convinced by its depiction of life and love on the ward; the ITA's annual report for 1959-1960 referred to it as a 'documentary-drama'.

It had a police series, Associated-Rediffusion's *Murder Bag*, which began in 1957 and two years later spun off into the better-known *No Hiding Place*. Raymond Francis played the lead as Chief Detective Superintendent Lockhart in both series. Faced with week after week of learning his extensive lines for live performance, he would often hide them on cards around the set – one week a cameraman replaced a card

Opposite page: Patrick McGoohan as secret agent John Drake in *Fair Exchange*, a 1964 episode of *Danger Man*.

Above: Jack Webb (left) as Sergeant Joe Friday and Ben Alexander as Officer Frank Smith in NBC's *Dragnet*, an imported series first seen on ITV in 1955.

Below: The 1965 cast of CBS's *Gunsmoke* – (front) James Arness and Amanda Blake with (behind, left to right) Glenn Strange, Ken Curtis, Roger Ewing and Milburn Stone.

that he had hidden in a drawer with one saying 'you will dry now.' He did. *No Hiding Place* was also notable for attempting to mount car chases in studio, and for featuring Johnny Briggs, who would later play Mike Baldwin in *Coronation Street*.

And from the off, ITV imported American drama series on film; police series *Dragnet*, and Western *Gunsmoke* (which first went out in Britain as *Gun Law*).

None of this was unique. The BBC, anticipating the arrival of ITV and getting its retaliation in first, had its own filmed police series, *Fabian of Scotland Yard*. It had a soap opera, the terminally drippy *The Grove Family*, who were supposed to be lower-middle class but in BBC style sported accents straight out of RADA – all except the stock caricature granny. The Queen Mother thought them 'so real' – possibly the only person in Britain who did. Once ITV was on air, the BBC even imported American Westerns.

But ITV had another string to its bow – something the BBC couldn't match. It was a huge hit with all the family, and gave the channel its first truly memorable theme tune. Riding through the glen, with his band of men, feared by the bad, loved by the good – it was *Robin Hood*.

Once again, it was Lew Grade who ploughed the new furrow with his ITC production company. He had seen American television, where, because of time zone differences across the country, prime-time drama was not performed live, but shot on film for flexible transmission – and even repeats. He saw the potential for generating income through future sales. But Grade had never produced a frame of film before. He was an agent, used to negotiating bookings and taking his percentage. This was unknown territory. Michael Grade:

Lew commissioned Robin Hood *and he went to a board meeting quite early on in the days of ATV and the board said to him, 'Lew, this* Robin Hood *series, you're not doing it are you?' And Lew said, 'Yeah, I've given my word, I've signed the contract. We're making it.' They said, 'But that's the programme budget for the first two years gone on one series! We haven't got any more money!' How Lew talked himself out of that problem I've no idea. But of course* Robin Hood *is still running today somewhere.*

Robin Hood was brought to Grade by Hannah Weinstein, an American radical who had fled America in 1950 as the shadow of the Communist witch hunts orchestrated by Joe McCarthy and the House Un-American Activities Committee fell across Hollywood. She set up a production company in Britain, Sapphire Films. *The Adventures of Robin Hood*, as it is properly called, was their first project.

She was able to employ other blacklisted Hollywood talent in direction, and particularly in writing. The symmetry is neat. In a series of stories about the outlaw robbing to the rich and giving to the poor, many of the writer credits are pseudonyms; behind them are American left-wingers who were in professional hiding because of their own alleged desire to redistribute wealth.

Lew Grade was himself a great fan of wealth redistribution – as long as it was coming his way. For *Robin Hood*, the company devised new ways of working economically. They built sections of walls and doors that could be quickly switched and rebuilt like children's building blocks to create room after room. A couple of cardboard trees on wheels made a forest. This economy did nothing to lessen the appeal of the series.

While some British viewers looked on American imports *Dragnet* and *Gunsmoke* as cultural pollution, *Robin Hood*'s adventures were different. Brian Tesler:

In some odd subconsciously-felt way they were ours. They weren't American shows, they were absolutely British shows, British performers as

Richard Greene starred as Robin of Locksley with Patricia Driscoll as Maid Marian in ITC's *The Adventures of Robin Hood.* The first of 143 episodes was originally seen in the UK on 25 September 1955, and then the following day on the American CBS network.

swashbuckling as Errol Flynn was in the movies. Great stuff.

Robin Hood eventually ran to 143 half-hour episodes. Grade's decision to invest in film production was vindicated when it sold around the world. The series spawned a host of followers, costume adventures set in days when there were wrongs to be righted, damsels to be rescued, and tights to be worn.

Weinstein and Grade soon turned their hand to *The Adventures of Sir Lancelot* (knights in armour), *The Buccaneers* (pirates in seaboots) and *Sword of Freedom* (Renaissance Italians in tights). Lew switched longbow for crossbow with *The Adventures of William Tell*. Associated-Rediffusion pitched in with *The Gay Cavalier*. The Americans at Columbia Screen Gems recognised a sturdy bandwagon when they saw one, and turned young English actor Roger Moore into *Ivanhoe*.

ITV's viewers had fallen in love with the romance of their history. But history was still happening. A Cold War was blowing. Lew Grade's next big hit series took the adventure out of the costume box and into a modern world of intrigue and espionage.

In *Danger Man*, first seen in 1960, Patrick McGoohan played John Drake, a troubleshooting American agent working for NATO. He was a downbeat hero who never bothered with the girl. He wrestled with his conscience and the existential problems of the agent's life, while also being very handy in a punch-up.

He cleared up other people's messes around a semi-fictionalised world, dealing with problems which often sprang from recognisable political tensions between East and West, or the first world and the third world. Troubles in the Soviet satellites, the legacy of post-colonial Africa, drug trading in the Middle East, and post-Suez relationships with oil-rich Arab states all occupied him.

But in reality, with Lew Grade's fingers on the purse-strings, the production didn't go far

Above: M9 agent John Drake (Patrick McGoohan) is on the trail in the *Danger Man* episode *Koroshi*.

Opposite page: Conrad Phillips was the eponymous freedom fighter in *The Adventures of William Tell*.

Below: Patrick McGoohan and Susan Hampshire film a scene for the *Danger Man* episode *Are You Going to be More Permanent?*

beyond the studio at Borehamwood. Scenes were often gratuitously set in whatever film set happened to be standing – places as bizarre as a nunnery or a ballroom. And almost every episode featured a forest, a jungle, or an exotic garden – all shot in the studio greenhouse. The minimal real exterior shooting was done with a second unit and doubles, directed by the then unknown John Schlesinger.

The first season of *Danger Man* ran to 39 half-hour episodes, and made McGoohan a star. Grade wanted to hire him to play the hero of the next adventure he had planned. But McGoohan, a deeply religious man, turned him down. The storylines he saw involved too much violence and too much kissing for his taste. It is widely believed that for the same reason he either turned down, or made it clear he wouldn't be interested in an offer to play, James Bond. Sean Connery got the movie role. For the television series, Grade turned to the actor who had followed *Ivanhoe* by working in Hollywood, playing an English cowboy in the TV series *Maverick*, and another English cowboy in the TV series *The Alaskans*. Roger Moore broke his typecasting by coming home to play 'the famous Simon Templar' – *The Saint*.

John Drake (Patrick McGoohan) fends off an attack by a kabuki assassin in *Koroshi*, one of only two episodes of *Danger Man* made in colour.

The Saint was based on the character created by author Leslie Charteris in a long-running series of books. Moore had tried, unsuccessfully, to buy the screen rights himself. They had sold instead to producers Robert Baker and Monty Berman. Now Grade was backing them – and he was as canny as ever with his cash. Roger Moore:

My agent called and said that Lew Grade wanted me to do The Saint. *So I read a script and I said to Lew, 'Are you sure this is a half hour series?' He said, 'Oh absolutely.' I said, 'It reads very long, this script.' He said, 'Well, you know, we'll shoot a lot more and cut it down and make it nice and fast.' And it really wasn't until we got to the press conference announcing thirty-nine episodes of* The Saint *that Lew said, 'We're going to do thirty-nine hours.' So I said, 'half hours', and the two producers, Bob Baker and Monty Berman, took me out saying, 'It's hour, not half hour.' Well, my*

Ken and Deirdre – the Burton and Taylor of
Coronation Street – tied the knot again in
2005, and drew a bigger audience than
Prince Charles's rival nuptials.

Patrick McGoohan starred as *Danger Man*, before creating the cult classic *The Prisoner*.

Benny Hill surrounded by
showgirls – a classic pose
that came to represent the
politically unacceptable face
of entertainment.

The downstairs contingent of *Upstairs, Downstairs*. Joint creator Jean Marsh is at the right hand end of the front row.

Emmerdale's Amos Brearly (actor Ronald Magill) and Seth Armstrong (Stan Richards). Pub landlord Amos was one of the founding cast in 1972, when the stories were more likely to be about sheep dip and scrapie than steamy sexual intrigues.

The uniquely imitable Alan Whicker in a typically exotic location.

One of the quieter moments in the groundbreakingly chaotic Saturday morning show *Tiswas*.

Leonard Rossiter's Rigsby raises a characteristically stingy glass in *Rising Damp*.

contract had been worked out for half hours. We made adjustments.

The Saint would become the most durable adventure series of the decade, running from 1962 to 1969. Grade sold it around the world, and it made Moore a huge star. He has clearly forgiven Grade for his attempts to bamboozle him over his fee.

Above: Simon Templar (Roger Moore) and Carmen (Annette Andre) explore a Welsh cave in *The House on Dragon's Rock*, a 1966 episode of *The Saint* directed by Roger Moore.

I had known him for years. He always referred to me as the nephew and I looked upon him as Uncle Lew. He had good taste for what the public wanted. He also had a tremendous sense of humour. He was at dinner once and he was sitting next to a minister who was complaining about the lack of substance in television. Lew mentioned some documentary-type programme and the minister said, 'Well I don't think you could actually call that a factual programme.' And Lew said, 'Well you couldn't call it bloody entertainment either, could you?' He wanted to entertain the public and he did; he entertained us well.

Below (left to right): Ewan Roberts, Roger Moore, Suzan Farmer and Laurence Payne in *The Convenient Monster*, a 1966 episode of *The Saint.*

Turning *The Saint* into a family entertainment required some changes from the original books. Roger Moore:

The Simon Templar we portrayed on the screen was a little more gentle than that in the books. We were not allowed, because of television codes, to do what Simon Templar had done in print, which was carry a knife called Betsy up his sleeve. He was not averse to using that. We played him rather more purist.

On the small screen he became the epitome of old-fashioned good manners. He tackled corrupt rulers, crooked lawyers, gangsters, spies and saboteurs, anywhere in the world where the locals were easily recognisable national stereotypes and a pretty young woman needed help.

On screen, he lived a glamorous life of fast girls and beautiful cars, which took him from his Savile Row tailor to the sophisticated haunts of the international playboy. In one episode, *The Ex-King of Diamonds*, he pitches up on the Cote d'Azur, to find all life's essentials on hand. 'Golden sunshine, golden money, golden girls,' he says to the audience as he eyes up a couple of bikini-clad lovelies and pulls out a wad of cash to hire a suitably swanky set of wheels.

On screen, the Saint's life was lavish. But off it Grade was still keeping his customary close eye on the budget. The character travelled round the world, but the production rarely strayed far from home, and the exotic locations were supplied on the cheap. Look again at the 'Cote d'Azur' and you see the boxy buildings of the Elstree studio offices, unconvincingly disguised by slapping a few French language signs around. And are those golden girls sporting goose-pimples with their skimpy swimsuits? Roger Moore:

Everything was shot on the backlot. And if it were the Bahamas, they would put 'Bahamas' up on the screen, put a rubber palm tree in front of me and as long as the rain wasn't backlit, you couldn't see that I was freezing to death. There was very little glamour attached to it.

Britain changed massively in the mid-Sixties. It became the country of the Fab Four and Mary Quant, George Best and Twiggy, World Cup Willie and the Pill. We were, briefly, the trendiest place on earth.

In the words of one pop song of the time, 'England swings like a pendulum do.' But the Saint never swung with it. His manners were unsullied by a decade of social revolution. He became as square as he was debonair, and his sharp suits turned into the uniform of yesterday's man.

By the end of the decade, and the end of his small screen run, in the episode *The Portrait of Brenda*, he was a tourist in the new scene.

'In Swinging London, whether you want to buy mauve hipsters or rent a man's chest wig for the weekend, the King's Road, Chelsea, is the place to look.'

Opposite page:
Roger Moore poses as the famous Simon Templar in a 1962 publicity portrait for *The Saint*.

Above: Ian Ogilvy took on the role of Simon Templar when ITC revived Leslie Charteris's literary hero for *Return of the Saint* in 1978. The most lavish television series ever made by ITC, over half of its 24 episodes were filmed on location in the South of France, Spain and Italy – a far cry from the original series' rainy Borehamwood backlot.

John Steed (Patrick Macnee) and his original partner Dr David Keel (Ian Hendry) investigate sabotage at a medical research laboratory in the 1961 *Avengers* episode *The Deadly Air*.

Looking was all he was doing. He was an observer, not a participant, in the changing times.

By the mid-Sixties, there was another, sharper adventure series on the block. For many viewers, it still epitomises the times. Forty years on, it still has a strong cult following. It was Steed and Mrs Peel; bowler hat and jumpsuits; the cream of English manhood and the cat who looked like she got it. It was stylish and sexy. It was *The Avengers*.

But it didn't start out like that. Few series in television history have gone through so many changes in style, in casting, and in production.

It began in 1961 with a title and a character. The title came from Sydney Newman, a contribution to ABC before he left for the BBC. The character was the eponymous hero of another ABC series, *Police Surgeon*, played by Ian Hendry. The series hadn't been a great success, but the company liked Hendry's action style and on-screen persona. Writer Brian Clemens was charged with finding a new vehicle for him. With a change of name, the police surgeon was transplanted as David Keel. Clemens and fellow writer Ray Rigby put him in cahoots with cynical and ruthless secret agent, John Steed, played by Patrick Macnee, and the pair were set to fight crime in a series of studio-bound stories.

There was none of the fantasy and fun that would characterise later series. No mad scientists – just a hard underworld that reflected the London of the Krays and the Richardsons. There were stories about counterfeiting, blackmail, and diamond smuggling. It was a grubby and grimy world and it looked it.

It looked particularly grubby and grimy because after a few live episodes production of *The Avengers* moved onto videotape. This had none of the gloss of film. The picture quality betrayed its use every time. But it gave television producers a much cheaper way of recording programmes in the studio. By the early Sixties Lew Grade was virtually alone in sticking to film in drama production.

Denis Forman has described video tape as 'rather more important than the invention of sliced bread'. It revolutionised television. But not all at once. It arrived in Britain in the late Fifties as a way of recording live performances – one take, no edits. No-one even knew that it was possible to edit it, until a Granada engineer took an oscilloscope, a razor blade, and a roll of sellotape and physically cut and spliced it, as a film editor would. It worked – but in the late Fifties and early Sixties it wasn't a popular idea. Tapes cost over a hundred pounds each – a huge figure then. They only made economic sense if they were wiped and reused. But cut a tape and its life was over.

(A huge proportion of the programmes made on video in the Sixties and Seventies were erased, their tapes reused. Sometimes the decisions about what would be worth preserving seem baffling. LWT mounted a huge production for the first manned moon landing in 1969. Arguably the most staggering event in human history. You'll look in vain for it in the archive library. It has been wiped. But the person who decided that programme had no future life did think it was worth keeping the musical gem *Cliff Richard Goes to the Movies*, in which Hank Marvin dresses for one number as Carmen Miranda, with full fruit salad on his hat. History may thank him one day – but not yet.)

There were also huge aesthetic arguments against editing. Television, it was said, would lose its essential excitement if, instead of giving the edge of live performance, it chased the false perfection of edited programmes. The public were supposed to love the slips and errors, and feel sympathetic towards performers who had to get out of difficult situations.

Seventeen of the first series of twenty-six *Avengers* episodes were laid down on video as live performances (with a few pre-recorded exterior scenes inserted). Most were wiped.

Hendry left at the end of the first run. The series that had been conceived as his vehicle would have to survive without him.

In the second series, Steed moved centre stage. With a rather better wardrobe, superior manners and expensive tastes, he began to turn into the memorably imperturbable dandy.

He was given two female co-stars. Six episodes featured night-club singer Venus Smith, played by Julie Stevens. Seventeen

Honor Blackman kick-started *The Avengers* when, as anthropologist Cathy Gale, she became Patrick Macnee's co-star from the fourth episode of the series' second season. In *Death on the Rocks*, Steed and Cathy tracked down a gang of diamond smugglers.

featured the character who kick-started the *Avengers* cult – Honor Blackman as Cathy Gayle. With a PhD in anthropology, a black belt in judo, a smart line in leather suits and kinky boots, there had never been a television heroine like her. Certainly, none had battered their way through villains like she did. Honor Blackman:

Cathy Gale was an intelligent, independent woman. It was the first time that they'd allowed a woman to be the intellectual equal of a man, and then she had the nerve to be able to defend herself, which was the last bastion of the male. So it was very exciting. It was a mould-breaking moment, before the feminist movement really got going.

Blackman herself had to brave a male bastion when she went to learn judo.

It was so funny because when I went for my very first lesson it was with the Robinson brothers down in Panton Street in their basement. I fondly imagined that I was going to have a private lesson. I went down the stairs into this basement and the smell of the sweat and the noise of everyone breaking falls and banging the floor was tremendous. There was nowhere for me to change because they'd never had a woman before. So there was a funny little curtain and they put me behind there. It was lined with grotty jock straps and I thought, well this is really charming.

Above: In October 1965, viewers were introduced to Steed's new companion, Mrs Emma Peel (Diana Rigg) in *The Avengers* episode *The Town of No Return*.

Blackman had walked into a man's world. She had also walked into a man's part. Her first few scripts had actually been written before Hendry announced he was leaving. The producers, not wanting to waste them or their own money, changed David Keel to Cathy Gale. A television legend was born.

Blackman stayed for a third series. The plots were largely straightforward espionage stories, but they were written and executed with wit, and there was a sexy interplay between the two lead characters that the viewers loved. *The Avengers* became a fixture in the top twenty

programmes.

Then Blackman left the programme to play Pussy Galore in the James Bond movie *Goldfinger* (a move alluded to in her last episode when Steed tells Cathy that he hears she'll be 'pussyfooting around the Caribbean'). The producers faced the difficult task of replacing the chemistry between Steed and Cathy Gale. They had a new character in mind – Emma Peel. The name was dreamed up as a variation on M Appeal – short for M(an) Appeal – which made it very clear what they required of the new actress.

Tara King (Linda Thorson) gets to grips with Shaw (George Innes) in *Bizarre*, the final episode of *The Avengers*, broadcast in September 1969.

Eventually they found their star; Elizabeth Shepherd. But after one episode was shot and cut together, it was clear that it wasn't working. According to director Peter Graham Scott, she was taking the whole thing too seriously, and the chemical reaction with Steed simply wasn't there. A replacement was needed. Enter – after extensive screen tests – Diana Rigg.

This new relationship was hotter than ever. And the programme went from strength to strength. With the American export market in mind, it moved from video to film. By the fifth series it was being shot in colour – an irrelevance to ITV's black and white transmissions, but important in the American market. The budget was pushed to ten times that of the Cathy Gale era. Mrs Peel swapped black leather for bright catsuits. And the stories were refreshed, too. More action, more locations, more imagination in plotting, more wit.

It was now the classic series of memory, in which a picture-postcard version of Britain concealed sinister plots; where fantastic conspiracies lurked behind the facades of castles, of gentlemen's clubs, of hi-tech industrial complexes, even in chocolate-box villages where roses grew round the door.

Murdersville, an episode in series five, opens at the sort of country pub that summer dreams are made of. But a figure reels out of the door, and is shot dead on the village green – the whole event causing nothing but wry amusement to the two domino-playing locals sitting and supping outside. The real and very pretty village of Aldbury in Hertfordshire is cast as the fictitious Little Storping In The Swuff – the sort of comedy name that indicates nothing is to be taken too seriously. The entire population turns out to be part of a lucrative assassination ring. Mrs Peel's investigations lead to her being dipped like a witch in the village pond, and imprisoned in the local museum by being locked in a chastity belt. She alerts Steed with a coded message in which she pretends they are married, and after he rides to the rescue the good end happily, the bad unhappily.

It is stylish, silly, fast and flirty – the essence of the best of *The Avengers*. Writer Brian Clemens:

> *The Avengers is like a Hitchcock movie, and I've always been a great admirer of Hitch. He was able to scare the pants off you, and then relieve it with a laugh. And I like to think we did that in* The Avengers.

But the party was nearly over for *The Avengers*. Diana Rigg left after the fifth series, to follow Honor Blackman as a Bond girl. Television wouldn't see her like as a heroine again for years. Her replacement was young Canadian actress Linda Thorson as trainee agent Tara King. Where her predecessors had been cool and knowing, she was a wide eyed innocent (though she carried a brick in her handbag to deal with the rough stuff). Steed now had a protegee, not an equal, an ingénue in the place previously occupied by a pair of divas. The chemistry was not the same.

Plenty of fans will say that the stories were better than ever. The pair of music hall veterans who murdered their victims with violent slapstick. The episode in which games were used to murderous end – snakes and ladders with real snakes, for one. But public enthusiasm waned, crucially in America. When the series was dropped there, ABC could no longer afford the expensive colour film production. *The Avengers* died in 1969 – but it died laughing.

While *The Avengers* had its success, Lew Grade was still in the adventure market. He backed Gerry Anderson's puppet series *Fireball*

John Steed returned to ITV in October 1976 with a new pair of associates, Purdey (Joanna Lumley) and Mike Gambit (Gareth Hunt), in *The New Avengers*.

Opposite page: Number 6 (Patrick McGoohan) and Number 12 (John Castle) plot the destruction of a super computer in *The General*, the sixth episode of McGoohan's enigmatic 1967 series *The Prisoner*.

XL5 (the first British TV programme to be sold to a major American network), *Stingray* and *Thunderbirds*. Young viewers loved them. Now they are grown up, many of them still do. They were futuristic and full of impressive explosions. As the *Stingray* title sequence told the watching world, 'Anything can happen in the next half hour!'

And, increasingly, anything could and did happen in Grade's ITC action adventures.

Below: The puppet heroes of Gerry Anderson's 1965 series *Thunderbirds* – (left to right) Brains, Lady Penelope, Scott Tracy, Jeff Tracy, Virgil Tracy, John Tracy, Tin-Tin Kyrano, Alan Tracy and Gordon Tracy.

Patrick McGoohan had been lured back for a further run of *Danger Man* in the mid-Sixties. As it ended in 1966, he came to Grade with his own production company to get backing for a series he created. Its seventeen episodes became a cult hit to rival *The Avengers* as a TV legend.

The series was *The Prisoner*. McGoohan played the lead himself, a secret agent now confined in a mysterious village (the already fantastic Italianate setting of Portmeirion in Wales) and referred to as 'Number Six'. Every week 'Number Two' would try to break him down – for reasons and ends which were never any clearer than anything else in the programme. The Prisoner would prevail, only to be confronted by a new

Above: Number 6 (Patrick McGoohan) with the Watchmaker's daughter (Annette Andre) in *The Prisoner* episode *It's Your Funeral*.

Below: Number 6 is given the option to lead or leave the Village in *Fall Out*, the concluding episode of *The Prisoner*. ATV switchboards were jammed after this episode was screened in February 1968.

Number Two in the next episode. But who was Number One?

Quite what went into the programme is impossible to say. What came out was a rich mixture of allusions to Freudian theory, dream analysis, drug culture, Kafka, European art house movies, Cold War espionage, and everyone's deep rooted fear of being chased along a beach by a giant balloon. The cocktail worked. It became required viewing for millions. Lew Grade left McGoohan to get on with it. Roger Moore :

All Lew knew was that it had viewers, it was successful. And I would say, 'What's going to happen?' and he'd say, 'Don't bloody ask me. McGoohan won't tell me how it's going to end.'

The eagerly awaited ending at last brought the Prisoner into direct confrontation with the hooded figure of Number One. McGoohan ripped away the hood to reveal a gorilla mask, then ripped away the gorilla mask to reveal his own face. There was a great deal more maniacal laughter than is usually considered polite. Depending on your point of view, the whole thing was either enigmatic, existentialist or just plain exasperating.

ATV's switchboard was jammed by viewers unsatisfied by this final revelation. Nick Elliott:

I think if we put on The Prisoner *now, it would be called cult or niche broadcasting. You might be very successful with it, particularly on Channel Four, but my judgement is that a programme like* The Prisoner *was too mysterious, too gobbledegook, too hard to understand to relate to an audience. If there were only two channels, and you were Lew Grade, you could probably put on what you wanted, and people would watch it because there was no multi-channel television for them to switch off. We can't do that today.*

Grade and ITC pushed further into the realms of fantasy. In *The Champions*, they asked viewers to buy the idea of three secret agents who were given superpowers by a mysterious Himalayan healer. In *Randall and Hopkirk (deceased)* they asked them to believe in a private detective agency in which one of the partners was a novice ghost. Most audaciously of all, in *Department S* and its spin-off *Jason King*, they sold the flamboyantly camp King as a heterosexual sex symbol.

These programmes rarely went down well with the critics. But they made a good profit, and won Grade the Queen's Award for Exports.

In 1970, Grade embarked on his biggest production to date – at the time, the most expensive series ever made for British television. *The Persuaders!* was to be like *The Saint* squared. Two maverick playboy crimefighters, one American, one English. This time, Grade was aiming for the big time. There would be real foreign locations, not back projection and backlot mock-ups. And he wanted two major league stars – Tony Curtis and Roger Moore.

But Curtis had never made a television series, and regarded it as a step down from the movies. And Moore simply didn't want to do any more television, and said no to the offer. It was going to take all of Grade's powers of persuasion. And more besides. Roger Moore:

> *I walked into Lew's office, he shoved a cigar in my mouth and he said, 'I've sold* The Persuaders!' *I said, 'But I don't want to do it,' so he put the cigar in my top pocket and he waved a cheque and he said, 'This is what I'll give you'. Eventually the cheque got to the right size and we did it. Not that I'm mercenary.*

Curtis, too, was persuaded, and soon learned that he might have to revise his opinion of the small screen.

Roger Moore:

> *When we started* The Persuaders!, *Tony still*

Above: In *The Champions*, Nemesis agents Richard Barrett (William Gaunt), Craig Stirling (Stuart Damon) and Sharron Macready (Alexandra Bastedo) are endowed with super powers by a lost civilisation in Tibet.

Below: Private detective Jeff Randall (Mike Pratt) is assisted by his ghostly partner Marty Hopkirk (Kenneth Cope) in *Randall and Hopkirk (deceased)*.

had a slight hang up about doing television, having come from movies. And we were filming outside the Hotel de Paris in Monte Carlo and two or three tourist buses pulled up outside the casino and disgorged thousands of Spaniards. And Tony got very edgy and he said, 'Oh Goddam tourists, they all want my autograph.' But they swept him to one side and came up the steps to me saying, 'El Santo, El Santo' [the Saint]. And then Tony realised how powerful television was. They recognised me from a distance, because they saw television every week in their homes.

The Persuaders! was a likeable series that knew it was fun. It is debatable how much intentional humour was in the stars' dodgy fashions and dodgy dance moves on dodgy Eurodisco floors. But no programme in which the protagonists' first meeting results in a fist fight over the issue of how many olives should be put in a particular cocktail could be accused of taking itself too seriously.

It sold internationally, and was popular in Britain. But Grade had staked a large budget to go into the peak-time arena in America. The show didn't do badly scheduled against top opposition. But it didn't do well enough. It was shunted out of its slot before the first run was over. There wouldn't be a second.

Instead Grade went on to spend and make huge sums on his epic series *Jesus of Nazareth*. Two stories are told about it. They are contradictory, but between them express a truth about his approach to making entertaining drama. In the first, he sees rushes of Jesus and his followers. 'Why,' he asks, 'are there only twelve Apostles?'

That was Grade the showman. The second is Grade the money man, as told by the director of *Jesus of Nazareth*, Franco Zefferelli. 'The television screen is only small,' he says. 'How are you going to fit twelve Apostles into the shot? Couldn't you do it with six?'

Showmanship and a return on the investment are still the twin, and often opposed, aims of most television production.

Below: Roger Moore (as Lord Brett Sinclair) and Tony Curtis (as Danny Wilde) in *To the Death, Baby*, an episode of *The Persuaders!*

Opposite page:
With a budget of around £100,000 per episode, ITC's 1971 action series *The Persuaders!* was the most expensive British television series made to that date. It was superseded by two later ITC series – *Space:1999* (£125,000 per episode) in 1975 and *Return of the Saint* (£150,000 per episode) in 1978.

8

DRAMA PAST AND PRESENT

Above: George Cole as Arthur Daley (right) and Dennis Waterman as Terry McCann in Euston Films' *Minder*.

BRIAN WALDEN:
You've really outlined an approval of what I would call Victorian values. The sort of values, if you like, that helped to build the country throughout the 19th Century. Now is that right?
MARGARET THATCHER:
Oh exactly. Very much so. Those were the values when our country became great, but not only did our country become great internationally, also so much advance was made in this country.

Weekend World, LWT, 16 January 1983

Above: James Lloyd as PC Steve Hunter in *The Bill*.

E VER SINCE THE avuncular George Dixon of Dock Green police station first greeted the BBC's viewers in 1955, the police drama has been one of television's classic formats.

They have been a constant in ITV's schedules. Chief Detective Superintendent Lockhart was ITV's top cop of the Fifties and Sixties in over three hundred cases in *Murder Bag*, *Crime Sheet* and *No Hiding Place*. His good-mannered approach to detective work was replaced in the early Seventies by the hard men of Thames's *Special Branch*. More recently the tough Glaswegian *Taggart* and the flawed genius *Cracker* (not in the force, but of it) have taken their place in the line-up of memorable detectives. For audiences today there is David Jason's portrayal of the dogged and downbeat Detective Inspector Frost in *A Touch of Frost*. Or there is the weekly helping of street crime and personal melodrama that is Thames Television's *The Bill*, now past its twentieth anniversary and still performing strongly. Paul Marquess (Head of Drama at Thames):

The Bill *is told entirely from the police's point of view. We are very rarely*

Opposite page:
John Thaw as Chief Inspector Endeavour Morse and Kevin Whately as DS Robbie Lewis in Carlton's *Inspector Morse*, based on the novels of Colin Dexter.

Superintendent Adam Okaro (Cyril Niri, right) and PC Steve Hunter (James Lloyd, back) in *The Bill*.

there when nasty things happen. We turn up just after the murder, the assault, or the rape, which is a brilliant pre-watershed crime format. The Bill *is the biggest drama production in the world. We shoot about sixty per cent on location, where the soaps might do five per cent. So we might have three units shooting at any one time. What you are getting is a flavour of real policing in the real street in contemporary London. And I think that goes right back to* The Sweeney.

The Sweeney, another Thames production (through its subsidiary Euston Films) was one of the few drama series that can justifiably be said to have changed television when it was first screened in 1975. It's easy to forget now that Seventies drama was a prisoner of the studio walls. But Thames had decided that studio drama was getting too expensive. Investing in lightweight 16mm film cameras and shooting out on location looked like a better deal. The result was a police series that for the first time got out and among the action on the streets.

It put the viewer in the middle of the police raid on the villain's home, or the armed assault on the wages van. It became famous for its car chases. But the budget barely stretched to the cars they needed. They used Fords, which the manufacturer donated. And they used cheap second-hand Jaguars – partly because real criminals liked their acceleration, and partly because they found they stood up to being rolled over and generally ill-treated.

It wasn't just the action that made the series stand out. When John Thaw as Detective Inspector Jack Regan pinned a villain against the wall and announced, 'We're the Sweeney, son, and we haven't had any dinner!' we knew we had seen nothing like it before. TV cops had come a long way since George Dixon controlled the underworld with a sharp word and a clip round the ear; they had started moaning about the job, drinking after hours, and having domestic lives. But none had ever put themselves about like this.

Regan was the policeman who refused to play it by the book in the days before that became a cliché of every detective series; caught between the need to get results on the streets, and follow the instructions of his superiors.

Cast, writers and crew spent time with real policemen – and real villains – to give their work the ring of truth. The title for the series came from a Flying Squad officer who told them that they referred to themselves in rhyming slang as Sweeney Todd. The research paid; Regan and his sidekick detective Sergeant Carter (Dennis Waterman) emerged as flawed and fallible; they drank, they swore, their private lives were a mess, they fought dirty and they didn't always get their man.

In the end Regan's unorthodoxy was too much. He was set up on a false corruption charge, and though finally exonerated, the hostility he

They're the flying squad and they haven't had their dinner – DI Jack Regan (John Thaw) and DS George Carter (Dennis Waterman) in Euston Films' *The Sweeney*.

Opposite page:
In *The Professionals*, CID detective Ray Doyle (Martin Shaw, left) was partnered with former SAS and Parachute Regiment hero William Bodie (Lewis Collins, right) in CI5, a covert agency specialising in criminal intelligence. The series ran to 57 episodes although one episode, *Klansmen*, was considered unsuitable for transmission and withheld from the original ITV screenings between 1977 and 1983.

had been shown by his superiors ended the series and his fictitious career. He went out in typically unrepentant mood, when refusing an offer of his old job back.

> *'And what do you bunch of bleeding double-dyed hypocrites want me to do now? You want me to crawl back to work and be terribly grateful I didn't get nicked for something I didn't do. Well, you can stuff it!'*

That last episode, *Jack or Knave*, written by Ted Childs, made it clear that other officers had been on the take. This was edgy material for a police series – but again it was a reflection of reality. There was stink in the air at the time. The police were beginning to investigate their own, and finding evidence of endemic corruption. It was a time of industrial unrest, of vociferous and sometimes violent support for extreme policies on both wings of politics, of international terrorism. If the police were embroiled in their own misdeeds, who was going to maintain order?

In 1977, LWT presented a new action series that offered a straightforward solution to dealing with bombers, gunmen, and other hard-case extremists. Shoot them.

The Professionals was devised by Brian Clemens in response to LWT's request for a counterpart to the BBC's popular American import, the buddy-cop series *Starsky and Hutch*. Clemens came up with a covert security force, CI5, which was answerable to no-one,

Above: CI5 controller George Cowley (Gordon Jackson) with his two toughest operatives, Bodie (Lewis Collins, right) and Doyle (Martin Shaw, left) in LWT's *The Professionals*.

and could use the most extreme measures to get rid of problems. Its two leading operatives, Bodie and Doyle, were the most testosterone-charged double-act on television. Brian Clemens:

> *The critics reviled it. Two tough guys acting tough, being tough, carrying guns and shooting people, and driving cars fast and skidding round corners – everything every young man wants to do. Maybe it was leaning a bit too macho, but women liked it too, because the boys were attractive. What* The Sweeney *didn't have, but we had, was glamour.*

Martin Shaw was cast as Doyle, the liberal ex-policeman whose sharpshooting prowess saw him drafted, somewhat reluctantly, into CI5.

His partner Bodie (no comfortable Christian names used in this series) was an amoral ex-SAS man and mercenary. Somewhat surprisingly, the fine-boned Anthony Andrews was the original choice, but when the two actors were found to look too alike on camera, Lewis Collins replaced him.

The difference between the two characters meant they often disagreed. Brian Clemens:

That's used in several episodes where Bodie wants to charge in and Doyle says, 'Hold on, there are kids in there,' or whatever. That brings a certain tension between the characters, otherwise they're just two guys agreeing with each other. You need that. They've got to be nitro and glycerine; they've got to strike sparks off each other.

Kevin Whately (left) as Neville Hope and Tim Healy (right) as Denis Patterson in *Auf Wiedersehen, Pet*, Dick Clement and Ian La Frenais' comedy drama which originally aired on ITV between 1983 and 1986.

They were volatile, but they were also close, closer than they ever were in any of their failed relationships with women. Some people have interpreted their macho buddiness as a homoerotic partnership – an idea later put to humorous effect by the Comic Strip on Channel 4. Clemens has a quick answer to anyone the question of whether they were gay: 'They weren't.'

Macho men in motors couldn't solve every problem in society. The optimism of the Sixties had evaporated as the Seventies brought industrial strife. The Heath government had been toppled in a climate of strikes and inflation. Labour had managed little better.

It was in this climate that Thames produced *Bill Brand*, an eleven-hour series by left-wing writer Trevor Griffiths. It charted the path of young working-class lecturer Brand (played Jack Shepherd) from local politics to Westminster. Its caustic view of the machinery of government made it one of the strongest serious dramas of the decade.

But drama could also reflect current affairs in a lighter mood. The Labour government fell to Margaret Thatcher's Tories. Recession and new industrial realities bred two classic ITV dramas that captured the period with wry humour.

Auf Wiedersehen, Pet, first seen in 1983, traced the fortunes of a gang of builders who had followed Norman Tebbit's advice to get on their bikes – or in this case on the ferry to the Hook of Holland – to find work on a German building site. The Central series, with scripts by Dick Clement and Ian La Frenais, helped to turn a bunch of little-known actors, Timothy Spall, Kevin Whately, Tim Healy, Pat Roach, Chris Fairbank and Jimmy Nail, into some of the best-known faces on television.

Minder began life with a well-known face. Thames seized on it as a new vehicle for Dennis Waterman, after the end of his run as Carter in *The Sweeney*. Writer Leon Griffiths had spent afternoons in North London drinking clubs where many of the clientele were duckers and divers, making a living on the edge of the law. His first version was a tough gangland film, but he revised it to focus on two of the characters, a second-hand car dealer with a dodgy lock-up, and his bodyguard.

The series began in 1979, but took a while to find its feet and its tone. When it did, Waterman's Terry McCann began to be eclipsed by his boss, Arthur Daly. As the scams and the slang became more comical, and the minor characters fleshed out, it was Arthur, played by George Cole, who became an unlikely national favourite.

Cole had previously played the spiv, Flash Harry, in the St Trinian's films, and there was a similar air of harmless humour to his Arthur. But it was unusual to see a criminal – albeit one who was never caught red-handed – become a popular hero. Perhaps it was Arthur's essential uselessness – whether getting paid for a deal in worthless roubles or landed with a crate of Japanese 'Scotch', and always in mortal fear of his unseen wife, 'Er indoors. Perhaps it was that in harsh economic times, many people felt that rules were there to be bent in order to make a living.

Arthur became popular enough for George Cole to become the television advertising

Above: Geordie trio Denis (Tim Healy, right), Oz (Jimmy Nail, centre) and Neville (Kevin Whately, left) relocated to Düsseldorf in the first series of *Auf Wiedersehen, Pet*.

Below: Used car dealer and opportunist Arthur Daley (George Cole, centre) with his right hand man Terry McCann (Dennis Waterman, left) and Dave the barman (Glynn Edwards) in *Minder*.

Opposite page:
Jean Marsh as chief
housemaid Rose Buck (left)
with Nicola Pagett as Lord
Bellamy's daughter Elizabeth
(right) in the first series of
LWT's *Upstairs Downstairs*
in 1971.

voice for a building society. *Minder* ran until 1994 – long after 'Er indoors at Number Ten Downing Street had left the building.

All these dramas, whatever their differences of tone and style, reflected the present back to their audiences. But the social problems of the Seventies had another effect. People began to look for comfort in a gentler past. ITV had a string of hit costume dramas. Its first great success came in 1971, with *Upstairs Downstairs*. The series was devised by actresses Jean Marsh and Eileen Atkins. Jean Marsh:

Above: The cast members
portraying the Bellamy's
domestic staff – including, at
the head of the table,
Gordon Jackson (centre),
Jean Marsh (left) and Angela
Baddeley (right) – record a
scene for the first series of
Upstairs Downstairs.

We were both very keen to write about something that we were passionate about. And we were both passionately angry about our pasts, that we hadn't been educated up to standard and that both sets of parents were working class. So we thought we would write in the immediate past and that, of course, was very easy to research. Eileen's father had been an under butler in a posh house. My mother had been a maid of all work in quite a big pub, and from that she took a step up in the world and became a bar maid. So we started to write about servants and it gelled when Eileen found a marvellous photograph of an aunt standing by a horse drawn bus with lots of other servants. And we thought they were obviously going on their trip out, so we would write each servant a story. But we gave that up because

Upstairs Downstairs –
the residents of 165 Eaton
Place in the 1920s:
(back row, left to right)
Daisy (Jacqueline Tong),
Ruby (Jenny Tomasin),
Edward (Christopher Beeny),
Rose Buck (Jean Marsh),
Mr Angus Hudson (Gordon
Jackson), Mrs Kate Bridges
(Angela Baddeley),
Frederick (Gareth Hunt) and
Lily (Karen Dotrice); (middle
row, left to right) Georgina
Worsley (Lesley-Anne
Down), Lord Richard
Bellamy (David Langton),
Virginia Bellamy (Hannah
Gordon) and Captain James
Bellamy (Simon Williams);
(front) Alice Hamilton (Anne
Yarker) and William Hamilton
(Jonathan Seely)

that meant it was finite, only the amount of servants that got on the bus. But by then we had settled on doing a version of below stairs. In fact, that's what we called it first of all: 'Below Stairs' or 'Behind a Green Baize Door'. It was only going to be about servants. And then gradually, of course, we realised servants had to serve somebody.

The series was taken on by London Weekend Television, under head of programmes Stella Richman. As it developed, it was shifted back the Edwardian era. Characters were developed above and below stairs; the Bellamy family in residence, and the surrogate family of domestic servants marshalled by the punctilious butler Hudson, and the formidable cook Mrs Bridges.

But half way through production, Richman was replaced by Cyril Bennett. He had no enthusiasm for the inherited project, and the programmes were left to gather dust. Michael Grade was later to join LWT:

Cyril told me this incredible story. There was a hole in the schedule on a Sunday at ten o'clock and Cyril said to his planning people, 'Have we got anything on the shelf?' and the planner said, 'Well there's this drama series that nobody's seen and nobody wants, but it's been sitting on the shelf for a year.' So Cyril said, 'What's it called?' He said, 'Oh, I don't know, it's called Upstairs Downstairs *or something stupid, you know', and Cyril said, 'Well the network's short, we'll stick it in, we'll get rid of it.' Cyril didn't even watch it and it went out with no publicity, no trails. We used to have to wait a week for ratings in those days and eventually the ratings arrive a week later and London Weekend's ratings, as usual, are somewhere below the toilet, right down there, and suddenly at ten o'clock there's this enormous jump. Cyril said, 'What's happened here?* Upstairs Downstairs, *get me the tapes.' So he sits down and he watches the tape, and says 'This is not bad. Anyway, we'll see what happens next week.' Next week, the ratings were even higher. The audience found it by osmosis; nobody quite understands how the audience smelt that show.*

Above: Hudson (Gordon Jackson) and Mrs Bridges (Angela Baddeley) ponder a problem in the kitchen. At the end of the series, the pair married and left to run their own guest house.

There was no button that that series didn't press. It appealed to everybody, and anybody with a television from the age of thirteen, fourteen, to ninety would enjoy it. It had no social barriers, no class barriers, it was a show made with real conviction and integrity. The British audiences loved the dual hierarchy, the hierarchy above stairs and the hierarchy below stairs and the two things mirroring each other.

Below: Downstairs at Eaton Place in the first series of *Upstairs Downstairs.*

According to Jean Marsh, who played the house-parlourmaid Rose, the dual hierarchy sometimes spilled over into the studio.

There were very rarely real tensions between actors. But there were arguments about the fact that the downstairs people had delicious food; there was actually a practical kitchen in the set and Angela Baddeley, who played the cook, would fry sausages and eggs and things. And we loved that. Whereas the upstairs people had game that had gone off by the time they got it.

It was painted with glycerine to make it look good. So they used to come over to our set and say 'Can we have some bread and cheese?' And we would sometimes say no!

The series never pretended that all the characters were happy – far from it. There were rumblings, rebellions and unfulfilled desires both above and below stairs. The Bellamys and their servants suffered war, they endured loss of life on the Titanic, they argued over votes for women. But neither the real family nor the surrogate family ever cracked. They got through. Jean Marsh:

I think that the people like drama in the past because we've recovered from all the tragic things that happen. So Upstairs Downstairs *showed the First World War, but we knew that the war ended happily – well, we won. We showed the Suffragettes – one committed suicide, they chained themselves to railings, they were force fed. But we knew it ended happily because women got the vote.*

In 1975, towards the end of its run, the series tackled the 1926 General Strike. Downstairs, opinions were divided, and arguments heated.

Granada's *A Family at War.*

Upstairs, Master James had fun volunteering to drive a bus. But when order was restored on the streets, it also returned to the house. They didn't all have to agree, but they could still get on with each other. To an audience experiencing strikes, terrorist violence, and newspaper headlines asking 'Is Britain manageable?' this was a massively attractive resolution.

But the attraction of the past began to turn into something that was quite contrary to Jean Marsh's idea of *Upstairs Downstairs*.

People have, in the main, quite an odd reaction to the past. I heard it a lot when Upstairs Downstairs *was on. They admired something that I find absolutely extraordinary. It was in a sense nostalgia, but it was a misplaced nostalgia. It wasn't nostalgia for the truth, and it's encapsulated by that extraordinary saying,*

'People knew their place'. Why would that be good? So you are born in a place, then you don't move. What's the point of education? You don't go up, you don't go down, you don't go sideways. You don't change your profession. You do what your parents did. To know your place is an odd thing to be pleased about. And it's not only posh people who think it. Working class people think things were better then when they knew this. Things weren't better then. They weren't better for anybody. It made sense to a duke who inherited millions of acres maybe, but even he wasn't allowed to be anything else.

ITV knew the past wasn't perfect and this was reflected in two series John Finch created for Granada. *A Family at War* (1970-72) spent fifty hours following the lives of middle-class Liverpudlians the Ashtons during the Second World War. *Sam* (1973-75) was a thirty-nine part series about life in a pre-war Yorkshire mining village. Neither would have had audiences yearning to hop into a time machine to experience the events first-hand.

But as the decade progressed, the past became glossier. The days of Empire returned, all of pomp and circumstance, doling out the lives and loves of the upper classes. *Edward VII; Lillie* (Langtry); *Jennie, Lady Randolph Churchill.*

The Ashton's eldest son David (Colin Campbell) was a docks worker who joined the RAF in Granada's *A Family at War.*

Above and opposite page: Anthony Andrews as Lord Sebastian Flyte (left) with Jeremy Irons as Charles Ryder (right) in *Brideshead Revisited*.

Below: Laurence Olivier as Lord Marchmain and Diana Quick as Julia Flyte in *Brideshead Revisited*.

As the Eighties approached, nostalgia became the national trait. We dressed in Laura Ashley's take on Edwardian style. Mister Kipling's exceedingly modern cakes were offered up as traditional artefacts. The Prince of Wales espoused ersatz neo-Georgian architecture. People restored the Victorian fireplaces they had once ripped out – some even rebuilt outside toilets. We read *The Country Diary of an Edwardian Lady*, then bought the notelets, the tea tray, and the pot pourri. Mrs Bridges became a food manufacturer's brand name. Heritage became an industry.

And the Tories lectured us all on Victorian values. If we would only turn back the clock, everything would be alright.

In 1981, Granada aired its adaptation of Evelyn Waugh's novel *Brideshead Revisited*. It presented the past on a scale more sumptuous than ever seen before. At a time when the BBC were reining in their expenditure on drama, it was a thirteen-part broadside across the airwaves.

Set in the decades before the war, its first episodes deal with the seduction of Oxford undergraduate Charles Ryder, first by Sebastian (and his teddy bear) and then by the rest of the aristocratic Marchmain family. From strawberries and fine wine under a summer sun, to Charles's first sight of their grand house (the glorious and perfectly cast Castle Howard), the viewer was equally beguiled. With Olivier and Gielgud the senior members of a stellar cast, with a plot that travelled from Oxford to London to Venice to Paris to North Africa to New York, with John Mortimer's script, and first class production and direction, there was a glow of luxury that enthralled all of its many viewers. Even the score was one of the most memorable ever heard on television.

At thirteen hours long (it takes longer to watch than to read the book) you knew that

Above: Tim Pigott-Smith as the sadistic, bigoted police officer Ronald Merrick in *The Jewel in the Crown*, Granada's 1984 adaptation of Paul Scott's *The Raj Quartet*.

Opposite page (top): Art Malik as Hari Kumar and Susan Wooldridge as Daphne Manners in *The Jewel in the Crown*.

Opposite page (bottom): Charles Dance (centre, as Sergeant Guy Perron) and Geraldine James (as Sarah Layton) in a scene from *The Jewel in the Crown*.

this was meant to be a series to savour, not to guzzle. Nick Elliott:

A lot of drama was stretched far too long in those days. If you try to look at them now, they often seem very slow. Now, we always try to cut everything down to be as fast as possible, for reasons of competition and the world we live in. I can remember bosses of mine in those days saying, 'Oh you ended that far too short, you should have gone on for weeks more,' because they just wanted to keep a good thing going. We just can't do thirteen parts of anything nowadays, people wouldn't stay with it.

Even in its day, television's *Brideshead* lost some of its grip over the second part of its run, and Olivier did deliver the longest death in the history of television drama (over half an hour). But for infatuated viewers it was the closest television ever got to Sidney Smith's definition of heaven as eating *paté de foie gras* to the sound of trumpets.

By then the stock in trade of the historical series were so familiar that Granada could parody them all in their comedy series *Brass*. John

Stevenson and Julian Roach's scripts scored hit after hit – from *Upstairs Downstairs* to *Brideshead*, via Kathleen Peyton's *Flambards* (Yorkshire 1979) and Catherine Cookson's *The Mallens* (Granada 1979) and, it seemed, every grimy urchin, cruelly wronged factory girl, ruthless mill owner, political dreamer, headstrong young heiress and downtrodden flat-capped lackey who ever crossed the small screen.

But Granada had another expensive historical treat planned – *The Jewel in the Crown*. Denis Forman was behind the project to dramatise Paul Scott's Raj Quartet, a cycle of four novels covering events in the closing years of British rule in India. It would mean five months shooting on location in the sub-continent. At the time Forman began to

consider it, no Western crew had ever filmed there. The undertaking was so ambitious that they tried it out with an adaptation of another single Paul Scott novel, *Staying On.*

When *Staying On* was a success, Forman pressed on with planning the series. The four novels were written with a complicated interwoven storyline. Forman pinned up huge pieces of wallpaper and started to break the events down into a linear narrative. He hired Ken Taylor to write the script and Christopher Morahan to produce. They assembled a large and top-quality cast, and tackled the logistical problems.

But there was one other obstacle: money. Its fourteen episodes were budgeted at just under half a million pounds each. Sales at home and abroad would cover half of that. They needed a sponsor – usually they turned to the big American oil companies. But this time they weren't interested. Denis Forman:

The Americans, over the years, sponsored all our major drama productions. I went to them with Jewel *and they said, 'No, I'm terribly sorry, India's a far off country of which America knows nothing. We've never been a colonial power, there's not a single element of this show that could be of any interest in America'. So I was like, 'Oh hell'. However, we ploughed on and made two episodes. We were committed, I think, to spending about four million and nobody really knew this except me.*

Forman kept the expenditure secret from his board, who would undoubtedly have taken a prudent line and pulled out early to cut their losses.

I knew the oil companies so well and I had such conviction about Jewel *that I knew when I showed this to Herb Schmertz of Mobil, that he would respond. So I showed these two episodes in the preview theatre at Golden Square and I must tell you, I heard his plaudits at the end with some relief. They put up all the money and it's been more successful in America than in any other country.*

The Jewel in the Crown stands as one of the finest of all television dramas. Its great sweep of narrative deals with complex and challenging subjects – racism, violence, and the collapse of Imperial confidence. It moved in uncomfortable territory.

But all around it, history continued to be presented with a comfortable glow. John Major's vision of Britain, expressed in a speech in 1993, encapsulated a wishful continuity between past and future:

Fifty years on from now, Britain will still be the country of long shadows on county [cricket] grounds, warm beer, invincible green suburbs, dog lovers and old maids bicycling to Holy Communion through the morning mist.

His words could almost be a director's notes on a shooting script for the Central Television programme which saw John Thaw's return to the police force. *Inspector Morse* came to ITV in 1987.

The values of heritage became the values of mainstream contemporary drama. The programme's leisurely pace, high production values, and quality casting gave it an air of nostalgia, even though it was set in the present day. Morse recognised the good things in life – intellect, high opera and a pint of proper English beer.

In one episode Morse and Sergeant Lewis sat supping outside a country pub in the village of Aldbury in Hertfordshire. *The Avengers* had visited the same village to turn it into Little Storping In The Swuff, and had looked with a knowing smirk at the picture postcard prettiness of Olde England. When Morse went back to shoot there, it was taken at its picturesque face value. And the Jaguar Morse drove wasn't abused like all those Jaguars in *The Sweeney*. It was, like the series itself, a treasured classic.

Opposite page (top): Kumar (Art Malik, left) is framed by Merrick (Tim Pigott-Smith) in *The Jewel in the Crown.*

Opposite page (bottom): Elderly missionary Barbie Batchelor (Peggy Ashcroft) in *The Jewel in the Crown.*

Above: John Thaw (left) and Kevin Whately (right) as Morse and Lewis of the Thames Valley Police with Morse's beloved 1960 Mark 2 red Jaguar in Carlton's *Inspector Morse*. The series ran from 1987 to 1993 but was followed by regular one-off specials until the airing of the final episode, *The Remorseful Day*, in 2000.

Above: PC Nick Rowan (Nick Berry) makes a call in Yorkshire's *Heartbeat*.

Opposite page: DCI Jane Tennison (Helen Mirren) in Granada's *Prime Suspect*, created by Lynda La Plante.

9

SISTERS DOING IT FOR THEMSELVES

I wrote about what I wanted to see on TV.
                                    Kay Mellor

IN 1980, VIEWERS of LWT's latest police series saw Detective Inspector Forbes chase a suspect through a multi-storey car park. So far, so typical of the time. But Inspector Forbes was grimly hanging on to a handbag. The series was *The Gentle Touch*, and for the first time a woman had been put into a position of power in what was a traditionally male preserve, both on television and in life. Lynda La Plante appeared as an actress in one episode:

> *Jill Gascoigne as Maggie Forbes was a major breakthrough with audiences. To accept a female officer, and believe her. Just her simply carrying a show, leading a show, was different.*

Maggie Forbes' stories were not concerned solely with her job. There was equal focus on her home life as a widowed mother with a son

Above: A copper with a difference – DI Maggie Forbes (Jill Gascoine) in LWT's *The Gentle Touch*.

to bring up. There had always been dramas which concentrated on what are usually termed 'female' subjects: family, relationships, domestic life (the equally stereotypical 'male' subjects include cars, guns, sport and work). These were the backbone of the soaps. They had been turned into some of ITV's most memorable drama. Certainly, nobody who had seen

Andrea Newman's torrid and tangled *Bouquet of Barbed Wire* (LWT, 1976), an everyday story of incestuous suburban folk, was going to forget it in a hurry. But something new was happening. As society changed, drama was changing with it.

The Gentle Touch had been created by a male writer, Terence Feely. But a new wave of women writers would achieve the full emancipation of television drama. Lynda La Plante led the way. Her first big success, in 1983, was *Widows*, in which a group of women pulled off an armed robbery which their dead husbands had failed to carry out. Led by the 'well 'ard' Dolly Rawlins, played by Ann Mitchell, they were far tougher than the usual wives and molls that female actors were allowed to play in crime shows. And they carried the plot. Nick Elliott:

This page: Frank Finlay as publisher Peter Manson in LWT's *Bouquet of Barbed Wire*, a tale of a father's incestuous love for his daughter. Sheila Allen (above) played Manson's wife Cassie, and Susan Penhaligon (below) was the daughter Prue.

When I saw Widows *I just thought, well that's a clever idea, I wish I'd thought of that... I didn't really think it was the start of a whole 20 years of feminist drama, the same as I did with* Prime Suspect.

With *Prime Suspect* in 1991, La Plante pitched a female officer into a male murder squad. Maggie Forbes had dealt mainly with domestic cases, and worried most about balancing the demands of work and home. La Plante's D.C.I. Jane Tennyson, superbly played by Helen Mirren, had to battle to lead the investigation, battle to get the respect of male officers senior and junior to her, and battle to get a result in the case. Sometimes you could hear 'the message' coming through the script like a voice through a loud-hailer, but it was a message worth shouting out. Nick Elliott:

I can remember Lynda's script arriving, and you used to have a committee of ten representatives of ten companies. It was very seldom that anything was more than seven for and three against. I remember that script getting ten-nil, and everyone just said, 'Wow, that script is fantastic.' And of course it was fantastic, for the dialogue and the excitement of a tense thriller. But actually it was a great shock to us to read a script that had a woman policeman taking on a whole work area full of men. It's extraordinary today to think that was radical but it was... Actually I think, today, ballsy women taking on male colleagues is so overdone it's kind of tiresome. But it was incredibly fresh and different in those days. And of course to some extent it reflected Lynda herself, who is a dynamic, bolshy

woman in her own right. And it was her experience. She was an actress in drama, and drama was male.

Helen Mirren (as DCI Jane Tennison), Tom Bell (as DS Bill Otley, centre) and Craig Fairbrass (as DI Frank Burkin, right) in the original two-part *Prime Suspect* serial shown in 1991. Three further serials and a series of three single dramas followed.

Drama production is no longer such a male preserve. What used to be a boy's club has been opened up to allow female members. And their influence has changed what appears on screen. Nick Elliott:

Television today is 50/50 controlled by women, and I would say that television drama has for years been more dominated by women than men. It wasn't back in the Eighties. Because women play such an important part in television drama decision making now, the idea of strong women characters, following Widows *and* Prime Suspect, *first was refreshing and gradually almost became overplayed. It was almost like, 'Well, we have done the criminal, we've done the police – oh well, they could have doctors or they could have scientists.' So you were putting strong female characters into almost every role you could find. We put a woman in the Fire Brigade in* London's Burning, *which was completely ludicrous at that stage. There were no women in the fire brigades – complete fallacy. But we put women into men's jobs everywhere. It was the big idea and like all big ideas when you over-use them, it gradually became a bit jaded. But I think that was Lynda's significant achievement.*

Helen Mirren collected the BAFTA Best Actress award for her role as DCI Jane Tennison in *Prime Suspect* on three consecutive years. Creator Lynda La Plante scripted the first and third *Prime Suspect* serials, but all of the other instalments were written by men: Allan Cubitt, Paul Billing, Eric Deacon, Guy Hibbert and Guy Andrews.

The movement towards strong female characters, and stories intended to have appeal to female viewers, has not slowed. Drama producers and commissioners have to recognise who constitutes their audience. Nick Elliott:

We do more female-oriented drama than we used to and perhaps than we should do. That's probably because they do turn it on. You can bash your head against a brick wall trying to make dramas for 16 to 34 year old males. You can make endless dramas for them, but if they only want to watch football or videos and Playstation, there's no point. Now, women do like television drama, they control the switches in many households. So you make it for a receptive audience.

We have had conscious attempts to do more male drama. But I'm not sure what a very male drama is. Maybe it's about business or something, but most drama about business is deadly dull. We do guns and violence for boys occasionally. We actually thought that Footballers' Wives *would appeal to men, but it doesn't very much. It appeals to young working class women. So you can aim at these chaps but they soon suss out that* Footballers' Wives *is not about football, it's about frocks and sex and things, and leave that to their girlfriends.*

Women writers didn't simply change the gender of leading characters.

They brought female characters who had previously been at the margins of drama and of society to centre-stage. In 1995, Kay Mellor's *Band of Gold* turned street prostitutes into leading characters for the viewers to care about. This was remarkable at a time when the only press stories you read about prostitution were based solely on the point of view of residents wanting to keep their kerbs clean. It took a change in Mellor's own perception to write it:

Kay Mellor's *Band of Gold* focussed on the lives of a group of Bradford prostitutes – including (left to right) Anita Braithwaite (Barbara Dickson), Rose Garrity (Geraldine James) and Carol Johnson (Cathy Tyson) – who became involved in the investigation of the murder of a young mother. The original six-part 1995 serial was followed by a sequel serial and a short series, *Gold*, in 1997.

The very first thing that made me want to write Band of Gold *was driving through Bradford. We were going to a party and we took a short cut through a fairly notorious lane for prostitution. I was looking out, the way you do, thinking – might see a prostitute when we're driving up here, it would be interesting, being a writer. What I wasn't prepared for was seeing this figure of a prostitute in the distance, and as we got nearer she bobbed down and peered in the car and it was almost like somebody had punched me in the stomach because she was so young – I would say 14, 15, she had that kind of lovely young skin. She was younger than my daughters, and I remember thinking, 'Whose daughter is she, whose sister is she, what is she doing out here on the lane selling her body?' It disturbed me.*

I got to the party, I couldn't stop thinking about it. I remember it got to

Above: The girls go to work on the lane in Kay Mellor's *Band of Gold*.

Below and opposite page: Appropriately named gardeners Rosemary Boxer (Felicity Kendal, right) and Laura Thyme (Pam Ferris, left) investigate murder most English in *Rosemary & Thyme*, a Carnival Films production for ITV.

about quarter to twelve and we drove back, drove all over looking for her, couldn't find her anywhere. We stopped somebody, another working girl, and said there was a young girl on the lane. And she went, 'Oh, that will be Tracy, she's gone down to Birmingham.' I said 'Is she all right?' she said, 'Oh no, she's got pimp problems.'

So that was it really, started my brain going, and I went back up there several times to try and find her again thinking she might come back but she obviously stayed in Birmingham. It didn't occur to me really to write it, funnily enough. I just thought I should give up writing and go up there and try and help these young girls that were on the lane.

Neither Mellor nor La Plante have shied away from showing violence and its effects in their work. Indeed, the nature of male violence towards women has been part of their subject. It's a difficult balance to strike: show too little, and the attempt to depict how repulsive violence is will be diluted. Show too much, and it can be gratuitous – even exciting to some.

It can sometimes seem that there is a war between the sexes being acted out in today's murder mysteries. Serial murder stories have taken many of ITV's programmes into increasingly bloody territory. Sex and violence – so often nonsensically roped together by campaigns to clean up television – are becoming ever more familiar companions. But this kind of blood and guts doesn't suit every programme. Some of ITV's murder mysteries are on their best behaviour. *Poirot*, *Midsomer Murders* and *Rosemary & Thyme* are cosier affairs altogether. Nick Elliott:

There's a tradition of Agatha Christie and murder as just a sort of parlour game. I have introduced Rosemary & Thyme *and even a sort of young person's* Rosemary & Thyme

called Murder in Suburbia. *We wouldn't want them to get too grisly.* Rosemary & Thyme *has a dead body under every rhododendron bush, and even I sometimes say that the actor whose wife had just been killed didn't seem terribly grief stricken. We don't take it that seriously. People reading Agatha Christie books aren't taking it seriously, it's a detection game. And it is a different world from the world of serial killers.*

Nothing succeeds in British drama like a murder. You've got perfect shape at the beginning, the middle and the end. And by and large you've got an upbeat ending. The murderer has been trapped and arrested and sent to prison. And it's all done and dusted and it's the shape that people like their dramas in. It's very tempting to do only murder dramas because you know you won't go far wrong.

David Jason was 1950s Kent farmer Sidney Charles 'Pop' Larkin in Yorkshire's *The Darling Buds of May*, which made Catherine Zeta Jones (as Larkin's eldest daughter Mariette) a household name. The series was based on the books of H.E. Bates – his son Richard was the series' executive producer and his great granddaughter, Daisy May Bates, appeared as Mariette's baby son John.

Sunday night has become the home to another type of entirely bloodless programme. They portray nostalgic versions of the Fifties and Sixties, the very years in which Sydney Newman pioneered television playwriting with a grittier voice. They are as comfortable as a warm bath. And they have been some of ITV's biggest hits of recent years.

The programme that set the trend was *The Darling Buds of May*. Yorkshire TV's 1991 adaptation of the H.E. Bates novels presented a 'perfick' rural idyll in 1950s Kent. David Jason and Pam Ferris played the Ma and Pa of a family who seemed to manufacture sunshine wherever they went. When they appeared in print in the Fifties, some critics were at first appalled by what they regarded as the immorality of stories of a family living on the edge of the officialdom, rarely bothered by red tape and taxes. If they had appeared in real life in 1991, the *Daily Mail* would probably have run damning headlines, warning its readers about the black-market PAYE-dodging cash-economy family, whose every caper mocked the hard-working honest citizen. But apparently such readers loved this happiest of series as much as the rest of the country seemed to. The appearance of Catherine Zeta Jones in jodhpurs can have done nothing to harm its appeal to the difficult 16 to 34 male audience.

The most successful inheritor of the Sunday sunshine slot is *Heartbeat*.

This time, the sun shines on a rural police station in 1960s Yorkshire. *Heartbeat* is all moorland, period cars, and yesterday's pop music. The clothes, the hair, the make-up and crucially the social attitudes reach the screen through a very modern filter. Keith Richardson is Head of Drama at Yorkshire, where *Heartbeat* is made.

I think people forget that the Sixties wasn't quite perfect. It was never quite that idealistic. But people like to believe it was, and we trade mercilessly on that. It's comfortable viewing, it's not confrontational, we have a cast that appeals to all ages. It's not frightening on a Sunday night.

Nick Elliott:

We totally reinvent the Fifties and Sixties. I mean, I lived in the Fifties and Sixties, and they weren't at all like we portray them. Coronation Street is complete fantasy, based in life in the Fifties and Sixties too, you know. We invent worlds which you can be escapist in. Doesn't mean to say you don't have death and pain and sadness in it. But it's all contained and it's all wrapped up at the end and it's probably going to come out alright at the end. The criminals will be caught. The ill people will get better – not always, occasionally there's death, and then we remember how we like the solidarity of the family around us and the village and the community. Yes – at 8 o'clock on a Sunday night, a lot of us like that very much.

There's not much in these programmes for the critics to get their teeth into, unless to make cheap jokes. They don't need to notice that it takes skill and craft to get these gentle series right. Nick Elliot agrees that they deserve more recognition.

Nick Berry starred as PC Nick Rowan in Yorkshire Television's *Heartbeat* from 1992 to 1998. Based on the *Constable* novels of Nicholas Rhea, the first series of *Heartbeat* was set in 1964 – 13 years later, the villagers of Aidensfield are still suspended in the Sixties.

Of course they do. And it isn't just the press, it's the whole of middle-class society. I always think of my mum, who came from a rather upper class family and used to have one of the early cars in Britain in the twenties and says, 'Well driving round the countryside, dear, was very nice before the oiks got cars.' And I try to think that that's like the middle class attitude of

Above: The cast of Yorkshire's *The Royal* – a medical spin-off from *Heartbeat* – pose in front of St Aidan's Royal Free Hospital in the seaside town of Elsinby near Aidensfield, in reality the Holbeck Road Nursing Home in Scarborough, North Yorkshire.

Opposite page: PC Nick Rowan (Nick Berry) helped to police the North Yorkshire village of Aidensfield in the early years of Yorkshire Television's *Heartbeat*. After Rowan moved to Canada to join the Mounties, he was replaced by PC Mike Bradley (Jason Durr) and then by PC Rob Walker (Jonathan Kerrigan).

journalists: they don't like the fact that people like me are making programmes for a mass audience, and that these oiks have invaded their television channels. And I don't care a penny that they don't like it. If I can get 11 million viewers with Rosemary & Thyme *I know I'm doing my job better than if I put on shows for poncy middle class critics, if I'm honest.*

But ITV's soft Sunday nights are facing a challenge. Nigel Pickard is the Director of Programmes for the ITV Network:

One of the issues for us is that our audience is quite old there. There is a sense of familiarity and they're used to it. But is that where ITV needs to be in three, four, five years time? We've got to start bringing on new drama in there. We have to mix and match with some younger appeal programming as well. I'm not suggesting for a minute that we replace Heartbeat *or* The Royal *and things like that. But how do you complement those shows? And how do you broaden the audience appeal?*

Over 50 years, ITV's drama output has changed radically in style, in tone, in production. It has responded to social forces and to technological advances. It will need to carry on doing so if ITV is to remain the country's favourite storyteller.

CROYDON
MEASURED FIELD STRENGTH CONTOURS (60 kW)

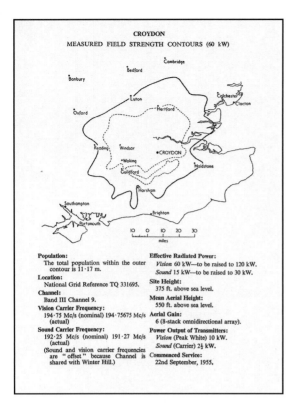

Population:
The total population within the outer contour is 11·17 m.

Location:
National Grid Reference TQ 331695.

Channel:
Band III Channel 9.

Vision Carrier Frequency:
194·75 Mc/s (nominal) 194·75675 Mc/s (actual)

Sound Carrier Frequency:
192·25 Mc/s (nominal) 191·27 Mc/s (actual)
(Sound and vision carrier frequencies are " offset " because Channel is shared with Winter Hill.)

Effective Radiated Power:
Vision 60 kW—to be raised to 120 kW.
Sound 15 kW—to be raised to 30 kW.

Site Height:
375 ft. above sea level.

Mean Aerial Height:
550 ft. above sea level.

Aerial Gain:
6 (8-stack omnidirectional array).

Power Output of Transmitters:
Vision (Peak White) 10 kW.
Sound (Carrier) 2¼ kW.

Commenced Service:
22nd September, 1955.

LICHFIELD
PREDICTED FIELD STRENGTH CONTOURS (60 kW)

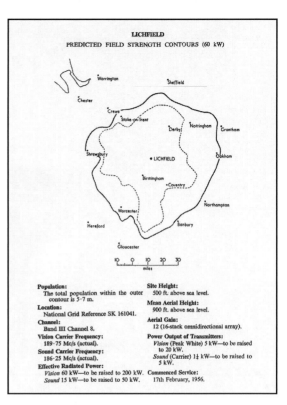

Population:
The total population within the outer contour is 5·7 m.

Location:
National Grid Reference SK 161041.

Channel:
Band III Channel 8.

Vision Carrier Frequency:
189·75 Mc/s (actual).

Sound Carrier Frequency:
186·25 Mc/s (actual).

Effective Radiated Power:
Vision 60 kW—to be raised to 200 kW.
Sound 15 kW—to be raised to 50 kW.

Site Height:
500 ft. above sea level.

Mean Aerial Height:
900 ft. above sea level.

Aerial Gain:
12 (16-stack omnidirectional array).

Power Output of Transmitters:
Vision (Peak White) 5 kW—to be raised to 20 kW.
Sound (Carrier) 1¼ kW—to be raised to 5 kW.

Commenced Service:
17th February, 1956.

WINTER HILL
PREDICTED FIELD STRENGTH CONTOURS (100 kW)

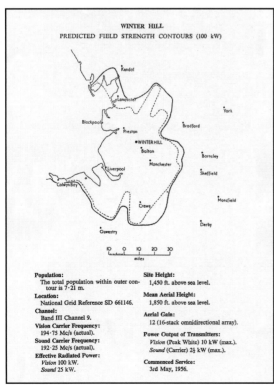

Population:
The total population within outer contour is 7·21 m.

Location:
National Grid Reference SD 661146.

Channel:
Band III Channel 9.

Vision Carrier Frequency:
194·75 Mc/s (actual).

Sound Carrier Frequency:
192·25 Mc/s (actual).

Effective Radiated Power:
Vision 100 kW.
Sound 25 kW.

Site Height:
1,450 ft. above sea level.

Mean Aerial Height:
1,850 ft. above sea level.

Aerial Gain:
12 (16-stack omnidirectional array).

Power Output of Transmitters:
Vision (Peak White) 10 kW (max.).
Sound (Carrier) 2¼ kW (max.).

Commenced Service:
3rd May, 1956.

EMLEY MOOR
PREDICTED FIELD STRENGTH CONTOURS (200 kW DIRECTIONAL)

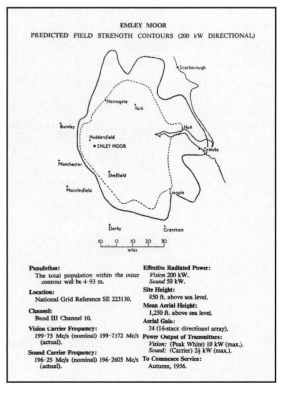

Population:
The total population within the outer contour will be 4·93 m.

Location:
National Grid Reference SE 223130.

Channel:
Band III Channel 10.

Vision Carrier Frequency:
199·75 Mc/s (nominal) 199·7372 Mc/s (actual)

Sound Carrier Frequency:
196·25 Mc/s (nominal) 196·2605 Mc/s (actual).

Effective Radiated Power:
Vision 200 kW.
Sound 50 kW.

Site Height:
850 ft. above sea level.

Mean Aerial Height:
1,250 ft. above sea level.

Aerial Gain:
24 (16-stack directional array).

Power Output of Transmitters:
Vision: (Peak White) 10 kW (max.).
Sound: (Carrier) 2¼ kW (max.).

To Commence Service:
Autumn, 1956.

10
THE DIFFICULT BUSINESS

Above: The campaign that made a catchphrase of 'Can you ride tandem?' – the tea-loving Brooke Bond chimps of PG Tips' long-running commercials.

I was in favour of commercial television from the start as the only way of putting some life into BBC television. I told my people we would come in after the second bankruptcy, as I foresaw a large expenditure before any possible return.

Cecil King, Chairman of *The Daily Mirror*

Below: Metallic Martians laughed at the primitive potato-peeling ways of Earth people in an enormously popular series of commercials for Cadbury's Smash instant mash.

Advertising is the lifeblood of ITV. Selling airtime to advertisers is what pays ITV's way. It's a serious business. ITV sells 1.6 million commercial slots a year, which bring in £1.8 billion – substantially less than the BBC's licence income or what is now paid nationally for subscription channels. It's a competitive market place.

Adverts play to millions of people, time after time. They have embedded themselves in our collective memory. Start to sing an advertising jingle on a crowded bus and someone will complete it (though probably silently in their heads, while they fumble for their mobile to report your behaviour to the police).

Television adverts have taught us to do the shake and vac, to tell Mummy about the honey, to go to work on an egg, and that graded grains make finer flour. They told us what beanz means, that everyone is a fruit and nutcase, to watch out because there is a Humphrey about, and that Martians don't mash real potatoes.

We learned what washed whiter, what eight out of ten owners said their cats preferred, what refreshed the parts that other beers couldn't

Opposite page: Diagrams indicating the measured and predicted field strength contours of the IBA's first four television transmitters – at Croydon, Lichfield, Winter Hill and Emley Moor – in mid-1956.

Above: Commercials for mild green Fairy Liquid told viewers that hands that do dishes can be as soft as your face.

Below: Sharon Maughan and Anthony Head shared a blossoming romance in a series of commercials for Nescafé Gold Blend coffee.

reach; that Esso sign meant happy motoring, that we could be sure of Shell, but that not everything in life was as reliable as a Volkswagen; which chocolate was the crumbliest and flakiest, which melted in your mouth, not in your hand, which helped you work, rest and play, and which you could eat between meals without ruining your appetite.

We rested safe in the knowledge that a Double Diamond worked wonders, that happiness was a cigar called Hamlet, that the lady loved Milk Tray, that he who drinks Australian thinks Australian, that a finger of fudge was just enough, and that hands that did dishes could be as soft as your face.

We loved J.R. Hartley so much that we tried to buy his book *Fly Fishing* for our Christmas stockings. We knew that the Germans said *Vorsprung durch Technik* but never had any idea what it meant. We heard Dvořák and remembered brown bread. We saw Labrador puppies and thought of wiping our bottoms. We knew when we'd been Tango'd.

Over the years we watched not one but two different families grow up on Oxo. We tuned in especially to see romance slowly blossom over cups of Gold Blend. We followed the love lives of Papa and Nicole, and saw her reprise the ending of *The Graduate* by jilting Vic Reeves at the altar to run away with Bob Mortimer.

Established film directors have found adverts a lucrative outlet for their skills. The list includes Lindsay Anderson (adverts for Iron Jelloids and Ewbank carpet sweepers among others); Stephen Frears (Harp Lager and the Co-op); Dick Lester (Smarties and Polos); Joseph Losey (Ryvita and Horlicks); Karel Reisz (Mars Bars and Campari); Ken Russell (Black Magic); John Schlesinger (Eno's fruit salts and Stork margarine); Mai Zetterling (Persil). Joan Littlewood made a series of adverts for the British Egg Marketing Board with Nicolas Roeg as one of her cameramen. Hugh Hudson, Alan Parker, and Ridley and Tony Scott all cut their teeth directing adverts.

We have seen stunning pieces of film-making. Griff Rhys Jones in Holsten Pils ads playing opposite long-dead Hollywood stars. Brilliant animation – Nick Park's hilarious talking animals in ads for electricity, or Richard Williams's ice-skating Cresta Bear desperately trying to stop in the centre of the frame to tell us 'It's frothy, man'. Hugh Hudson's British Airways adverts with hundreds of high-school children manipulating coloured cloths to make the shape of a giant face. Tony Kaye didn't manage to make the lion lie down with the lamb, but to get a dog, a cat and a mouse to curl up contentedly in front of a Real Fire was clever enough.

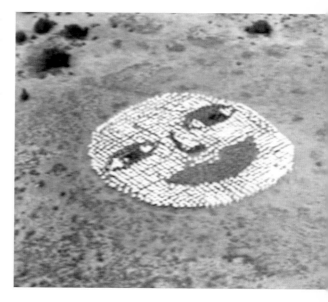

Above: Hundreds of high-school children formed a giant face by manipulating coloured cloths in Hugh Hudson's memorable commercial for British Airways.

We have watched adverts pillage movies, television and the visual arts – sometimes for comic effect, sometime simply ripping them off. We have seen them get indulgent and pretentious on bloated budgets. And we have seen adverts influence the programmes around them. They forced the writers and directors to tell stories in seconds, not minutes; to learn to use a quick image, not windy dialogue, to establish a scene; to cut quickly from shot to shot. Television drama wouldn't have grown up the same way without them.

ITV aired its first advert on its opening night at 8.12 p.m. An eagerly expectant nation discovered that it was not polluted by the message on the airwaves. In fact, as it was Gibbs SR toothpaste that had won the draw to see which ad would lead the way, and as at the time up to a third of Britons didn't brush their teeth, it almost certainly helped to make the country cleaner, not grubbier. 'It's Gibbs SR toothpaste, the tingling fresh toothpaste that does your gums good, too.' So the first voice-over began. That first ad also included the first sleight-of-hand. The block of ice in which the tube of tingling toothpaste appeared in close-up was actually plastic. The producers found that you couldn't read the name through real ice.

Advertisers were paying a premium for time on that first night. The intention was that the

Below: Director Tony Kaye persuaded dog, cat and mouse to curl up together in front of a Real Fire.

Above: From 1957, Mary Holland starred as Katie in a series of adverts for Oxo stock cubes.

Below: ...and all because the lady loves Milk Tray. Gary Myers was the daring 'Man in Black' who braved danger to bring the lady her chocs in a long-running television and cinema campaign.

profits would be donated to charity. In fact, the banquet at the Guildhall cost so much that the evening made a loss. If anyone had been looking for omens, that fact might well have made them worried. They would have been right.

ITV needed to perform. It needed to attract an audience, and to attract advertisers who wanted to sell to them. It was born into a country with a growing appetite for television. In the wave of reconstruction that followed the war, many people were living in new housing. Usually better than anything they had had before, it meant that they no longer had to go out at night to escape their surroundings. And new houses probably also meant higher rent – so there was less to spend on beer and cinema tickets. With companies realising that there was money to be made by renting out televisions, the set in the corner was no longer a middle-class status symbol. It was becoming part of the furniture – ubiquitous enough for dentists to be concerned that prolonged viewing by children lying on the floor, chin cupped in hands, would cause buck teeth.

But nobody knew how many viewers would tune to the new station. By 1955, there were four and a half million television licence holders (and who knows how many evaders?). The BBC's television signal could reach 90% of the population, and the best estimate is that its evening programmes averaged about five million viewers. Some were very popular: *Ask Pickles* (a sort of prototype *Jim'll Fix It*, heavy on winsome infants, jolly pensioners and cuddly pets), *The Grove Family*, *Dixon of Dock Green* and the imported American format *What's My Line?* were big-hitters. But did viewers watch the BBC because they loved it, or because it was all there was? 'Auntie' was complacent. Brian Tesler was then a BBC producer:

We didn't think that ITV would work. I mean, how could it? It was only going to be in three areas, London, the Midlands and the North. It was bound to have crass, vulgar, down-market programming that was going to be interrupted continually by these irritating little commercial jingles. The public would see that, and so it couldn't last. And to people like me, colleagues who had come from university straight to the BBC, the thought of working for the cut-throat, ruthless, commercial television world was pure anathema. So we didn't think it would succeed at all.

Others sounded a warning. Two months before ITV's debut, Brian Inglis wrote in *The Spectator*:

The BBC has been unable to develop valid standards of self-criticism; bubble reputations have remained unburst because there has been no cannon's mouth, no enemy gunners, to explode them. What will happen when the cannon is loaded this autumn?

In his speech at the opening night banquet, Postmaster General Charles Hill expressed his hope that the 'famous elder child' – the BBC – would work alongside ITV 'the lively youngster'. In fact, the BBC did its best to strangle the lively youngster at birth. That very night BBC Radio, the senior service, killed off its popular radio character Grace Archer. Twelve million had tuned in to listen to *The Archers*. As the fictional village of Ambridge reacted with shock, people were seen in the streets in tears. But ITV could hold its own. When an ITN reporter interviewed a policeman on duty outside the Guildhall about the lack of crowds, he gave the response they wanted to hear. 'I would imagine everyone's at home, hoping for the best and waiting for the arrival of ITV Television.'

After the glamour of the gala, the next day was the first day of ordinary business for Associated-Rediffusion. Friday 23 September opened at 10.45 a.m. with the serial *Sixpenny*

Above: Doing the Shake 'n' Vac put the freshness back in a memorable commercial for powder carpet freshener.

Below: A woman disposed of of her unreliable partner's expensive gifts except for the VW Golf in a commercial which was so successful that Volkswagen sold an extra 37,000 cars.

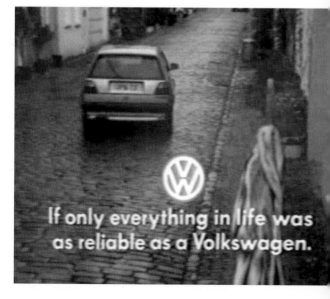

VW

If only everything in life was as reliable as a Volkswagen.

Corner, the thoroughly pre-Womens' Liberation magazine *Hands About the House*, and an interview with an American actress who had just published her autobiography. These programmes were targeted at housewives, and were soon dubbed by one wag 'The opiate of the Mrs.'

After a short programme for toddlers, transmission closed at 12.30 p.m., and opened again at 5.00 p.m. for children's programmes. There were no programmes between six and seven: ITV inherited the BBC's 'Toddlers' Truce', a break intended to allow parents to get their children to bed without distractions. The evening programmes ran from seven to eleven, and included *Take Your Pick*, the imported American cop show *Dragnet*, and the first ITV programme to be built round its star – comedian Reg Dixon in *Confidentially* (the title of his signature song).

Broadcasting was permitted for a maximum of eight hours per day, and slightly less on Sunday, when there was a break from 6.15 to 7.30 p.m., for people to attend evensong. (There was also a rule to forbid children's programmes between 2.00 and 4.00 p.m., so they wouldn't be tempted to skip Sunday School). The BBC had the same rules, but tended to broadcast only five hours per day. There was to be a long-running argument over broadcasting hours. For ITV, more hours represented a chance to sell more adverts and make more profits. For the BBC, it meant more programmes to be funded out of their fixed licence fee.

When ITV opened in London, 188,000 homes were equipped to receive its programmes (older televisions had no facility to change channels – you watched the BBC or nothing). By the end of 1955, it had reached 495,000 homes, as more televisions were sold. The transmitter at Lichfield opened on 17 February 1956, taking ATV (Monday to Friday) and ABC (weekends) to the Midlands. Winter Hill opened on 3 May, carrying Granada (week) and ABC (weekend) west of the Pennines. The sister transmitter to serve Yorkshire, Emley Moor, was delayed until November that year. By the end of 1956, some 2,656,000 homes could tune in to ITV.

It was soon clear that most of them did so, most of the time. It is usually said that ITV was averaging somewhere between 79% (which it claimed) and 65% (which the BBC admitted) of the audience. A poll in March 1956 showed that 60% in London and 58% in Birmingham said they preferred ITV of the two services, against only 16% in either who opted for the BBC. A teacher from an inner-London Secondary Modern school told the papers that the pupils overwhelmingly opted for ITV, and regarded watching the BBC as 'sissified behaviour'. ITV provided every one of the chart of the top 20 programmes in its first full year of broadcasting, 1956, and kept its monopoly until 1963.

More recent academic research has questioned some of these figures, and the data from which they were derived. They may not be taking proper account of the people with older sets, for whom the BBC was the only option. It is difficult to know how many viewers held on to those BBC-only sets, and how many changed them. But even this current and continuing analysis doesn't disguise the fact that the first ITV companies

had no problem attracting viewers, or that the public deserted many formerly favourite BBC programmes *en masse*.

Above: The elaborate graphic of the on-screen Associated-Rediffusion clock, seen only in the London area from 1955.

But attracting advertisers and earning income was a different matter altogether. It soon became clear that the advertising agencies regarded television as no more than a sideline, an occasional extra to the tried and trusted medium of print. The plan was for the ITV companies to sell six minutes of adverts per hour. In practice, they were barely selling half that.

The companies were haemorrhaging cash – and going under. The whole project was on the verge of collapse. It looked as if ITV wasn't going to live to celebrate its first birthday.

Alarm bells sounded everywhere. Redundancies were planned and in some cases implemented. To save costs, Associated-Rediffusion dropped morning broadcasts by Christmas. The four companies lobbied for substantial reductions in the rent they paid to the ITA for use of the transmitters, which would have left the Authority with severe problems in paying for the programme of transmitter construction on which ITV's expansion to other regions depended. ABC tried, and failed, to get out of putting money into the ITN news service.

ATV looked for backing from *The Daily Mirror*. ATV staffers would later tell the story of the day in April 1956 when an empty office was decked out with carpet, furniture and chandeliers. At lunchtime, ATV Chairman Prince Littler greeted the Mirror Group Chairman Cecil King. After he left with his entourage, the men of the studio props and set crew who had brought in the trappings of luxury stripped them out again. The story may or may not be true; what was certain was that King had soon paid out for a 25% stake of ATV. King had once said he was going to wait for the second ITV company to go bankrupt and then buy them out. His decision not to wait that long turned out to be very shrewd.

At Associated-Rediffusion, the newspaper was the problem, not the solution. By July 1956, A-R had lost £2.7 million. It was too much for Lord Rothermere, Chairman of the *Daily Mail* stable Associated Newspapers, who held a 50% share. He wanted out. A-R Chairman John Spencer Wills was made of sterner stuff. He represented the other half of the company, Rediffusion. He was a money man, and he understood the long haul. When Rothermere asked him if he would be interested in buying him out, Wills held his nerve and bought out almost all of Associated's holding at a 25% discount.

The problems at Granada were compounded by the delayed opening

Above: ATV Chairman and theatre impresario Prince Littler.

of their Yorkshire transmitter. Denis Forman:

We went on the air in May 1956. We had been promised two transmitters, but only one was ready. Therefore our audience was about half of what we'd expected. The budget for building the studio and getting the show on the road had been greatly exceeded. It was, I would think, double. And by the first two or three months after we were on the air, there was not much money left. In fact, cash ran out in July '56. Wages were delayed for one week and then the next week after that, and everyone knew what was happening, but this was vociferously contradicted, of course, by the management. We said, 'No, no, no everything's alright, just an administrative hitch,' but we knew there was no money left and it was quite, quite scary.

Within days, Sidney Bernstein told Granada that he had signed a great deal to save the company. How great it was is debatable. It certainly had a significant effect on ITV.

Bernstein had been to see Wills at Associated-Rediffusion. The deal they had struck was this: Granada would make as few programmes as it could get away with – 15% of its output was the figure stipulated in its contract with the ITA. It would pass these on to Associated-Rediffusion, who would also show them and cover the production costs. Associated-Rediffusion would supply Granada's other output (apart from ITN's news coverage), either with its own productions or with bought-in programmes. Associated-Rediffusion would be entitled to nearly all of Granada's advertising revenue, on a sliding scale dropping from 90% of the first million to 85% beyond four million. The deal would run for four years.

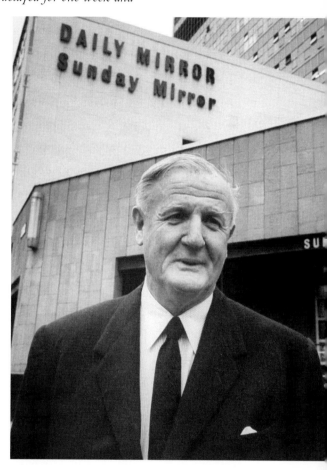

Above: Mirror Group Chairman Cecil King.

How canny was this on Bernstein's part? He saved his company, and did so without diluting the family shareholding by bringing in another major investor (if any such investor would have been willing to come in to a company in Granada's condition). But as Granada (along with the rest of ITV) quickly started to perform better, it cost them heavily – an estimated £8 million of lost income over the course of the deal. They tried to wriggle out of it when it really started to bite. Denis Forman:

> *It was absolute murder for people like Sidney and Cecil to sit and watch this money being shovelled over to Rediffusion. It was very painful indeed.*
>
> *I was sent in to see if it could be renegotiated. Of course I failed completely. Then John Wills, who was a very forceful industrial giant, came to Sidney's office and there the topic of reneging cropped up – that's his word – and there was a furious row and nothing happened, the deal went through for the four years.*

Wills had stood firm behind not only his own company, but Granada as well. He would profit immensely from his nerve in doing so.

But this deal was not the way the ITV companies were supposed to work together. They were meant to be in a cut-throat market of their own, buying and selling programmes to each other, and making up their own individual transmission schedules (with the approval of the ITA). 'Competition with a vengeance' Robert Fraser had written in his memorandum to Kenneth Clark in 1954. It had become clear to anyone with a business head that some degree of co-operation over programme making would be desirable, even necessary, to the companies' economic well-being. But this pre-arranged, wholesale and guaranteed swapping of programmes between two of the four contractors was utterly contrary to the notion of a competitive market.

It is not clear how much anyone at the ITA knew about this deal. It was kept secret from the business community, and the City only started to ask questions about what was going on when Granada's balance sheets for later years showed less profit than other companies. The ITA asked to see the written agreement as late as 1959.

The ITA reacted with fury when the news came out. But if they were aware of the deal beforehand, there was nothing they could sensibly have done. To lose Granada in July 1956, after it had been on air for only two months, would have been a disaster. ITV's economic credibility could have been destroyed: the whole plan for a commercial network might have imploded. The ITA lawyers might have pursued the matter and successfully argued that the agreement was in breach of the Broadcasting Act, which required the companies to be 'independent as to finance'. But their only sanctions would have been to require the agreement to be torn up, to impose heavy fines, or – in extremis – to revoke Granada's licence. Any one of these measures could have destroyed Granada's television

Above: Roy Thomson, the Canadian proprietor of *The Scotsman* newspaper, was awarded the franchise for Central Scotland. His station, Scottish Television, came on air for the first time in August 1957.

adventure – exactly the result the Authority needed to avoid. The Bernsteins could simply have returned to their cinema chain.

It was in the middle of this perilous economic squeeze, in the summer of 1956, that Roy Thomson, the Canadian proprietor of *The Scotsman* newspaper, heard that he had been awarded the franchise for Central Scotland. He had expressed an interest in 1954, and held his nerve now. He had planned to take a 60% share of the broadcaster. But so few people were willing to come in with him – because of the state of the existing companies, and perhaps partly because of his outsize personality – that Thomson ended up with 80%. Scottish came on air in August 1957.

Thomson struck a deal with ATV to supply programmes to Scottish. This sort of affiliation between one of the original four companies (who were charged with producing between them most of the programmes for the network) and the smaller newcomers became a pattern. The ITA could do nothing to stop it, as the deals were not exclusive and did not preclude the smaller companies from buying elsewhere. But it was another nail in the coffin of the notion of cut-throat competition.

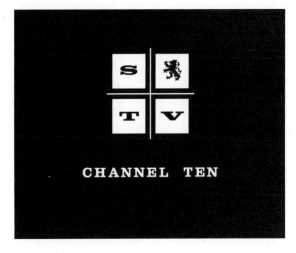

Before the end of 1956, there was a sudden upturn in television advertising. The national economy was improving. Agencies and manufacturers were beginning to appreciate what the new medium had to offer. The television companies had made the fastest losses in British industrial history. Now the tide turned. Granada's deal started to look expensive. Rothermere's bailing out started to look foolish.

The licence for South Wales and the West of England was awarded to a group led by Lord Derby, and involving *The News of the World*, impresario Jack Hylton, the *Liverpool Post and Echo*, The Imperial Tobacco Company of Bristol, and a whole society scrapbook full of prominent Welshmen. Little of the money came from industries in the area to which they were broadcasting, but the range of people and

SOUTHERN TELEVISION

PRESENTS

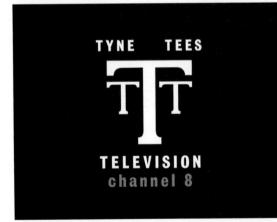

PRESENTS

companies involved showed how attractive a stake in ITV was starting to look. TWW (Television Wales and West) began transmission in January 1958.

Having jumped off the Associated-Rediffusion ship, Rothermere tried to hop on the next one along, joining the Rank Organisation and the *Daily Telegraph* group to apply for the licence for the South of England. With nine applicants in all for this region, the ITA had a real choice for the first time. Rothermere's group was one of several made up of national industries. Other applicants had much stronger roots in the local area. But Rothermere and his associates were chosen, and Southern Television was born. Just how minimal were their ties with the region became clear when they tried to set up their offices and production centre in London. The ITA insisted they had to set up inside the area to which they were broadcasting: Southern Television chose Southampton. Transmissions commenced in August 1958. Over 80% of the UK's population were now within the reach of ITV.

By the end of their second year, Southern posted profits of over one million pounds. In 1962, Southern paid a 650% dividend to its shareholders: six pounds ten shillings back on every pound of original investment. ITV's finances had taken off. Where most businesses were happy to take one pound gross profit for ten pounds of income, the ITV companies averaged six pounds of profit out of every ten pounds received. At ATV, the one shilling founders' shares had risen to £11.00 within a year – not a bad punt. 'These days they call us tycoons,' Lew Grade later commented. 'If there hadn't been that turn round in 1956, we'd have all been called martyrs.'

The rest of the ITV broadcasters were conceived and born into this profitable world, filling the gaps between established transmitters and companies: Tyne Tees in the North-East (January 1959); Anglia in East Anglia (October 1959); Ulster in Northern Ireland (October 1959); Westward in the South-West (April 1961); Border in the margins of England and Scotland (September 1961); Grampian in North-East Scotland (September 1961); Wales (West & North) in that area (September 1962); Channel in the Channel Islands (September 1962). Channel faced problems when the people of Alderney realised that the transmission mast that was to be erected on their island was only to relay pictures from mainland Britain to Jersey and Guernsey. They would have the eyesore, but wouldn't be able to watch the broadcasts. There was a vote against it in the island's parliament, and public demonstrations, before they were won round.

The bigger worry was whether the smallest regions would be commercially viable. Channel had only 100,000 potential viewers, Border less than half a million (where as London and the northern regions had 12 million each, and the Midlands seven million). In the end the only company to go bust was Wales (West & North), which was expected to originate too many Welsh language programmes for it to be viable. The company was subsumed in TWW in January 1964.

The rest of the regions performed well enough for questions to be asked in print and in parliament about the size of their profits. Each region had a lucrative monopoly within its borders. They held what Roy Thomson at Scottish called 'a licence to print money'. His words were going to come back to haunt them.

11
QUALITY CONTROL

*One of these consultants came up once to lecture us at Granada. He started
his lecture by saying, 'The purpose of a company is to make money.' I said,
'Stop there. That's not the purpose of Granada. The purpose of Granada is
to make good programmes and to make good money. Remember that.'*

Denis Forman

IN JUNE 1962 copies of the Report of the Pilkington Committee
thudded through the letter boxes of television's great and good. The
committee had been charged in 1960 with looking into the future of
broadcasting in Britain – which meant of course that it conducted a
thorough examination of its past. The committee's chairman was Sir
Harry Pilkington, an industrialist. Among its members were the
sociologist Richard Hoggart, who was one of the first academics in
Britain to allow that there was such a thing as working-class culture, as
well as one of its most perceptive interpreters. Other members included
figures from the worlds of business, education, and law. There was 'a
housewife', the actress Joyce Grenfell, theatre director Peter Hall (who
resigned), and footballer Billy Wright. A motley group and, one might
feel, one not entirely qualified for the job.

As well as evidence from broadcasters, advertisers and other involved
parties, they had heard the opinions of hundreds of individuals and public
bodies, from the Plymouth Brethren to the Royal Horticultural Society;
from the Association of Assistant Mistresses in Secondary Schools to the
Billericay Constituency Liberal Association; from the British Women's
Advisory Council of Burley-in-Wharfedale to Mr Graeme Shankland
and Associates, Architects and Town Planners. Many were special interest
groups (cranks might be unkind) who were treated as though they were
the voice of the general public, millions of whom had been thoroughly
enjoying ITV's output. Now the committee had pronounced – and its
conclusions were going to rock the ITV companies to their foundations.

Above: *On the Buses* was
one of LWT's most popular
sitcoms, despite being
peppered with innuendo that
would have horrified the
Pilkington Committee.

Opposite page:
ATV's *Tiswas* would also
have been frowned upon by
the members of the
Pilkington Committee.
Chris Tarrant (left) and Sally
James (right) presented the
anarchic Saturday morning
children's show.

MISS JOYCE GRENFELL

MR. RICHAF

Members of the 1962 Pilkington Committee – (left to right) Elwyn Davies, Secretary of the University of Wales, actress Joyce Grenfell, and academic Richard Hoggart. They concluded that much of television was preoccupied with the superficial.

The report grouped its comments under two headings – 'disquiet' and 'dissatisfaction'. Commercial television, far more than the BBC, had blame heaped upon it. The disquiet was that there was a failure to recognise how TV supposedly influenced morals and behaviour; dissatisfaction over the range and quality of programmes, and the late hour of minority interest broadcasts:

> *Much that is seen on television is regarded as of very little value. There was, we were told, a preoccupation in many programmes with the superficial, the cheaply sensational. Many mass appeal programmes were vapid and puerile, their content often derivative, repetitive and lacking in real substance. There was a vast amount of unworthy material, and to transmit it was to misuse intricate machinery and equipment, skill, ingenuity, and time.*
>
> *The BBC know good broadcasting; by and large, they are providing it.*
>
> *We conclude that the dissatisfaction with television can largely be ascribed to the independent television service.*

How fair was this? Denis Forman is in little doubt:

Those in authority decided that television should be looked at as a whole and should be reported on by a committee of the great and the good, two of whom didn't have television sets, so that was a good start. They came out with a report which was absolutely stunning in its condemnation of ITV and not really very surprising in its praise for the BBC. If you look at it today, you will see it is a rotten report on technical grounds in that it deals with philosophy and does not deal with detail. Not a single company is mentioned in ITV. Not a single programme is mentioned.

The report lumped ITV's programme output together, and found it wanting.

There *were* bad programmes, of course. Television has always had bad programmes. It still does. Some are born bad, some achieve badness, some have badness thrust upon them. Some are shoddily conceived and under budgeted (and as Pilkington and his cohorts took evidence, Tommy Steele went into print complaining that while he insisted on a month's rehearsals for his ATV entertainment shows, all around him the small screen was showing cheap, hurried, botched and inferior productions).

Benny Hill appeared with Ilona Adams in a TV adaptation of the Folies Bergére revue *Paris by Night* produced by ITP for ATV/ABC and screened in September 1956. Hill later told the viewing public that he refused to compromise his standards by guesting on other shows.

Some stretch their talent too thinly to cope (Benny Hill, who at the turn of the Sixties worked for both ITV and the BBC, told the viewing public that he appeared rarely on screen because he wouldn't compromise his standards by accepting guest slots on other shows written by whichever jobsworth happened to have been hired by the producers – even though this meant he couldn't see a way of making a living by TV alone). Some programmes see the Fates conspire against them, with bad weather, bad timing or plain bad luck.

The ITV companies were expected to provide a balanced diet; among the entertainment there were supposed to be current affairs programmes, arts, religion, science and children's broadcasts. They had scored some notable achievements.

In 1957, Associated-Rediffusion beat the BBC to the first educational schools broadcasts by several months. When the restrictions on the early Sunday evening 'God slot' were lifted in 1956, it was ITV that gave Britain its first weekly religious discussion programme. Two years later, it was ITV that tried to take Christianity to a younger audience with *The Sunday Break*, which aimed for a youth club ambience of jazz, dancing and competitions.

Granada had pushed the coverage of current affairs way beyond anything on the BBC – as we'll see in a later chapter.

There were children's programmes, of the sort you might find on the BBC, and of the sort you would not. There was great concern over the possible effect of television on children, and many people felt it should be no more than an extension of nanny's tender ministrations. ITV sometimes fitted the bill – in its first week Rolf Harris presented *The Big Black Crayon*, and later Muriel Young told stories in the company of glove puppet Pussy Cat Willum. But ITV also had the rough and tumble of the American cartoon *Popeye*. The head of children's programmes at the BBC declared that he wouldn't touch it if it was offered to him on a plate.

And ITV had culture – classic plays, art and music. But they had soon found that, whatever the right-minded liberals of the day might hope, these were not the most popular with the viewers. In their first cash-strapped months A-R's programmes with the Halle Orchestra and ATV's extracts from *Hamlet* had been among the cultural treats featured in peak time. Audiences deserted them in droves. *Hamlet*'s dropped below ten per cent of the viewing figures. Its impact on culture-watchers was not enhanced when the live broadcast over-ran and ATV ended it before the last scene to go to an advertising break (which legally it needed to cross to before the hour turned). It is said – perhaps apocryphally – that ATV

boss Lew Grade rang the production office to ask what happened. 'Oh,' he was told, 'they all died in the end.'

In those early, financially perilous days, ITV was not helped to fulfil its higher cultural role by the Establishment. The 1954 Television Act had acknowledged that these programmes would not pay their way by attracting sufficient advertising (indeed, religious programmes were not allowed to have advertising breaks at all), and had set up a contingency fund of £750,000 to help to finance their production. But the Treasury

Jennifer Vyvyan as the Governess and Tom Bevan as Miles in the A-R production of Benjamin Britten's opera *The Turn of the Screw*, based on the ghost story by Henry James.

and the civil servants under Postmaster General Charles Hill (speaker at ITV's opening gala) wrapped it in yards of their best and stickiest red tape and not a penny of it was ever spent – not much help for Hill's 'lively youngster' there. Kenneth Clark tendered his resignation over the freezing of this fund.

In the circumstances, it was not unreasonable for the ITV companies to draw their horns in and concentrate on their more popular programmes. As Clark pointed out, they had to get an audience and get on their feet before they could really worry about the class of the fare (though in private he badgered the broadcasters to remember their legal and contractual obligation to provide a range of programmes, high as well as low).

What was more open to criticism was the lack of eagerness shown by most of the companies to push their horns out again once they were awash with money. It can't be denied that some companies, and some programmes, did scramble very readily for the lowest common denominator. Not all companies were the same. Tyne Tees was notorious for avoiding minority programmes and putting out cop shows or westerns instead. Granada continued to aim for quality and intelligence with many of its productions (though it has been pointed out by other commentators that under their agreement Associated-Rediffusion were in effect paying for Granada's aspirations, which may have made them rather easier to maintain).

Granada had become used to seeing any press criticism of the ITV companies being followed by the words 'except Granada'. But the Pilkington Report lumped them all together.

Many of the original supporters of the creation of ITV had based their support on faith in the people. Given the chance to exercise choice, the working people would surely choose for themselves just what the liberal intelligentsia would want to choose for them – *Hamlet* and the Hallé. But all the wishful thinking in the world could not make it so. When the liberal intelligentsia found they were wrong, they tended to criticise ITV's output, not their own predictions.

Robert Fraser attacked this view in a speech in 1960:

If you decide to have a system of people's television, then people's television you must expect it to be. It will reflect their likes and dislikes, their tastes and aversions, what they can comprehend and what is beyond them. Every person of common sense knows that people of superior mental constitution are bound to find much of television intellectually beneath them. If such innately fortunate people cannot realise this gently and considerately and with good manners, if in their hearts they despise popular pleasures and interests, then of course they will be angrily dissatisfied with television. But it is not really television with which they are dissatisfied. It is with people.

This was the deeper issue underlying Pilkington's declarations. Should television reflect taste or try to lead it? With Hoggart influencing their report, possibly writing most of it, they decided that broadcasting was supposed to have a purpose. And it wasn't to be trivial.

> *Our own conclusion is that triviality is a natural vice of television, and that where it prevails it operates to lower general standards of enjoyment and understanding. It is, as we were reminded: 'more dangerous to the soul than wickedness.'*

Denis Forman:

> *The whole thrust of the report was that one must decide what are the purposes of broadcasting and the committee decided that the purposes of broadcasting were to educate, enlighten and improve the British public.*

ITV bosses were incensed. At Westward, Peter Cadbury held a bonfire party and burnt a giant mock-up of the report.

The Beaverbrook *Express* crowed. Other papers sided with ITV. The *Mirror* (with its shareholding in ATV) ran the headline: 'Pilkington tells the public to go to hell'. The *Sketch* said, 'If they think you're enjoying yourself too much – well, they'll soon put a stop to that'. In the *Sunday Pictorial*, columnist and Labour MP Woodrow Wyatt turned his criticism on the critics:

> *You 'trivial' people, to borrow the Pilkington Committee's favourite phrase. How dare you prefer watching commercial television to looking at what Auntie BBC so kindly provides for you. The ITV programmes are 'naughty' and 'bad' for you. They are produced by ordinary men and women who like the same things as you do. Pilkington is out to stop all this rot about you being allowed to enjoy yourself. You trivial people will have to brush up your culture.*

The attack was withering. But the report would not wither away.

Its most crucial recommendation was that the third television channel should not be given to ITV. It had been widely assumed since 1954 that there would be more than one ITV channel. This was another blow to the idea of competition within commercial television.

It also recommended the abolition of 'admags'. These programmes existed outside the limits of six minutes of advertising in an ITV hour. Personalities including Jimmy Hanley, Noele Gordon and Kenneth Horne would tell viewers about commercial products. The ITA had allowed them to be aired, saying they were not adverts but consumer information programmes. But they had the editorial independence of today's shopping channels – one enthusiastic puff after another. They were soon removed from the ITV screen.

Pilkington's most radical recommendation was not followed. It would have ended ITV as we know it. Finding the regional companies so lacking, the report suggested that the ITA should take over the job of scheduling, and commission programmes from the individual companies. The ITA, like a prototype Channel 4, would take the advertising revenue and dole it out to pay for productions. This was supposed to safeguard programme standards, and steer ITV towards intellectual respectability. Better such then-sitting ITA members as Sir John Carmichael KBE (former member of the Sudan Civil Service and member of the Scottish Gas Board) or Mrs Isabel Graham-Bryce (Chair of Oxford Regional Hospital Board) than Lew Grade and Sidney Bernstein to decide what broadcast? One can only imagine how many weeks it would have taken to kill ITV.

But Pilkington set a climate in which ITV's schedules would be more strictly monitored and quotas of public service broadcasting more strictly set and enforced. Denis Forman regards it as ITV's great fall:

Before Pilkington it was like the Garden of Eden; nobody knew about sin, we just made programmes and people laughed and loved them. After Pilkington we had to have a quota of how many quiz shows, how many hours of American programmes. It put all kinds of forms of cultural censorship onto independent television.

But it also made life easier for Granada's programme-makers.

It was very beneficial to us because there were a lot of our programmes which the other companies wouldn't take because they were too highbrow. Now the authority insisted they took them because they were serving the purposes of broadcasting, so it suited us very well. We had nothing to grumble about, but by God, Lew had.

This was a watershed in ITV's history. Pilkington's ideas informed the Television Acts of 1963 and 1964, which increased the power of the ITA – now invested in Charles Hill (who served as its chairman from July 1963 to August 1967). As he put it in a speech:

The Act of course strengthens the authority in relation to its old functions:

quality, decency, impartiality, taste. It strengthens the authority's powers in relation to future programming. Yes, the authority is stronger.

Hill set about using his powers. He visited Glasgow to see Scottish Television's blunt daytime entertainment programme, *One o'Clock Gang* in the studio. He axed it, reportedly with the words: 'My God, how long have you been getting away with this?'

ATV drama *Crossroads* originally ran five nights a week when the Crossroads Motel in King's Oak first opened its doors in 1964. By the time production was assumed by Central in 1982, the programme's frequency had been reduced to three episodes a week on the instructions of the IBA.

The Gang weren't the only ones to feel the weight of the Authority in the aftermath of Pilkington. In 1967 the ITA persuaded Lew Grade and ATV to reduce *Crossroads* from five episodes a week to four, in the hope that this would improve the programme's quality. (They would try the same thing again 12 years later, reducing it from four episodes to three. Neither move had much discernible effect).

The companies' profits had also come under prolonged scrutiny. The Treasury had introduced a flat levy of 11 per cent on their income from advertising. The new Television Acts went further, introducing a sliding scale of charges, intended to safeguard the smaller companies while taking a bite out of the larger bank balances. After long debate, it was announced that it would be levied not on profits but on income (nett of the commission paid to advertising agencies, a figure known as the Nett Advertising Revenue, or NAR). The first £1.5 million of income would be untaxed; the next £6 million taxed at 25 per cent; and above that 45 per cent. It was intended to take £17 million out of the companies, leaving them with profits (on which normal business taxes would still be due) of just over £15 million.

Norman Collins called it a 'licence to lose money' and said it would put ATV out of business. Beaverbrook, as supportive as ever, said that the Express Group would happily take over if that proved to be the case. In time, the tax would bite; by 1970, Scottish was paying a three quarters of a million pound levy on its income, even though it was two million in the red overall. Thomson's licence to print money had expired. But no companies were driven to bankruptcy by the new tax; by handicapping their monopoly on television advertising, it put them more on more of a par with the rest of industry.

1964 might have brought even worse news for some of the companies. The first licences for broadcasting expired. They had to reapply. Eight new applicants joined the round. But after long debate, the existing licence holders were reinstalled. The ITA saved the shocks for next time. It wasn't long coming.

Those 1964 licences were due to run until the still-expected introduction of ITV2, planned for 1967 at the latest. When it became clear that technical and financial circumstances were going to preclude that, another round of applications for new licences was announced.

Some changes were announced in advance. Only London would continue to be split between weekday and weekend contractors; the Midlands and the North would become seven-day contracts, like the other regions. But Granadaland would be split into two areas, east and west of the Pennines. Sidney Bernstein threatened to 'go to the United Nations' over the decision, but he could do nothing to check the ITA's power.

There were 36 applicants for the 15 regions, ten of them for the new Yorkshire licence. Many of the incumbents treated the process as a formality. The attitude proved fatal to some.

TWW's grip on Wales was not helped by their insistence on running management operations from London. The ITA had become increasingly

keen on local involvement in their regional contractors. Now they got a new applicant, led by Lord Harlech, which promised regional operations and regional talent. They gave them the job. TWW's chairman Lord Derby banged off outraged letters and telegrams to all concerned, protesting that they had had no warning, demanding that they should have some right to appeal. The *Guardian* summed the position up:

> *TWW has obviously been sadly upset to discover that the Television Act of 1964, as interpreted by the ITA, means what it says. Television franchises do not last forever.*

This page: With Alan Whicker as a board member and major shareholder, Yorkshire Television first went on the air on 29 July 1968. The company produced many successful shows for ITV including (above) *Emmerdale Farm* and (below) *Rising Damp*.

TWW's shareholders had to be content with a tenfold dividend on their investment over ten years. The company slunk into a corner and sulked, eventually handing over to the new Harlech group almost four months before they were required to.

The other new contracts began in July 1968. Yorkshire was won by the group who, in typically straightforward northern style, became known as Yorkshire Television, and who set up in Europe's first purpose-built colour studios in Leeds. The Midlands was given full-time to ATV, who

lost their weekend London slot. ABC was now homeless, having lost its weekends in the Midlands and the North, and applied for the London weekend as their first preference. The ITA might have moved them in, and left Rediffusion in place in London during the week. But the London decision had been complicated by a bright, new applicant.

The application was put together by David Frost, who was already famous as the front man of the BBC's *That Was the Week That Was*, and of his own interview programmes on Rediffusion. He recruited the Head of BBC1, Michael Peacock, as prospective Managing Director. He lined up experienced programme makers, including Frank Muir, head of situation comedy at the BBC, and Doreen Stephens, its head of children's programmes. Rediffusion's Controller of Programmes, Cyril Bennett, was set to join them if their application was successful. So was Rediffusion's head of sales. Former head of ITN Aidan Crawley was to be Chairman. The money was in place. It seemed that the only person Frost failed to bring aboard was John Freeman, whom he wanted as Deputy Chairman. The former presenter of the legendary BBC interview series *Face to Face* was now the British High Commissioner in New Delhi. Frost flew to India to court him, but though interested, Freeman put his diplomatic career first. David Frost:

This page: LWT went on air on 2 August 1968 and soon became a channel notable for programmes as widely varied as *Weekend World* (above) – hosted by Brian Walden (left) and Peter Jay (right) – and *On the Buses* (below) starring Reg Varney (right) and Bob Grant.

We had a feeling that the people running ITV should be the television people, rather than the businessmen or the financiers or the investors and so on. The television people should have a damn good go at running television themselves. So it was a question of bringing together the best people in television.

The ITA wanted a weekend company that even Pilkington would approve of; a group who would provide programmes for the sort of people who only watched television on Saturdays and Sundays and wanted to find quality when they turned the dial. If they had posted their invitation for applicants as a lonely hearts advert ('Discerning, slightly authoritarian, let down too often by cheapskates and vulgarians; seeks long-term relationship with suitor who appreciates the finer things in life; opera, laughter, children and intense political discussions') they could not have got a better response.

Frost's group set out their stall in their application:

The first, and inherent, principle of the Company's programme philosophy is a respect for the creative talents – for those who, within

sound and decent commercial disciplines, will conceive and make television programmes. The second is respect for those who watch them, the audience...

These programme-makers have been united by a common belief that the quality of mass entertainment can be improved while retaining commercial viability. Independent television has the capacity to be as complete a public service as the BBC.

The ITA fluttered their collective eyelashes and swooned. Lord Hill wrote of the then London Television Consortium's bid:

> *It is an understatement to say that the Authority liked this application. Even allowing for the fact that promising is so much easier than performing, it was difficult to resist the thought that here was a group which would bring us new thinking, fresh ideas, and a lively impetus to weekend broadcasting. It had to have its chance whatever the repercussions.*

The Consortium won the franchise, and became London Weekend Television. Hill was heard pointing out Peacock at a party as 'the man who will save independent television'. But the appointment was soon going to turn into a crisis.

Meanwhile, there were the repercussions to deal with. The ITA forced Rediffusion and ABC into a shotgun marriage to run weekday broadcasting in London. The result was Thames Television, which became a powerhouse of ITV production, with popular and quality series across the board; from children's programme *Magpie* (which always felt like it fancied taking the BBC's *Blue Peter* round the back of the bike sheds to show it who was boss) to long-running sitcom *Bless This House*; from the landmark archive series *The World at War* to TV detective *Van Der Valk*; from *The Sweeney* to Tommy Cooper; from *The Naked Civil Servant* to *Bill Brand*.

Formed by the merger of Associated-Rediffusion with ABC, Thames Television was launched on 29 July 1968 and soon became an ITV production powerhouse with shows such as *The Sweeney*, starring John Thaw (left) and Dennis Waterman (right).

But it was a bitter reward for Rediffusion's John Spencer Wills, who had done so much to keep ITV afloat in its first year. He had certainly made a mistake by choosing to treat the ITA high-handedly when they interviewed him about the new licence application. The ITA not only forced his company into partnership; it gave the controlling interest in Thames to ABC.

LWT did not start well. To soften the financial blow to Rediffusion, the ITA required them to set up their first home in Rediffusion's Wembley complex, and to keep on the workforce – far more than LWT had intended to employ. Peacock and Frost fell out when the former found out how much the latter was paying himself to appear on screen on Friday, Saturday and Sunday nights. The first night of transmission was blacked out by a strike after seconds on air.

It didn't get better. LWT had swept in on a promise to provide a much-needed improvement on existing programmes. The existing programme-makers didn't like that. The Grades and Bernsteins of the broadcasting world didn't think they needed any lessons.

Brian Tesler was Director of Programmes at Thames:

> *LWT was considered by the rest of the network, particularly the seven-day contractors, the old hands, as a callow upstart with highbrow aspirations and no commercial nous.*

They very quickly went about alienating the ITA as well, by scheduling *The Franchise Trail*, a satire about the whole business, for the first weekend. Peacock postponed it as inappropriate for its opening salvo. But the blushing bride of the ITA was perfectly aware that it had woken up on honeymoon to find the bridegroom farting in bed.

More importantly, LWT's brave new television world alienated the viewers. They were charged with putting together the network's weekend programmes. Their idea of peak-time broadcasting included *Saturday Specials* such as Stravinsky's music-drama *The Soldier's Tale*, avant-garde agit-prop drama from Jean-Luc Godard, a tribute to Jacques Brel, and *Georgia Brown Sings Kurt Weill*. All admirable. All wrong for the slot. With the BBC wheeling out its top light entertainment on Saturdays,

Above: Laurence Olivier was the narrator of Thames Television's award-winning 1973 documentary series *The World at War*.

from *Dixon of Dock Green* and *Doctor Who* onwards, LWT's Saturday night schedules lost something like a sixth of ITV's audience.

They got no help from the other ITV big guns. Why put their best shows up against Auntie's finest? With seven-day contracts, they were happy to let the BBC rule Saturday nights, and keep their own big-hitters for the rest of the week, when they could make up their advertising income. But LWT only had two and a half days to make its money in. Losing Saturday night hurt them.

Arguments within the company began to rip it apart. Controller of Programmes Cyril Bennett announced that the first duty was to survive, and pushed the populist buttons. Leslie Crowther and the Tiller Girls spearheaded a return to light entertainment. But the company was trying to make up lost ground, and was still being flattened by the BBC.

In March 1969, Peacock told the LWT board that they had to get ratings up high enough to justify the airtime cost to advertisers, satisfy the ITA, and make the staff proud to work there. In September, the board forced his resignation. He had given up a glittering BBC career – and blown it. Other senior programme-makers followed.

Peacock's resignation was front-page news. There were questions in Parliament. The group that the ITA had appointed no longer existed; where did that leave the ITA, and LWT? Should their licence be revoked?

LWT was in a mess. There was a power struggle between senior management. It was in financial difficulty, building new studios on the south bank of the Thames that had to be paid for. Other big ITV companies sniffed around the prospect of a takeover.

A solution was on his way. But he turned out to be another problem.

In October 1969, David Frost had interviewed the Australian newspaper tycoon Rupert Murdoch. It was ITV's first live colour programme. The content was pretty colourful, too. Frost and his studio audience laid into the morals and conduct of the man who owned the *News of the World* and was about to take over the *Sun*. Murdoch ended the broadcast in fury, and is reported to have turned to his entourage and told them he was going to buy LWT.

He got his chance before the end of 1970. With the company struggling, he bought existing shares, and injected capital in return for new ones. He became the biggest power on the board.

Stella Richman had succeeded Cyril Bennett as Controller of Programmes. In January 1971, she reported to the board that they faced 14 'insurmountable problems'. Murdoch fired her. As was often his way,

Newspaper tycoon Rupert Murdoch so disliked the treatment he received in a live interview for LWT that he bought the company.

where he thought things were being run badly, he stepped in himself. Senior management figures were kicked upstairs, sideways, or out of the company altogether. Murdoch was effectively in control, and began to decide what programmes would be broadcast.

Now the ITA reacted with alarm. They weren't happy to have foreign shareholders. Programme policy was not supposed to be influenced by newspaper owners. They would never have awarded the licence to LWT under these conditions. They told LWT's board that they would be within their rights to revoke the licence immediately, but instead gave them six weeks to put a new management in place and effectively reapply for their contract. Murdoch went to the ITA and spoke for 90 minutes about what he regarded as their public assassination of his character. But his coup was over.

Frost was at last able to bring in John Freeman, who was appointed Chairman and Chief Executive on 9 March 1971. Murdoch remained on the board, but no longer in control. The ITA had made an enemy who would be back to haunt it.

Freeman revamped the management. Cyril Bennett returned. In 1972, LWT moved into its new white office tower and studios on the South Bank. It symbolised a turnaround, which was only slightly marred by the discovery that the studio doors were too low to accommodate the double decker bus that starred in the hit sitcom *On the Buses*. They made do with a single-decker with a custom built plywood and cardboard superstructure that could be lowered on from the studio grid.

Other programmes grew far less rickety. In 1975 LWT won seven BAFTAs – more than the rest of ITV put together. *The Stanley Baxter Moving Picture Show* won four; Peter Barkworth won best actor for *Crown Matrimonial*; *Aquarius* and *Weekend World* won one each. With successes across the board, in entertainment, drama, arts and current affairs, LWT had finally fulfilled its promise.

Above: LWT was forced to abandon original highbrow aspirations in favour of more popular entertainment such as the 1970 *Tommy Cooper* sketch show.

Below: Elaine Stritch played American author Dorothy McNab and Donald Sinden her butler Robert Hiller in four series of LWT's *Two's Company*.

12

JOINING THE CLUB

There was a Programme Controller's meeting every Monday. I used to take Valium before I went in.

Brian Tesler

ITV WAS CREATED AS an agglomeration of regional companies. But not all regions were created equal. All were required to bring local news and local perspectives to their viewers. But only a few were responsible for providing the vast majority of programmes to be seen across the network. And those who held a place at top table guarded their privileges fiercely.

In the early days it was the first companies, the Big Four, who had the

Above: An engraving from Hogarth's *Rake's Progress* – likened to the meetings of the ITV Programme Controllers Group.

Top: Weather girl Wincey Willis on TV-am's *Good Morning Britain* programme.

Opposite page: Richard Wilson as barrister Jeremy Parsons QC, a regular figure at Fulchester Crown Court in Granada's *Crown Court* series which ran from 1972 to 1984.

commercial strength to carry the responsibility. The bosses of ATV, Associated-Rediffusion, ABC and Granada dealt with each other by phone or face-to-face, thrashing out prices, programme exchanges, and suitable slots in the schedule. Denis Forman recalls the working relationship between Lew Grade and Cecil Bernstein:

> *They talked to each other on the telephone and one would offer the other a programme. Cecil would say, 'What do you want from us Lew?' and Lew would say, 'Well, Cec, I reckon two thousand pounds.' Cecil would say, 'You're out of your mind, Lew, what are you talking about?' I would often be a silent witness of these conversations because there was this earpiece on Cecil's phone and he had me listening in. Lew knew I was listening on the earpiece and after they argued for about ten minutes, they got it down to six hundred. Lew would say to Cecil, 'Cecil, what does Denis say?' I would say, 'Well, Cecil I think that six hundred and fifty's pretty fair.' Cecil: 'Lew, Lew, Lew, Denis says six hundred and fifty is pretty fair'. Once the deal was done, no correspondence ensued, nothing was confirmed in writing, the deal was done and that was the deal. Cecil called his secretary and she would note it and pass it to the accounts department. This went on for, I should think, five or six years and Granada and ATV never had a contract from each other.*

This page and opposite: Programme exchanges between ITV's Big Four enabled series such as ATV's *Danger Man* (above), ABC's *The Avengers* (below), A-R's *Do Not Adjust Your Set* (opposite top) and Granada's *Coronation Street* (opposite below) to be seen in other ITV regions.

This kind of gentleman's arrangement existed more or less between the other companies – though paperwork was involved. Forman remembers ABC's Howard Thomas as a little shifty to deal with. The most difficult was A-R's Tom Brownrigg, a retired naval captain who ran his company as though it were the fourth branch of the services, all rank and protocol, but with no feel at all for choosing or scheduling programmes. In meetings he would refer to other individuals by their company names, so Cecil Bernstein was 'Granada' to his face. But the gentlemen and their successors made their deals until 1968, when the arrival of Yorkshire turned the Big Four into the Big Five.

Now there was a new system, in which the Controller of Programmes of each of the five would meet each week. The gloves came off. Denis Forman:

> *It was a rough house. I was Chairman of the first meeting and there was in fact a physical encounter between two programme controllers, which gives you an idea of the degree of emotion that we had at these meetings. They were about to have a fight.*

He declines to name the two involved, as 'one of them is still alive'.

This atmosphere persisted through later generations of Programme Controllers. After one meeting, it was necessary to remind one of the most senior figures in television that it was neither polite nor conducive to good business practice to refer to his counterpart as a 'motherf★★★er'. Brian Tesler, who took tranquillisers to get through the roughhouse, remembers it well.

> *There's a very vivid engraving by Hogarth in his* Rake's Progress *sequence, of a gambling scene in a little 18th century back room. It's a scene of uproar, there are gentlemen sprawled round a table and they're obviously having a furious row – fists are raised, faces bulging, apoplectic anger, people shouting, people threatening. One of them actually picking up a chair and hitting somebody else over the head with it. Two and half centuries before its time, that engraving was a remarkably accurate depiction of an ordinary everyday meeting of the Programme Controllers Group of ITV. We were there fighting our respective corners. We were making our own programme offers, we were trying to avoid other people's programmes. We were making our suggestions for the way the schedule should run and resisting other*

Above: Ben Kingsley presents his case in Granada's *Crown Court*.

Below: Grace Mulligan presents a rustic spread in *Farmhouse Kitchen*.

people's. Exciting and electric I think you could say. But we were all programme makers and in the end we wanted the best programmes to get onto the air; we wanted the best possible schedule. You had to be able to argue not only persuasively but loudly. You had to have a bit of a brass neck but in the end the schedule was right. The programmes were more or less in the right place. The respective costs of the programmes were just about right.

The Big Five contributed programmes to the network in proportion to their share of the overall nett advertising revenue (their NAR). It worked for them, and by and large it worked for the schedule, which continued to offer popular and successful programming. But it didn't work for all of the companies who weren't part of the Five. Some, like Scottish, were happy enough to contribute little to the network, pay for the supply of programmes, and count their income from the advertisers. But others were frustrated at the paucity of opportunities to get programmes onto national television, to see them bankrolled by the system, and to make money from international sales.

When ITV expanded into daytime programmes, after restrictions on broadcasting hours were lifted in 1972, there were some opportunities. The Big Five, the Majors, took some slots for themselves; Granada's *Crown Court* with its real jury hearing fictitious cases across three episodes a week; Yorkshire's *Emmerdale Farm* – all sheep, no sex, in those days; *Farmhouse Kitchen* with Dorothy Sleightholme resembling Beatrix Potter's Mrs Tiggywinkle; and *Indoor League* with Fred Trueman, like as not pint in hand, bellowing his enthusiasm for groundbreaking television coverage of bar-billiards, skittles, shove ha'penny and darts. But there was room, too, for Scottish with its village drama *Take the High Road*; Border with the comfortable quiz format of *Mr and Mrs*; and Southern with the story of sheltered flat-dwelling folk in *Together*. Southern also had some success finding takers for *House Party*, a format in which a group of women would gather to discuss topics of burning interest such as how one's son was getting on in the Navy, the best recipe for flan, or the numerous varieties of elastic and their proper uses (illustrated with examples from a big box of the stuff). It seemed to seethe with subtextual jealousy and rivalry, and had a cult following among students.

Southern had long been one of the more enterprising of the smaller companies when it came to finding holes in the schedule to fill. They covered opera from Glyndebourne, which the Authority loved (so much so that they insisted that its coverage of Verdi's *Macbeth* have a peak-time slot in the 1972 Christmas

Above: Fred Trueman hosted the bar games show *Indoor League*.

Below: Yorkshire's long-running drama set in a farming community began in 1972 as *Emmerdale Farm*.

schedules, to the fury of the commercially-minded companies). They enterprisingly converted a boat to become Britain's only floating Outside Broadcast unit, and were able to trump the BBC on events such as the return of Sir Francis Chichester from his round the world voyage – not only picking him up miles from home, but also manoeuvring to be able to shine their lights directly into the BBC's cameras when he reached the

harbour. They made a popular series of programmes in the countryside with Jack Hargreaves, who was also one of the regulars on the children's series *How?*, which offered all manner of information (and had the distinction of being lampooned by Monty Python in their 'How to Do It' sketch). Southern were regular contributors of children's programmes, with *Worzel Gummidge*, *The Famous Five* and *Saturday Banana* (allegedly a misprint of Saturday Bonanza) among their network sales.

But some people thought they could be doing more. The chance to try out the theory came when the licences were up for renewal in 1980.

EMMERDALE

Please drive carefully through our village

Worzel Gummidge was one of Southern's most popular series. Based on the books of Barbara Euphan Todd, the programme starred Jon Pertwee (centre) as the eponymous scarecrow with Geoffrey Bayldon (left) as the Crowman and young actors Jeremy Austin and Charlotte Coleman as John and Sue Peters.

The ITA had by then become the IBA (Independent Broadcasting, not Independent Television, after it took on responsibility for the new commercial radio companies in 1972). But its function was still the same, as judge, jury and sole authority in the round of applications. It was a beauty contest, with incumbents and aspirants striving to put up the most alluring plans. This round saw cosmetic surgery to several parts of ITV.

ATV survived the competition, but was required to move its headquarters from London to the Midlands, set up a dual service to give separate local coverage to the east and west of its area, bring in local investors, and rename itself as Central.

Westward was not so fortunate, a casualty of a virtual civil war in its own boardroom. It was replaced by TSW, which came on air when the new licences became active in 1982.

The biggest change came with the advent of breakfast time television. The IBA advertised for contractors who could supply a service of news, information, and current affairs. The award went to one of the eight applicants that offered all that and more. It had the Famous Five – Anna Ford, David Frost, Robert Kee, Michael Parkinson and Angela Rippon. Their chairman, the experienced broadcaster and diplomat Peter Jay, impressed the Authority, though there were some doubts about whether

Above: TV-am's Famous Five – (left to right) Robert Kee, Angela Rippon, David Frost, Anna Ford and Michael Parkinson – on the *Good Morning Britain* set for the first edition which aired on 1 February 1983.

there was an adequate company structure behind the star names. TV-am began its broadcasts from its Camden Lock studios in February 1983.

It became a notorious misadventure. The BBC had got in at breakfast time two weeks before with Frank Bough, Selina Scott, and the celebrated chemistry of the couch. TV-am opened with teething troubles, botched stories, and confusingly erratic schedules. The presenters smiled through, but the smiles faded at the end of the first week, when it became clear that they were losing the ratings battle with the BBC by two-to-one. With 800,000 viewers, TV-am were just hitting enough viewers to keep them solvent. Three weeks later they were down below half that. Jay was forced out by major investors. Ford and Rippon spoke out in his favour and were sacked by new Chief Executive Timothy Aitken. Parkinson joined the criticism of the way the company was being run, but Aitken

realised he was their biggest asset and called a truce.

In May, a new Editor-in-Chief was appointed, with a deal that would give him a fifty per cent bonus if he could get a million viewers. Greg Dyke set to work.

I spent a year at TV-am. It was without doubt the funniest year of my life. I've never laughed so much. It was a total shambles. It was so bad that people who weren't there will never believe the stories. Who else had ever been running a television station when the electricity board turned up and said, 'If you don't pay the bill in 20 minutes, we're going to turn you off'? When the newsagent wouldn't deliver papers any more to a news organisation because we hadn't paid the bill? When researchers had bailiffs coming round their house, because they'd signed for a hotel bill and nobody ever paid it? And when, every so often, we used to have to put out another little note saying, 'Due to computer error, unfortunately your wages won't be in the bank this weekend,' and everybody knew what it meant?

Even the IBA's research had told it that it was advertising for the wrong service, that early in the morning viewers wanted news with entertainment, cartoons, cookery and keep fit. Dyke drafted in breezy weather girl Wincey Willis, keep-fit teacher 'Mad' Lizzie Webb, and Jeremy Beadle, and lightened and brightened the tone overall.

The story of American breakfast television might have made illuminating reading. NBC had set it off in 1952 with *Today*, but the show had only been saved from disaster by the popularity of J Fred Muggs, the chimpanzee whose infamous if unwitting intervention in

American coverage of the Coronation had given so much ammunition to the anti-ITV lobby. Dyke found his own animal star already working at the station; he became known as the only rat ever to join a sinking ship. Greg Dyke:

We played Roland Rat between nine and nine thirty in a half-term week and there was quite a big jump in the figures. I suddenly realised that the way into breakfast television was through the kids. So we then decided that we would play Roland Rat right across the summer, combined with doing this bizarre thing we called 'By the Seaside' where we took Chris Tarrant out on the road doing all sorts of strange things on the beaches around Britain. We had six weeks of the most wonderful weather – I mean but for the sunshine we would be dead. And that turned the thing around.

Audiences grew, but TV-am's income was blighted by a strike by the actors' union Equity, which put the squeeze on the supply of adverts. The company was still on the financial edge.

They gave me bonuses on ratings; they didn't pay them, but they gave them to me. There was one day when we were going to go into liquidation – if the unions had voted against changing the pay structure, something like that, we were going to go into liquidation. I thought, these guys owe me twenty thousand pounds, what can I take that's worth twenty thousand pounds? I looked around, of course they didn't own anything. And then I found out the only thing they owned was the barge on the canal out the back, so I stole the keys to the barge and if they'd gone into liquidation, I was going to chug off on the Grand Union Canal. I don't know what I was thinking of.

In November 1983, Australian media mogul Kerry Packer bought into the company. He sent his executive Bruce Gyngell in to represent him. The following May, Gyngell took over as Managing Director. The appointment would later have huge repercussions for ITV, as we'll see in

Opposite page: The changing face of TV-am's *Good Morning Britain*. After the Famous Five (top) were dropped from the line-up, Nick Owen and Anne Diamond co-hosted the show – they were joined by Roland Rat (centre) in 1983. The programme was presented by Mike Morris and Lorraine Kelly when TV-am finally went off the air on 31 December 1992.

Above: Bruce Gyngell became Managing Director of TV-am in May 1984.

the next chapter. For now, it had huge repercussions on Greg Dyke.

I liked him a lot but we were never going to get on. The first day he was there, he insisted we went out for lunch and we had to play numerology with our birth dates over lunch. I don't know what he did with them, but he took my dates and his dates and then he said, 'Greg, this is wonderful, we are going to get on so well'. I was fired within a month.

With Gyngell insisting on taking control of editorial policy, backed by the board, Dyke was pushed into offering his resignation. He bequeathed TV-am an audience of one and a half million.

He soon found himself at the last of the recent licence winners, as TVS's Director of Programmes.

Southern had thought they were impregnable. They gave Glyndebourne to the IBA. It was only a few years since the Authority had written that they 'probably lead the regional companies in the professionalism and range of their output'. They were a model of their kind.

But in the beauty contest, other people had prettier models, and presented them better. The area covered by the licence was being extended. It was a plum, with the most affluent audience in the country. Southern remained complacent. The three shareholders – Rank, Associated Newspapers, and DC Thomson – were all based outside the region but had consistently ignored warning noises about bringing in local investment. They put in an application running to just a handful of pages – the IBA tried to help them out by inviting them to try again.

There were six other applicants. When the award went to a group led by local programme-maker James Gatward, Southern were left asking, in the name of their popular series, *How?*

The IBA gave them no reasons; it didn't have to. Southern's Chairman David Wilson wrote a letter of protest:

For the first time in the history of independent television, a company had been summarily dismissed without previous warning or complaint... When we were interviewed we were courteously, even gently, treated by the Authority... We were not invited for a second interview... We cannot believe that a decision of such importance affecting the lives and futures of hundreds of people can have been taken purely on assumptions that a new group of people looked as though they might provide a better service... The Authority performed an act of arbitrary power based on a secret process of

assessment, exercised without the opportunity for defence, questioning or appeal… This can be no proper way to conduct affairs of this importance – it surely defies every concept on natural justice.

They got a reply – but still no explanation. The Prime Minister, Margaret Thatcher, asked Lady Plowden, the outgoing chairwoman of the IBA who had presided over the decision, why Southern had been axed. 'I can't possibly tell you that,' was her answer. Plowden's successor, Lord Thomson, was soon heard to be suggesting that there had to be a better way of deciding. The idea would occupy political minds for the next decade, and produce a new system that was even worse.

Gatward's company TVS set up offices in portakabins in Southern's car park, and prepared for the 1982 handover. David Wilson made an emotional speech at Southern's farewell gala:

For over 25 years Southern has been and still is a fine company… but we are to be killed off… for reasons we know far too little about. The agony of that decision may now be passing… but there remains the rage, the bitterness, the sense of injustice… and that will not pass. History may vindicate us, but there is little comfort in that at this present time.

Top turn Richard Stilgoe sang a barbed song about 'Portakabin TV', which ended, 'We would change things if we could, but Southern was so good, we've decided to keep everything the same'.

But Gatward wasn't going to keep everything the same. With Dyke in place, the company began an offensive to join the Big Five, lobbying politicians and broadcasters.

Greg Dyke:

We were not good at being subservient and that's what the system required you to do. You had to sit there and thank the Big Five for providing such a great schedule and you just had to pay them. We were never going to be like that, so we decided we would try and become the sixth major.

James Gatward:

We had the best demographic profile in the country, most desirable. We were the third largest earning of revenue in the country equal to LWT. We were behind Central and behind Thames. But we were definitely ahead of Granada and definitely ahead of Yorkshire.

Greg Dyke:

It was a bizarre thing: we had the lowest ratings in ITV and because of it, we were probably the richest company. Because if people wanted to advertise in your area, which they did in the south of England because it was very rich, they had to advertise more times to hit the right number of people. Because the supply of advertising time was finite, they just had to pay more. It's a complete contradiction of what business is supposed to be about – the worse you did, the richer you got.

However rich they were, the Big Five treated their programme proposals no differently from the rest. James Gatward:

I was not happy sitting back waiting to be called to the table to doff my cap and say, 'Yes, will you please take this drama which stars the biggest stars we could make available in the UK?' And five guys would sit there and think, well, no – I mean this could do us out of revenue. And so we were denied access. We had six hours of drama a year when we started, that was our allocation. That is crazy for a company our size.

Gatward's attempts to persuade the Big Five to set a sixth place at their table failed. Brian Tesler remembers that Gatward then opened an offensive on another front, and that he was Gatward's guest when he lunched Home Secretary Douglas Hurd, and tried to persuade him to end the stranglehold of the Big Five.

Gatward says he has no memory of such a lunch:

The thought of being responsible for changing the legislation, that's very flattering, if it were true. I can't believe it's true. And if Brian believes it's true then surely he should have done more to allow us into the network to be the sixth major, as I wanted, rather than fighting us all the time.

Whether Gatward was responsible or not, the system did change. The 1990 Broadcasting Act led to the introduction of the ITV Network Centre, where Commissioners for each genre were responsible for choosing the programmes for ITV.

Gatward was not there to see it. TVS had bought out the American company MTM. They thought they were getting a lucrative programme library; they found they had taken on a money pit. Gatward was ousted from the company he had created. TVS failed to get its franchise renewed.

13

BAD RELATIONS
(and how to deal with them)

Q: What's the difference between an Arab oil sheikh
and an LWT video tape engineer?
A: The oil sheikh doesn't get London weighting.

Anon, 1970s

ITV HAD ITS FIRST strike before its first broadcast, when the preparation of Associated-Rediffusion's new headquarters was halted. The unions were determined to be recognised; they and many of their members had experienced the exploitation endemic in the casualised British film industry. They weren't going to be taken again. The grip they established on the ITV companies was savagely effective. They protected jobs, imposed manning levels, pushed up pay rates, refused to work with new technology.

In some cases they were cleverer than the management; they knew, as the bosses evidently could not predict, that if they got a deal in which overtime rates doubled, redoubled and doubled again on long shifts with anti-social hours, and also got a deal in which they could set their own rosters, the combination would be enormously lucrative.

In other cases, they simply had management over a barrel. Equipment needed skilled operators. They could halt production. They could halt transmission. Once airtime was gone, it could never be made up; the advertising revenue was lost forever. According to Brian Tesler, 'the unions ran Independent Television.' Michael Grade was another executive at the sharp end:

Many was the night I was in a studio on my knees begging the technicians to let us finish something – you know, the clock was ticking to 10 o'clock and we needed one more shot which would have taken us to five past ten

Above: Anne Diamond soldiered on to present TV-am's makeshift service during the ACTT strike of 1987.

Opposite page: Joanna Lumley and David McCallum as time agents *Sapphire and Steel* in the ATV science-fiction serial. Transmission of the programme's first series was disrupted by strike action in early August 1979 when the ITV network was blacked out for 11 weeks.

and they just said, 'No, we're going home.' Plugs would be pulled.

No-one who worked in the first 30 years of ITV lacks a story about labour relations and working practices. The drama shoot in Germany that needed a plum pudding, which could have been bought on site – the union insisted it had to be flown out from London, with a props man. The studio shoot with a toaster modified for a stunt – the electricians refused to plug it in because it was a prop, the props men refused to plug it in because it was electrical; an actress plugged it in and the studio crew walked out. The shoot in America on a boat with room for only camera, sound and director; the union insisted that an electrician had to be flown out to spend three weeks on expenses in a hotel. The cameraman who had first pick of shoots and could insist that foreign trips had to be arranged around his holidays; no matter the availability of the subjects, or the fact that directors who reluctantly worked with him knew they were lucky if his shots were in focus. Greg Dyke:

My first ever shoot, as a young researcher, I turn up and a car comes up. Big car with only a driver and nobody else in it. So I said, 'Who's that?' They said, 'That's the electrician's driver.' I said, 'Well where's the electrician?' And they said, 'Oh, he likes to bring his own car, so he can claim the mileage as well.'

Sir Denis Forman, chairman and managing director of Granada Television (1974-1984).

It is too easy simply to point the finger at the unions. The whole economy was dogged by sometimes vicious disputes for years; ITV was nearer the rule than the exception. Certainly, there were abuses of power by the ITV unions at their worst – but British industry is also full of stories of abuses of power by management. And many of the people who were responsible for running ITV recognise their own collective failings. There was a lack of resolve, and a lack of solidarity. It was impossible to get the different companies to hold together. Denis Forman:

The biggest delinquent here was Lew [Grade,] who was producing shows

Jeremy Irons and John Gielgud were among the cast of Granada's lavish adaptation of *Brideshead Revisited*.

The Bill in a bit of bother on the streets of Sun Hill.

Typically irreverent caricatures from *Spitting Image*.

Charlie Williams became a household name with his regular appearances on Granada's *The Comedians*.

Sergeant Lewis (Kevin Whately) and Inspector Morse (John Thaw) on the case.

Niamh Cusack and Nick Berry starred in the early series of cosy Sunday night drama serial *Heartbeat*.

Cracker's Fitz (Robbie Coltrane) was a latter-day Sherlock Holmes, solving crimes but prey to his own demons.

Chris Tarrant graduated from *Tiswas* to ask *Who Wants To Be A Millionaire?*

Cilla Black sizes up three more potential Mister Rights in *Blind Date*.

Simon Cowell
shows aspiring
pop stars just
how tough
showbusiness
can be.

Ant & Dec (never knowingly seen standing the other way round) are the current kings of Saturday night.

for America in the Seventies. If he was running out of time at midnight, he'd pay them double time, treble time and then go around with pound notes in the studio, anything to get the show finished. He was our weakest link, without any doubt. But getting 14 or 15 companies to take a firm and sensible stand on policy was very difficult. Most of them were pretty gruff Tory boards and they would say, 'Stand firm, management must manage,' and when they saw what it was costing them they went white in the face and crumpled. Big fight to start with and then immediate crumple when they saw they were losing ten million a day.

Greg Dyke was a vociferous union representative in his younger days:

I'll never forget when two of us, myself and a bloke called Andy Forrester, were negotiating on behalf of the producers and directors. We walked into the management and demanded 20 per cent increase in wages. And I think they offered us five per cent. And we stomped around and said no. So they offered us 18 per cent. And I remember we looked at each other, and we thought,

The Protectors, an action-adventure thriller series produced by Gerry Anderson for Lew Grade's ITC, was one of ITV's most popular teatime programmes, running to 52 episodes between 1972 and 1973. Filmed on location all over Europe – including Paris, Rome, Malta, Madrid, Venice and Salzburg – the series followed the members of an international private detective agency led by Harry Rule (Robert Vaughn, centre), the Contessa di Contini (Nyree Dawn Porter) and Paul Buchet (Tony Anholt).

how fast can we get out of this room? So we threw in a few other things and said we wanted televisions and videos on top of the rise. They agreed to that as well. We always joked and said it was the pop-up toaster deal because we think if we'd asked for a pop-up toaster we'd have got that as well.

In spite of lean years in the British economy, the monopoly on television advertising kept plenty of money flowing through ITV. The levy on income changed in the mid-Seventies to a levy on profits. Two thirds of company profits over a quarter of a million pounds went to the Treasury. Add that to other taxes, and it meant that the cost of any wage increase was borne almost entirely by the taxman's share. So it was relatively painless for managements to settle. Greg Dyke:

The management, as you discovered later, were paying tax rates of 95 per cent, 96 per cent. Now if you're paying tax rates of 95 per cent, 96 per cent and you give in to a demand from the unions, it only costs you five per cent. And the combination of how easy it was to take any of the ITV stations off the air, combined with the tax rates the managements were paying, gave the unions enormous power. But I think you've also got to accept that most of the managements were pretty gutless.

Greg Dyke, former TV-am editor in chief, Chief Executive of LWT and programme controller of TVS, became chairman of GMTV in 1993.

But the managements decided make a stand in 1979. With inflation running at over 13 per cent (and on its way to 18), the unions demanded a 25 per cent pay rise. The companies could have afforded it, but chose to try to limit the rise to ten per cent, and offered nine. It was rejected. The companies came back with 15 per cent. Alan Sapper of the powerful ACTT union responded in a television interview:

15 per cent is not reasonable when you compare the profits of the companies. They're enormously rich and wealthy and [have] made incredible profits over the last four years, and therefore we do feel that our claim of a substantial increase is fair and reasonable.

The unions restated their demand. It was the start of August, 1979. ITV managements had always tried ensure that if disputes were going to happen, they happened in summer when advertising was at its slackest for the year. They dug in.

Michael Grade was LWT's Director of Programmes at the time:

In their stupidity, the bosses of ITV at that time decided this was the ground on which to fight. So they said no. The unions went on strike and ITV closed down for 11 weeks. There was a test card. I went to the South of France and said, 'Ring me when it's all over', nothing I could do. We were off the air with a blank screen. So, we sat it out for 11 weeks and eventually, of course, we came back begging for mercy. And we reached a settlement that was much higher than what they'd been asking for and what they were striking over in the first place. That was kind of Custer's Last Stand. It was a nightmare and I think that's when everybody realised we were living in an Alice in Wonderland world, but we were powerless to do anything about it.

The next decade would see power shift dramatically, and the change had

In November 1987, changes in agreed working practices at TV-am prompted a strike by ACTT members. The strike turned into a lock-out when Managing Director Bruce Gyngell decided he could continue to broadcast without them.

already begun. In May 1979, Margaret Thatcher was elected Prime Minister. Over the next five years, three Employment Acts attacked the closed shop and secondary picketing. In television it became more difficult for disputes to spread from union to union, from site to site, or from production to transmission. A strike in one area could be contained.

Add this to the way that the machinery used in transmission had become simpler over the years, and the blank screen became much less of a threat.

Brian Tesler:

That made possible the concept of a management service. If the unions refused to put out a service, and we had enough people in management who could put it out instead, we would still be able to earn advertising revenue. We'd still have our programmes taken by the rest of the network. That was the beginning of the breaking of the unions.

Bruce Gyngell, Managing Director of TV-am, kept *Good Morning Britain* on the air during the 1987/88 ACTT strike by calling in favours and screening vintage American series such as *Batman* (opposite page).

The first big test came at Thames in 1984. A strike was called over the use of new cameras and editing equipment, and overtime payments to transmission staff. It lasted two weeks, but Thames was only off the air for a day. The management had planned ahead, and trained up people from their finance, personnel and other departments to keep broadcasting. They were able to keep a service of sorts on air. Mrs Thatcher sent them a message of support. For once, the unions gave ground in the settlement that ended the strike.

The key dispute came three years later, at TV-am. It started small: the management tried to change agreed working practices, and reduced a film crew from five people to three. ACTT members voted to strike. Action began on Monday 23 November 1987. TV-am boss Bruce Gyngell told them they would never come back. The strike became a lock-out.

With no producers, no technicians, no cameramen, and no floor managers, Gyngell took control, mustered all available untrained hands, and ran the output himself. He told reporters:

I'm not a union basher. I'm out to set up practices and conditions which we are used to in Australia, It's a matter of pushing or dragging the ACTT into the 21st century.

He called in favours, and pulled together a stack of vintage programmes like *Batman* and the adventures of dolphin *Flipper*. Within a fortnight they had managed to add some live studio coverage each day,

presented by Anne Diamond. One of her first guest interviewees was Margaret Thatcher, brimful of anti-union solidarity. Adam West, who had played Batman, was booked to appear but refused to cross the picket line. Flipper was presumably unavailable.

The makeshift service was riddled with fluffs and gaffes, missed cues and people talking to the wrong camera. But the hours of live transmission increased, dusty repeats reduced.

Gyngell presented the locked-out ACTT workers with a ten-point plan for revised working conditions – revised in TV-am's favour. They rejected it. On 16 February 1988, Gyngell sacked all 234 of them, and banned the ACTT from the company.

TV-am found it hard to recruit new workers, but continued their often patchy broadcasts. TV-am's reputation had been hurt by its programming, but its pocket had not. In the year to January 1989 the company made profits of over £20million, more than 50 per cent up on the previous year. The ACTT and the management only reached a settlement in September 1989.

The unions had lost their power to shut down transmission. They were also losing ground in production. This development had its roots in the opening of Channel 4 in November 1982.

The frequency for a fourth channel had been available throughout the Seventies, but no-one had decided what to do with it. At first, it was assumed that it would be handed over to the old idea of a competitive ITV2 – companies offering the same mix as ITV, and fighting it out for advertisers. Then the word 'complementary' started to be put around; why not a service owned by the same companies, an equivalent to BBC2 which could offer contrasting and sometimes specialist programmes? Finally, fashionable ideas of open access to the airwaves became influential – the channel should be available to anyone to make programmes about anything. There wasn't much sensible thought about how to pay for this new idea.

In the end, the Conservative government decided that the new channel wasn't going to be competitive, or complementary, or open; it was going to be 'distinctive'. It would offer programmes the other channels didn't, chosen by a group of commissioning editors; and as many as possible would be made by independent production companies – that appealed to Mrs Thatcher's belief in the competitive market. And they thought very hard about how to fund it.

ITV could do it.

For a decade, the ITV companies would bankroll the new channel, in return for selling its advertising and keeping the income. There was some alarm about the drain on resources; in the end the ITV subscription would rise from £132m in 1983/4 to £270m in 1991/2. There was further worry that in the long term ITV would have its first competitor for advertising revenue; the lucrative days of monopoly were over.

But the companies benefited too. The independent producers were able to start from scratch in agreeing practices with the unions. And ITV

London Weekend Television
Director of Programmes
Greg Dyke (left) and
Chairman Christopher Bland
(right) in 1987.

was able to use the new agreements as a lever in disputes.

Greg Dyke returned to LWT in 1987, as Director of Programmes:

When I first got back to London Weekend, we commissioned a drama called
Betty, which starred Twiggy. It was one of the first independent productions
and it was being made at Shepperton. The set was built, when suddenly the
unions, including Equity, all said, 'You can't make this under the agreement
that this independent's got, you've got to make it under the ITV agreement.'
Now that would have been a disaster, it would have cost twice as much. And
I realised this was a moment, this was a turning point, so I cancelled the
whole thing – cost us a million pounds. I went public, said, 'We will not be
held to ransom by these people.' It was funny because it was the only year
that I ever got a Christmas card from Margaret Thatcher.

We said, 'That won't happen again,' and we then said to our own drama
department, 'Right, not only are we not going to do Twiggy, but we're not

Opposite page:
Prime Minister Margaret
Thatcher was interviewed
live on LWT's *Weekend
World* in 1985.

going to make any other drama in house unless you change these agreements. We'll make them all through independents.' And they folded.

Dyke and the LWT management were ready to push reforms of working practices through the company.

I remember sitting in a meeting with the unions when we were beginning to say quite aggressive things to them, and they accused us of trying to lock them out. And that was the moment when it changed, that was the moment when I knew it was all over. For years the managements sat in meetings with the unions and the unions threatened to walk out, and the moment it changed was when they said, 'Well you're threatening to lock us out.' And of course we were, I mean it was quite true. We had set up an alternative transmission base and we pretended it was in Holland and we all walked around with books called Teach Yourself Dutch. *I don't even think there is a language Dutch, but we all tried to pretend we were learning to speak Dutch. In fact, all the tapes were stored in somebody's garage and we'd found somewhere in London where we could transmit from. We had a whole plan that if they tried to take us off air we would go to our alternative transmission base.*

It was Christopher Bland, who was Chairman of London Weekend, really who changed it, because every time the people who ran the facilities management said, 'We want to take on the unions in this little bit,' he said, 'Don't be ridiculous, I'm not taking on a little bit, because you take on a little bit, they take you off air and you're paying everybody else in the company'. He said, 'If we're going to have a bust up with the unions, we're going to have it right across the board.' So in the end we planned and organised the potential bust up, not them.

It never really happened because by then they knew the writing was on the wall. They knew things had changed. And it was amazing the speed at which the unions went from being all powerful to being irrelevant.

Things had changed. But in spite of her Christmas card to Greg Dyke, Mrs Thatcher was still not a fan of ITV's management practices. She hadn't seen all the developments inside the companies. But she remembered what she had seen.

One of her memories was of a massive diplomatic gaffe on ITV's part. In November 1985, LWT's *Weekend World* arranged a live interview at Downing Street. Mrs Thatcher had dealt with plenty of foreign news crews, and knew it took no more than three people to get a picture on

screen. LWT sent 53. No matter that they were putting interviewer Brian Walden onscreen as well as her. And no matter that it was such an important live event that they had sent an entire second crew to cover the first one in case of accidents. There were, as Mrs Thatcher was heard to mutter 'an awful lot of people in this room'.

Her relationship with ITV came to a head at a Downing Street seminar on commercial broadcasting in September 1987. Representatives of ITV, Channel 4, and advertisers were invited. And so was Michael Green, who had made millions running television facilities but had been frustrated in his attempts to buy into broadcasting – and had told Mrs Thatcher so. Michael Grade was also there, now as a representative of the BBC:

Everyone knew she was out to get ITV and of course she was a very powerful personality. We were all in rows of seats and she sat there at a desk with Douglas Hurd who was the Home Secretary, who was responsible for broadcasting. She had her handbag and some note paper there and she listened and we did our turn and somebody else did their turn. Then we got to ITV. At this point she opened her bag and got her pen out. Bill Brown of Scottish Television got up and did his ITV piece. And she's listening to him, and tapping on the desk. And then suddenly in the middle of his speech, she put her hands on the desk and stood up, she leaned across the desk and she pointed at him and she said, 'You, gentlemen, are the last bastions of restrictive practices.' The room was shaking. I was pleased to be working for the BBC at that moment, I can tell you.

The agenda was to reform Independent Television, to find the 'better way' to allocate the licences that had been an issue since Lady Plowden had declined to tell her why Southern had been ousted. She got her idea of how to do it from another person in the room, Professor Alan Peacock.

Thatcher had appointed Peacock to lead a committee to look into the BBC. Its task was to take evidence on the relative merits of funding it by licence fee, or scrapping the licence and introducing advertising; to carefully weigh up the relative merits of the two systems; and to decide in favour of advertising. But the 1986 report had given her the answer she didn't want to hear. No adverts on Auntie.

But the Peacock Committee stretched their brief to look at ITV as well. And they didn't like what they saw. They wanted efficiency; they saw waste. The problem was that the levy ITV companies paid on profits gave them little incentive to be more efficient; if they saved money, it would almost all have to be paid out in tax.

But, Peacock suggested, it would be different if they paid upfront. Then the outgoings would have been dealt with, and any saving would be the company's. So why not put the licences out to competitive tender next time? Highest bid wins (as long as the business plan stands up to scrutiny). The more they pay, the more they need to cut costs. Restrictive practices would be driven out by economic necessity. The Peacock Committee were clear:

…the successful bidder would then have monopoly profits creamed off in advance of operating the franchise, and the subsequent earning of profits would depend on close attention to economy on the use of resources.

There were immediate worries in the industry about what would happen to programmes if there was no check on content. Wouldn't they be driven downmarket? TVS ran press adverts in 1988 featuring a stripping 'Italian housewife' as seen on deregulated Roman TV, and warning that cheap programming on British satellite stations might take us the same way. And critics of the 'highest bid' policy warned that the prospect didn't apply just to satellite stations.

Home Office minister David Mellor managed to get the bidding system amended. By the time the 1990 Broadcasting Act became law, it included a clause to say that applicants in the forthcoming licensing round would be disqualified if their programme plans did not meet a quality threshold. Another clause contained another safeguard; the highest bidder could be turned down, even if the threshold was met, and the licence awarded to another applicant in 'exceptional circumstances'. It sounded reassuring, though no-one had the faintest idea what 'exceptional circumstances' meant.

The new licences would come into force in 1992. Interested parties had until 15 May 1991 to submit their bids to the Independent Television Council. The ITC had succeeded the IBA when the 1990 Act came into force, and was intended by government to act with a lighter touch. They were no longer officially the broadcaster, only a regulator.

There began the most elaborate bidding round in ITV's history. In previous licence rounds, it had only been realistic to expect incumbents to be ousted if they had a real weakness in programming or business structure (even if the incumbents were blind to it). Now every one of the 15 licences was up for grabs.

The incumbents had the advantage of knowing the inside figures. The new contenders had the advantage of being able to cut costs by proposing a lightweight business, in the manner of Channel 4, commissioning programmes from independents rather than producing in-house. Some sitting tenants tried to avoid being sitting targets by slimming down their workforce – LWT became a notably leaner meaner machine in the years leading up to the applications.

Who was bidding? Everyone wanted to know. Interested companies circled each other, trying to find who was planning to pitch where. Potential rivals became partners, or were offered sweeteners to keep their distance. Current companies took minority stakes in new bids (as the new law allowed them to); Granada snapping at Tyne-Tees; Tyne-Tees and Yorkshire snapping back at Granada. Secrecy was paramount; information about other bids could be worth tens of millions.

David Frost was involved with Richard Branson in three bids. He told reporters:

There are two approaches that we're debating: one is the months and months of computer models that have been prepared, and the other is to just close your eyes and take a pin.

Greg Dyke:

I got a wonderful letter one week from a guy who said, 'I know what they're going to bid and if you want to know, just place an ad in the Evening Standard on Friday saying, 'Something for the weekend sir?' and then I'll know you're interested.

Thirty-seven different groups submitted forty different bids. Some had prepared whole applications with different financial offers, and waited until the last minute to decide which to run with.

At the ITC, Chairman George Russell opened the first envelope. TVS had bid a staggering £59.76 million to retain their licence.

The new bidding system was supposed to produce a more transparent process, a 'better way'. It was intended to provide straightforward criteria for the decision-makers. But almost every choice seemed to be an anomaly.

TVS were disqualified; the ITC thought their revenue projections were unrealistic and their bid unsustainable. Their franchise went to Meridian, the next highest bidder, at £36.5 million. One of two other failed bids for the region was from the Frost-Branson group, who had spread their efforts too thinly across three areas, and were ruled out of all of them for not passing the quality threshold.

Another of their applications failed to oust Anglia, who retained their franchise with a highest bid of £17.8 million.

In the south-west, licence holder TSW were also judged to have made an unsustainable bid, and lost out to Westcountry Television's lower offer.

Channel, Grampian, Granada, Ulster and LWT all won against higher bidders, who were ruled out on quality. LWT knew they weren't going to outbid their rivals (who turned out to have put in a figure of £35 million), and that they were relying on the quality threshold saving them. They debated whether to bid a token sum, but decided not to risk embarrassing the ITC, and eventually won their franchise back for a respectable £7.5 million.

Harlech, Yorkshire and Tyne-Tees all believed they would have to bid high to win. They bid so high that the ITC seriously considered rejecting the business plans of each in turn and disqualifying them, before deciding in their favour.

Border, Central and Scottish were all unopposed. Border decided to bid £52,000. Central and Scottish gambled everything on their deductions that they had no rivals, and went for bids of just £2,000. (They would have gone for £1,000, but the law required bids in multiples of a thousand pounds, and they were worried that the ITC might decide that the figure one was not a multiple, and reject them. Two undoubtedly was a multiple; the extra thousand pounds each spent was sound investment).

Michael Green (right) was managing director of Carlton Television when the company ousted Thames as contractor for the London weekday ITV franchise. Carlton went on air for the first time on 1 January 1993.

The biggest prize was the London weekday licence, where Thames were the incumbents. The Frost-Branson group scored their third elimination here, leaving Thames and Michael Green's group Carlton in competition. Thames bid over £32 million. The ITC looked at their programme proposals and decided they were exceptional, but that having exceptional programmes did not constitute exceptional circumstances. Carlton, commissioners not producers, won with a bid of £43 million. The stalwart of the ITV schedules was out, though it continued to trade profitably as an independent producer.

Of the 15 regional franchises eight had gone to applicants who had been outbid, three had been chosen unopposed, and only four had gone to highest bidders against competition. Three of those four had been serious candidates for rejection on the grounds that their business plans were over-optimistic.

A better way?

Several of the losers demanded meetings and explanations from the ITC. They got their meetings, where they were told the ITC was not required to explain anything. TSW chairman Brian Bailey decided to seek a judicial review, on the grounds that the ITC's decision was 'unfair and irrational'. Their application went from High Court to Appeal Court to the House of Lords, who ruled that whether or not the ITC's judgment was sound, it was their job to make it and there was no legal mechanism to appeal against it. Not the most ringing endorsement of the new process.

There was one other franchise decision. Bruce Gyngell knew he was the Prime Minister's favourite broadcaster. He had delivered the unions on a plate. TV-am was a model of efficiency and profitability. He believed they were untouchable on the quality threshold. If ever there were exceptional circumstances, they related to his company. The new law hadn't been designed to target him.

TV-am bid £14 million, Daybreak Television £33 million, and Sunrise Television £34 million. Sunrise got the job, and became GMTV. The power behind it was LWT. Greg Dyke had his revenge on Bruce Gyngell.

I put together the bid that took away TV-am's franchise. I remember thinking that's game, set and match to us.

Not everyone was happy to see Gyngell go. On hearing the result, Mrs Thatcher wrote him a letter. Gyngell read it out to the television news cameras:

Dear Bruce,
When I see how some of the other licenses have been awarded I am mystified that you did not receive yours, and heartbroken. You of all people have done so much for the whole of television – there seems to have been no attention to that. I am only too painfully aware that I was responsible for the legislation.

She never said 'sorry'.

Opposite page:
Inspector Morse – starring John Thaw (right) and Kevin Whately – is arguably Carlton's best known drama series, although the company has also brought viewers *Peak Practice* and *Kavanagh QC*.

THAT'S ENTERTAINMENT!

Above: Tommy Cannon and Bobby Ball starred in nine seasons of their *Cannon and Ball* series for LWT.

14

I didn't choose television. Television chose me. I could string two words together. I was a bit of fun and a bit of scouse rough and everybody liked me. I was normal. I could have been the kid next door. And then I turned into the auntie next door. And now I'm the granny next door.

Cilla Black

THE CREDITS HAVE just rolled on another live edition of *Ant & Dec's Saturday Night Takeaway*. Games have been played, practical jokes pulled, prizes won. The stars have thanked the audience, who are now filing out of the studio, popping the balloons that descended on them

Above: On *Blind Date*, contestants from the previous week's show returned to relate their holiday experiences to host Cilla Black (right).

Opposite page: Bruce Forsyth dances with Juliet Prowse on a special one-off edition of LWT's *Bruce Forsyth's Big Night* screened in April 1980, two years after the original run of the series ended.

209

Above: Anthony McPartlin and Declan Donnelly – formally known as pop duo PJ and Duncan – are the hosts of *Ant & Dec's Saturday Night Takeaway*.

Below: Chris Tarrant was a regular target for the Phantom Flan Flinger on ATV's *Tiswas*.

during the show.

Declan Donnelly is talking to the puppeteer who has operated their guest star, Kermit the Frog. Still buzzing from the show, Dec is thrilled to have appeared with the green glove-puppet. The Muppets, he says, were one of the programmes that he and Ant McPartlin grew up with, and their energetic knockabout comic style has influenced their own programme. And it's not the only influence from ITV's entertainment past that has fed this current hit.

ANT: *There's nothing particularly ground-breakingly different about our style. I just think we're obviously more modern in our approach, in how we do things.*
DEC: *The roots of* Saturday Night Takeaway *are very much in shows like* Sunday Night at the London Palladium *– having the audience as part of the show and the games.* Game for a Laugh *was a huge influence on us as kids. And you draw on those influences.*
ANT: *It's very much like watching old* The Price Is Right, *you know – 'Come on down'. I remember watching the audience on that and they went crazy, and that was exactly the same kind of atmosphere we wanted to create. If you watched as a viewer, you wanted to say, 'I want to be there next week and experience that atmosphere.'*

Tiswas, Chris Tarrant's early-Eighties Saturday morning show, is another influence on their style. *Tiswas* ended the requirement for kids' television to be polite. Flans being flung, Spit the Dog – the vent act with no words but a great line in phlegm – parents in cages being drenched in water, and Tarrant yelling, 'This is the stuff, this is what they want.' It looked like a huge kids' party running out of control, with a bunch of entertainers who were often terrible but occasionally inspired. It was the original zoo television, and a huge influence on many programmes that followed.

But for all the mix of influences, Ant and

Dec needed a new twist to find a working formula – a competition to win the contents of an advertising break.

DEC: Saturday Night Takeaway *is a show that we have wanted to make for years and years and years. When we were growing up we were both huge fans of that kind of light entertainment zoo, anything can happen, live hour on a Saturday. We had a crack at it with a series called* Slap Bang *which didn't quite work, but it was same thing, a lot of mini formats within a bigger format. Granada, who we made the show with, had an idea for a spine of a new show called* Win the Ads.

ANT: *And having failed with* Slap Bang, *we realised you need that one hook for the viewer. You get the* TV Times *and you see it's the show that, oh yeah, you can win the ads, I get it. And then, once people have got that then you can reduce that slightly and have fun in other areas.*

Entertainment shows are notoriously difficult to get right. Production teams who embark on what looks like a surefire hit can be left picking over the bones, wondering what went wrong. One of the great ITV successes of recent years is Celador's *Who Wants to Be a Millionaire?*, presented by Chris Tarrant. It started, says Tarrant, as a game dreamed up on his Capital Radio show with his producer Dave Briggs. 'We did a thing called Double or Quits, which was basically a very raw version of *Millionaire*. You started off for a pound, and played for however much you could win.' But who knows how successful it would have been if the television translation had not been reworked just before going on air. Chris Tarrant:

Ant & Dec's Saturday Night Takeaway developed from a game show idea titled *Win the Ads*, a competition to win the contents of the show's advertising breaks.

We did two pilots of Millionaire. *My bit didn't change much. I think we refined the gormless stare I do at a camera, and making the contestant sweat a bit.*

What completely changed between the first pilot and the first transmitted show – it was only a few weeks later – was the music, the lighting and all that stuff that is actually designed to increase the drama. Paul Smith and Co., the producers, actually realised at the time that's what they were doing, making it look much more modern, not making it look like an old-style game show that could be 20, 30 years old, and putting in music and lighting that would heighten the drama for people at home, and frighten the shit out of the person in the chair. They got rid of this quite dreadful song, that I think dear old Peter Waterman wrote. No disrespect to Pete, it was sort of what you wrote for that kind of show, until Millionaire. *It was winning lots of money, holiday, living on an island, yachts, it was all that, it was like, urgh. But actually, a year before, it would have seemed perfectly reasonable, because that's the sort of song you had with shows like that. And suddenly Paul Smith said, 'No, we don't one of those, we want, da, da, da, all that stuff.' But until then there was this quite dreadful old song, that's probably still hanging round waiting for a show to go with it.*

Who Wants to Be a Millionaire? has circled the globe as a package, remade in other languages, but with the same set, the same music, and the same lights – even the same catchphrases. Chris Tarrant:

These key phrases, like, 'Is that your final answer?' or 'Do you want to phone a friend?' just sort of happened. We never sat down and thought, let's have catch phrases.

I was in Kazakhstan, of all places, and I'd been fishing for about a week, and I was looking pretty grim, and evil smelling, and I'd dived into the only hotel in town when I came back in from the wilds, had a bath, turned on this little black and white telly, and even before the picture had come up, there was this music going, da, da, da, and I thought, Oh God, not here as well. And this bloke, a bloke not that unlike me, wearing a very similar suit and this sort of gormless face, and all that, handed this man a cheque for getting the right answer. And then he went to him, blah blah blah, and I thought, I know exactly what he's doing. 'I don't wanna give you that.' I just thought, how weird is that? Thousands of miles from home, and culturally a million miles from home, on the Chinese border, there's a man doing something that Dave Briggs and I dreamed up in a studio in Elstree seven years ago. Very odd.

Who Wants to Be a Millionaire? has been licensed in over a hundred countries. It's the Holy Grail of twenty-first century television: a format that can be sold and reproduced all round the world. The market was different 50 years ago, but ITV had its formats then, too. *Take Your Pick* and *Double Your Money* came from Radio Luxembourg. *People Are Funny* was American. The *Beat the Clock* games that were part of the success of *Sunday Night at the London Palladium* were also based on an American show.

With the early *Palladium* programmes, ATV effectively turned their cameras on a stage show. Granada had its own rival entertainment series, based not on the variety theatre but on the atmosphere of a London nightspot. *Chelsea at Nine* brought viewers the sophistication of Yehudi Menuhin, Charles Laughton, Marcel Marceau, Stephane Grappelli, the young Daniel Barenboim, and Maria Callas. They also had their resident song and dance troupe, the Granadiers, who covered current hit songs so successfully that they got their own show. In one edition they trolled on in a rickshaw while trilling 'Living Doll', Cliff Richard's first number one hit. But ITV also gave its viewers the real Cliff.

Oh Boy!, created by producer Jack Good, was British television's first rock and roll show. Cliff was one of its regulars, starting down the bill in 1958, and reaching the top of it a year later. Cliff began by singing other people's songs, in a style that made him every inch Britain's answer to Elvis. Cliff Richard:

Oh Boy! *was the forerunner to every pop/rock show that ever happened since that time. And it was the genius of Jack Good that created a very fast, pacy, show, where we, then young singers of our time, sang other people's hits. Because Elvis wasn't likely to come over and do* Oh Boy!*, and neither were any of the other stars from the States, we got the privilege of singing their songs. And they'd say, 'And here's Cliff, singing Elvis's hot stuff.' And I would do his song. Of course, I got a chance to sing my own stuff too. But I presented myself on television — as did Adam Faith, Marty Wilde, Billy Fury, Dickie Pride — and that's where it all began for me. So it naturally means a great deal to me.*

Cliff Richard made his name as the featured artist on Jack Good's *Oh Boy!* The show was scheduled on Saturday nights in direct opposition to the BBC's *Six-Five Special*, also created by Good, and led to its demise.

There had been variety shows with pop numbers in them before. But *Oh Boy!* was rock and roll from top to tail, fizzing with energy. Cliff Richard:

Everything was live. There were no tracks. We didn't have the facility for tracks in those days. So we just had to come on, spend a week rehearsing,

(From left) Bernard Manning, Mike Reid and Tom O'Connor were joined by (from right) Duggie Brown, Jim Bowen, George Roper and Colin Crompton in the original 1972-74 editions of *The Comedians*. Revivals of the format in 1979, 1984 and 1992 were less successful.

and then get out there, heart beating, and do it live. And it started with a bang, and it went out with a bang, week after week after week. It was fast and furious. That was down to a woman called Rita Gillespie, who was the lighting director, and Jack Good with his direction. I remember one instrumental that Lord Rockingham's Eleven, the band that we all sang to, did. He filmed it so that every single bar was a different shot. I think it was the first time that had ever been done – in fact, I'm not even sure it's been done since! Maybe parts of a song would have been filmed like that, but this was the whole number. You just look at it and think, 'This is impossible.' And, of course, we didn't have hundreds of cameras in those days, so cameras were flying around.

Pop shows became a regular feature of the ITV schedule. In 1961, ATV's *Thank Your Lucky Stars* began a six-year run. It featured a jury giving marks to new records, and made a celebrity of Midlands teenager Janice Nicholls, and her catchphrase 'Oi'll give it foive'. But by now the edge of live singing had been replaced by modern technology. Cilla Black:

I was a pop singer and Thank Your Lucky Stars *was a plug show. And if you did the show you were guaranteed that your record sales would go up. You would go down to Birmingham, they'd call you at some unearthly hour, nine o'clock. I was rock and roll, and we rock and rollers like to sleep all day, and then we'd party all night. You know, I'm an energy vampire. So nine o'clock in the morning, that was tough. And you're only miming. It was not live then. So you mime to your record, and you had to spend the whole day there. And do the show at nearly seven o'clock at night – with an audience, but what a waste of time. I mean all you're doing is miming, for goodness sake, and can't the camera guys get the shots right? Can't the director do it right, in all that time? I used to sing with the record. Because you had to get all the breathing right. It's quite an art, actually. As a singer, I do it differently every time, especially on stage. So you'd have to have a few practices in your dressing room with your little tape. Hey, if you're a pro you can do it.*

By the late Sixties, the theatrical variety format was pretty much dead. But variety performers were still the bedrock of television entertainment. They moved into the studio, with shows made for the camera. For viewers, it was less like a seat in the front row at the theatre, more like having the performer in your living room. At Granada, producer Johnny Hamp raided the northern club circuit for stand-up comedians, recorded chunks of their acts (the clean sections), and intercut them to make quick-fire gag sessions. *The Comedians* made stars of Frank ('It's the way I tell 'em') Carson, shy Ken Goodwin, black Yorkshireman Charlie Williams, weedy Colin Crompton and robust Bernard Manning.

Duggie Brown was just one of *The Comedians* who went on to appear at *The Wheeltappers and Shunters Social Club*, a fictional northern variety club in the Granada series of the same name which ran from 1974 to 1977.

The last two were regulars when Granada set up their own club on air – *The Wheeltappers and Shunters Social Club*. Hamp put acts on stage in a tinsel-dripping parody of the real circuit. There were established stars (Gene Pitney, the original rock and roller Bill Haley), novelty acts (baton twirlers and violently acrobatic dancers), and young faces who would become very familiar (Paul Daniels, Cannon and Ball). Manning played the compere, forever joking about how cheap the turns were, and Crompton played the shambolic club chairman, interrupting proceedings with his bell to make announcements: 'The pies 'ave come. Put plenty of pepper on 'em, they came by themselves.'

It was a long way from *Chelsea at Nine*. It played well in the north. But it did nothing to alleviate LWT's entertainment headache. By the time the *Wheeltappers* finished their three-year run in 1977, London was the only region in which surveys found that people preferred the BBC to ITV. The BBC was still rolling out one big gun after another on Saturday night.

Bruce Forsyth and Anthea Redfern – his assistant on *The Generation Game* who became his second wife – defected from the BBC in 1978 to appear in *Bruce Forsyth's Big Night* for LWT.

In 1978, LWT's Michael Grade came up with a plan to simultaneously capture the audience and rip the heart out of the BBC's early evening Saturday schedule. For seven years, Bruce Forsyth had been presenting *The Generation Game*, delivering audiences of up to 20 million to the BBC. Grade thought he could tempt Forsyth across with a show that would allow him to show off the full range of his talents. 'I sat down with my Controller of Entertainment, David Bell, and I said, "We've got to reinvent variety".'

Grade and Bell concocted a format for a two-hour show, *Bruce Forsyth's Big Night*, which included song, dance and guest interviews from Bruce, international star performers, short sitcom segments, sketches and games. Forsyth, feeling *The Generation Game* was getting tired, signed up. Floated on a huge wave of publicity, and massive expectations, the first *Big Night* attracted 14 million viewers. But it was an ambitious production, launched without a pilot, and the next few weeks saw changes in the format and the start of a drop in the audience.

Grade had thought that *The Generation Game* relied on Forsyth. But the BBC recast it with an act whom Grade, previously a talent agent, had discovered in a drag club: Larry Grayson. As the two shows went head-to-head, the press joined in. Michael Grade:

> *The press saw this as David against Goliath. We had Goliath and the BBC had David. And ours was an experimental show, it was work in progress.*

And the press killed us. They just decided they were going to destroy Bruce.

Having built the show up before it aired, the papers began to knock it down. Bruce Forsyth:

They said things like Elton John had walked out of the show because of me. Completely false. Elton walked out of the show because his guy who was sent to put his piano track down hadn't done it properly and Elton came in

and said I can't work with this. Elton came to apologise to me actually, and say 'Bruce I'm sorry about letting you down.' I said, 'No, you're not letting us down. If your music isn't right then that's your livelihood, that's your job. And if it isn't right then that's fine.' He said, 'What were we going to do?' I said, 'I was going to get round the piano and try to sing one of your songs the way you do, the way you phrase it.' And he said, 'That sounds fun, come on, let's do it.' And in the end he did the show. But as far as the press were concerned, he walked off the show because of me. Now that's unfair.

Bruce Forsyth dances with special guest Juliet Prowse in a big song and dance number in a one-off edition of *Bruce Forsyth's Big Night* screened in 1980.

Michael Grade:

The press was telling the world that this is a disaster – every day a front page story, so-and-so quits or this is dropped or crisis meeting at London Weekend. Anything to keep the story running. We couldn't deal with the artillery coming in. We just weren't allowed to get the show right. The show would have come right in the end, there were some good things in it. There's no question we lost our nerve, but part of that was driven by how much more punishment can we inflict on Bruce? He was taking it. He was very loyal. He never once said to the press, which he could have done to get himself off the hook, 'Well, London Weekend promised me this, promised me that, they've let me down.' He could have very easily dumped it all on me and London Weekend Television and I'd have forgiven him for doing it.

Bruce Forsyth:

And then the papers said the show was axed, and the show wasn't axed. The show was booked for 14 weeks and it did well for 14 weeks. Okay, they didn't want to continue with it, well that's fine. Probably it was the right thing to do. I think another 14 weeks of a live show that was complicated may have been a bit too much to take on. But because they said it was axed, you know, in great big headlines, I said to Michael 'I'd like to do two minutes to camera and just give them a bit back, because I've had enough.' When you feel everybody is against you or the press is completely en masse against you, you either fight and get on with the job or you just say, 'I've got a bad leg,' or you faint in front of the cameras and you pack it in. I decided to fight and I just wanted Michael to give me the chance to fight back with two minutes on screen, just to put the record straight.

Forsyth addressed the cameras, giving voice to his opinions on the way the press had treated his *Big Night*. Viewers at home heard him say:

With all that pre-press, it made people think that when the show started, that glitter was going to come out of the set, and it was going to be so sensational. And it's like everything else, when people tell you, 'Oh you must go and see that.' When you go and see it yourself, you're a bit disappointed…

And several minutes more in the same vein. But, as Forsyth now points out, the show had eventually recovered:

In its defence I'd just like to say that we got back the viewers and we did finish up with 14 million, which in the Seventies, Eighties was a very respectable figure. Only one newspaper quoted that we got back to 14 million.

Over on the BBC, *The Generation Game* sailed on with Grayson at the helm. Audiences loved his camp ineptitude when demonstrating the games on the show. Saturday night had a new queen. ITV continued its strategy of building shows round variety stars. Russ Abbott, who had won on *Opportunity Knocks* as one of the Black Abbotts, and appeared in sketches on *Big Night*, got his own series. So did Cannon and Ball, who had lost on *Opportunity Knocks*, and recorded sketches for *Big Night* that were never transmitted.

But Saturday night entertainment was about to change. In 1980, the BBC made a pilot of a programme called *Gotcha!*, in which members of the public took part in games and had tricks played on them. The show was presented by Paul Daniels. One of Daniels' sidekicks was the show's writer, Jeremy Beadle:

Bill Cotton, who was then the boss of the BBC, saw the pilot and said, 'So long as I am controller, the BBC will never ever transmit anything so vulgar.'

Beadle and his partner Jeremy Fox developed the idea further, and took it to senior LWT Entertainment Producer Alan Boyd. Boyd had produced *The Generation Game*. Now he thought he had a new show that could take on the old one. He gave it a title, *Game for a Laugh*. Jeremy Beadle:

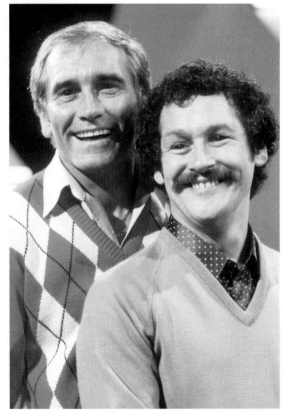

Thomas Derbyshire (left) and Robert Harper, former welders from Oldham better known as the comedy duo Cannon and Ball, broke into television as part of *Bruce Forsyth's Big Night*. They were given their own series on LWT in 1979 and became familiar ITV faces throughout the Eighties.

The show worked for one reason… Alan Boyd. There is no two ways about it. He was the producer, he did the thinking. I learned fantastic tricks from Alan Boyd.

Boyd set about casting the presenters. He didn't look to the usual pool of experienced hosts and stars. Beadle again:

Watching us watching you – the original hosts of LWT's *Game for a Laugh* were Matthew Kelly (left), Henry Kelly (back), Sarah Kennedy and Jeremy Beadle. Later hosts included Rustie Lee, Martin Daniels, Lee Peck and Debbie Rix.

He already had Matthew Kelly and Sarah Kennedy and so he was looking for a father figure and someone suggested Henry Kelly, who was an ex war correspondent. Slightly unlikely piece of casting for light entertainment Saturday evening – Irish, full of charm. But then none of them wanted to do the practical jokes, and so Alan Boyd mysteriously and wonderfully said, 'Do you want to do them yourself?' so I said, 'Yes, please.' David Bell, who was Alan's boss at the time – another brilliant name in the list of light entertainment producers – he turned around to Alan and said, 'You will never make a star of a man with a beard,' and Alan Boyd made two stars of two beards.

One thing that people don't know about Game for a Laugh *is that we made every show twice to begin with, and then Alan Boyd would cherry pick the best moments. Now that is a luxury afforded to few, but it laid the groundwork, he wanted to get it right and, by golly, he got it right. A hole in one. If I was to pick out a defining moment of British light entertainment, I would say the day Alan Boyd transmitted his first* Game for a Laugh. *It changed the viewing habits of the British public. For the first time in television history, the BBC lost Saturday nights and ITV owned it and haven't looked back.*

From its first night in September 1981, the mix of programme elements, the four presenters, and the care in production that extended to making sure that the audience shots always featured clean-cut faces to maintain the show's fun atmosphere, all combined to give ITV a winner. By November *Game for a Laugh* was the sixth biggest show on ITV. *The Generation Game* dropped from first to ninth in the BBC lists in the same two months. In December, Larry Grayson announced that he was quitting. Jeremy Beadle:

I knew we had a big hit show. What I didn't realise was just how big and how big an impact that show was to have on the future of television. Although it's not been recorded and there are only a very few, very serious writers who've actually picked up on it, when the history books are written, without a doubt Game for a Laugh *will be remembered as a watershed programme.*

Come on down – Leslie Crowther appeared to select contestants at random on the Central game show *The Price Is Right* which ran for five years from 1984. The show was later revived in 1995 by Yorkshire as *Bruce's Price Is Right*, hosted by Bruce Forsyth.

Game for a Laugh showed that entertainment shows didn't need variety stars to be successful. The public could become the stars. TV bosses realised that they could save money on musical rehearsals, top-of-the-bill guests, and all the paraphernalia associated with big production numbers.

ITV chased its success. In 1984, Central hired Leslie Crowther to front American import *The Price Is Right*. Contestants had to guess the retail price of the prize goods. It was simple, but many thought it was not

wholesome. The *Daily Mail* described it as 'Unspeakable vulgarity, ghastly materialism and unedifying greed' whilst *The Guardian* labelled it 'The noisiest, most money grabbing show so far.' The noise was the point. The people taking part were the show. When Crowther shouted, 'Come on down,' to members of the audience, he knew they were going to perform for him. The researchers had already been down the queue waiting to get into the studio, chatting them up and picking out the extroverts.

In the same year, Beadle presented LWT with another 'people show', *Surprise, Surprise*. Its mixture of fun elements culminated in often emotional reunions between estranged relatives and friends.

I knew that Game for a Laugh *was coming to an end, so I produced this piece of paper which was called* Surprise, Surprise. *It was the best of* Game for a Laugh, *it was the best of* This is Your Life, *all mingled into a programme that's full of surprise, and a lump in the throat, and makes you laugh. They made the pilot while I was on holiday. I was slightly upset about that, but it became a national show, fantastic success.*

Surprise, Surprise was presented by Cilla Black. Nigel Lythgoe:

Cilla was a huge success because she was an ordinary person. She was the auntie who was the life and soul of the party, if you like, or your mum, or your wife. She was an ordinary person, it was felt by the public, anyway. And she was. She had a great wit about her, a great charm, and when you saw Cilla's face, it was a bit like seeing Beadle's, but you didn't want to hit Cilla.

Cilla Black:

It was a feel-good show. We used to do Cillagrams, which took two days shooting. We took over the whole of Holyhead because the Lord Mayor of Holyhead wrote to me and said, we've got such bad street cred, nobody comes here. Could you come and do a Cillagram for us? So we re-wrote the tune

Opposite page and above: Cilla Black appeared in her first television series for over eight years when she agreed to host LWT's *Surprise, Surprise* and make dreams come true for ordinary members of the public. Cilla was initially partnered by Christopher Biggins and then by Bob Carolgees. Gordon Burns hosted a segment of the show entitled *Searchline* which reunited friends and families.

*'Hooray for Hollywood' to 'Hooray for Holyhead' and it was fabulous. The
Mayor met me from the train, and we did this Cillagram in the main high
street, where I was walking along with all the people in the background
singing, 'Hooray for Holyhead, don't go to Benidorm, come here instead.' It
was a fabulous day.*

*But then we got all the letters after that, because all the shops were looted.
Because all the people that were working there in Woolies and Marks and
Sparks and everything, all came to 'Hooray for Holyhead'. And as we were
marching up and singing, all the scallies were going in and pinching
everything in sight. I know it's a funny story but I felt so sorry. But an awful
lot of people went to Holyhead after that. They did.*

There were casualties of this new style of entertainment. Stanley
Baxter had been one of ITV's strongest performers for years. His
programmes had won four BAFTAs when LWT turned their fortunes
round in 1975, and had followed up with the biggest prize in television
entertainment, the Golden Rose of Montreux. But his programmes were
conceived on a grand scale, with musical extravaganzas and parodies of
Hollywood movies and TV dramas. In 1985 LWT cancelled production
of his new series. Baxter left for the BBC. Shortly afterwards, he was
followed by Russ Abbott.

LWT's 'people shows' continued to dominate Saturday night. In the
year of Baxter's departure, LWT imported an Australian dating show. But
they were worried that a programme in which boy met girl and the pair
were whisked away on holiday together might have too many suggestions
of sexual promise to play in a family slot. They needed a presenter who
would tone down the smut. They missed the mark spectacularly.

The pilot show, *It's a Hoot!*, was put in the hands of presenter Duncan
Norvelle, a straight comedian whose stage persona out-camped even
Larry Grayson. As he simpered his way through the show, it wasn't just
the nervous fluffs in his performance that must have raised doubts in the
minds of the production team. When one contestant told him he smoked
a lot, Norvelle may not have been responsible for the gag line 'You're a
bigger puff than me.' But when he pretended to flirt with one of the male
contestants, and made as if to drag him off the set for his own purposes,
he broke one of the cardinal rules of traditional British comedy: gay men
were only a hoot as long as there wasn't a hint of real sex about them.
Norvelle was meant to diminish the smut level – instead, he raised it in
directions the show couldn't take.

Alan Boyd realised that he was already working with the ideal

presenter. Cilla Black had seen the original programme in Australia. Boyd played her the pilot tape, and asked her to take over. Cilla Black:

I had Surprise, Surprise*, and I'm of the old school and I thought I can't possibly do two shows. I'm BBC trained, I can't do two shows. I didn't want to be Cilla overkill on television.*

But she agreed to Boyd's request. As *Blind Date*, the programme became one of ITV's most durable entertainment programmes. And far from overkill, running two programmes in tandem confirmed Cilla Black as one of the most popular television presenters ever. She made the show flirtatious and funny, but never smutty. Cilla Black:

Blind Date *ran for 18 years. It's very unusual to run that long. I'm very proud. I actually think it was because of the changing of the faces every week. I never used to rehearse with the three kids on the stools ever. I never met them before the show. So the first time they met me is when I walked*

On the dating game show *Blind Date*, Cilla Black played matchmaker as young men and women selected a member of the opposite sex to join them on a prize holiday. They returned the following week to describe the experience and offer frank criticism of their partners.

Contestants Maryanne, Melissa and Helen strike a *Charlie's Angels* pose on a November 1996 edition of *Blind Date*. Cilla Black (right) hosted the show for 18 years from 1985 – it was cancelled when she decided to leave the series in 2003.

over to them. 'Hello Number One, what's your name? Where do you come from?' And one girl said she'd been a big fan of Blind Date since she was seven years of age. And that was the first time it hit me that we'd been going that long. And I said, 'Well how old are you now?' And she said, 'I'm 19'. And I thought 'Wow'. And I think that was one of the main reasons that it was a big success. It was a family show. If you were a kid you could sit there and play the game. I mean I used to do it, sit there with the three boys, because I used to watch rehearsals, and think, oh no I don't fancy Number Two at all. And then Number Three – you'd go behind the sofa and you'd literally chew the pillow thinking, 'Oh, this is so embarrassing. Who's going to pick him?' And inevitably, the girl, because they didn't see, would pick Number Three. And you've just been chewing the pillow, saying, 'Please God, don't pick him.' It had that element. Everybody could play the game at home. And they also had their dreams. There have been a lot of people watching Blind Date that have actually got in contact with the people on the show. And I had three marriages on Blind Date. All still very happy. It was just another feel-good show. You didn't have to think. You didn't have to worry. You just switched on your telly, you watched, you sat back. You enjoyed.

15

MY MOTHER-IN-LAW...

I think the sitcom is probably in a similar position to the England football team. If you get one bad game suddenly everyone is absolutely tearing into it.

Frank Skinner

I N JANUARY 1956, ATV screened a new programme put together by impresario George Black. *Strike a New Note* was intended to find fresh entertainment talent for ITV. Among the viewers who tuned in was Nicholas Parsons.

I watched it and it was terrible, but there was one chap in it called Arthur Haynes who I thought had a great television personality but rotten material.

Above: Les Dawson appeared in his own Yorkshire Television series *Sez Les* which ran to 71 editions between 1969 and 1976.

Top: Gareth Hale and Norman Pace as children's television presenters Billy and Johnny in LWT's *Hale and Pace*.

I happened to see the show the second week and it was even worse, and the following morning my agent phoned me and said, 'Nicholas, have you seen a programme called Strike a New Note?' *and I said, 'Yes, isn't it absolutely appalling?'. He said, 'They want you to join it,' so I said, 'When do I begin?' You know in showbusiness we don't ask, we like to work. Nowadays the show would have been off immediately, but in those days Independent Television had just begun, they were losing a fortune, they were fighting to keep everything on the air, so when they had a show going, they had to keep it running in order to try and build up some audience. After six shows George Black got rid of everybody else, kept Arthur and myself and said, 'I think you two should do sketches together.'*

Opposite page: Arthur Haynes topped the bill on ITV for a decade in 15 seasons of ATV's *The Arthur Haynes Show.* His best known character was the aggressive know-all tramp Hobo Haynes.

The programme was renamed *Get Happy,* and featured material by young writers, including the little-known Johnny Speight. Writer, comic and straight-man clicked, and eventually became the key talent in *The Arthur Haynes Show.* It gave ITV a comedy hit that lasted for over 150 programmes from 1957 to 1966, with an approach that matched the channel's signature style. Nicholas Parsons:

I played the figure of the establishment, being a doctor or an MP, a ministry official, a vicar or a bank manager — something like that. Arthur was always the epitome of the working man, he was a very aggressive Mr Know-all character, with a wonderful tramp character and a very violent East End character as well. And it always finished up with him getting the better of me and putting one over. Once he appeared in the sketch everybody knew I would be on the receiving end of some embarrassment or distress.

Above: Unmarried siblings Nellie (Hylda Baker) and Eli Pledge (Jimmy Jewel) inherited the Lancashire firm of Pledge's Purer Pickles in Granada's *Nearest and Dearest.*

Working-class audiences loved the triumph of the little man over the Establishment — even when Haynes's little man was belligerent and acerbic, and Parsons's authority figure played for sympathy. This class-conscious humour became a staple of ITV's comedy.

Frank Skinner is now writing his own ITV sitcom, *Shane*:

I am generalising, but when I look back on ITV sitcoms, versus BBC sitcoms, I think of quite a clear class divide. I think of the BBC as

Butterflies, *and the lead character was always a graphic designer in a very beautiful house, and his wife wore a lot of Laura Ashley. When I think of ITV I think of the characters in* Nearest and Dearest *in a pickle factory with a bloke calling his sister a knock-kneed knackered old carthorse. And her saying, 'It's ten past, I must get a little hand put on this watch.' It felt to me like it was more of a kind of music hall tradition. People like Arthur Haynes were very much of that tradition anyway. It was grittier in lots of ways.*

You can rattle off quite a few proper working class sitcoms: George and Mildred, Rising Damp, The Dustbinmen *and* On the Buses.

No-one ever summed up the working man's lot better than Reg Varney as Stan Butler in *On the Buses*. The programme ran for 74 episodes, from 1969 to 1973, a fixture in ITV's top ten and the top dozen on all channels. It was voted the favourite show of 1970 by readers of the *Sun*. And it spun off into three movies; the first was the biggest box-office film in Britain in 1971, even pushing James Bond into second place.

Michael Grade became the Head of Light Entertainment at LWT during its run.

On the Buses *was one of the biggest situation comedy hits of all time in the UK. It was a tabloid sitcom, very vulgar, very crude, but it was working class life. Reg Varney was magnificent as Stan Butler, the bus driver. Ronnie Wolfe and Ronnie Chesney who wrote it were originally sketch writers, gag writers, who drifted into sitcom, so their taste was very much music hall, but distilled music hall, sight gags, double entendres, or mostly single entendres, a sort of earthy, seaside, vaudeville comedy, but character-based with a nice little plot through each episode. They were great craftsmen. It was music hall comedy, but it gelled and it captured the public's imagination in a way that very few ITV half hour comedies have ever done before or since.*

'I 'ate you, Butler!' – Stephen Lewis was the petty-minded Inspector 'Blakey' Blake in the LWT sitcom *On The Buses*, a primetime hit for the fledgling station which clocked up 74 episodes between 1969 and 1973.

The programme still has a devoted following and a fan club, some of the members too young to have seen it first time around. When Reg Varney, now 88 years old, was taken to meet some of them, it was clear that they responded to the way that the series represented their own experience of life, and that of millions of other viewers. One person asked:

Do you think the Butler family were a family people could identify with? You're scrimping and saving trying to make ends meet – you had to take the washing machine back after a couple of days, and I think that's what people identified with. It was the hardship of those times.

Varney's reply:

That's right. Well I could play that type because that's what I come from – bloody hard times, really. So it was nothing for me to act that type of life because that was my life.

Like Haynes, Varney had worked the music halls, where the humour was based on a rich tradition of stock comic types. These characters have a pedigree that runs through centuries of comedy – the seaside postcard, the *Punch* cartoon, the Harlequinade, all the way back past Shakespeare and Chaucer to the Roman comedies of Terence and Plautus (which were the basis of Frankie Howerd's BBC series *Up Pompeii*). They were familiar. And familiarity was the point; audiences knew how and why they were expected to find them funny.

Varney's Everyman Stan was far from the only stock character in *On the Buses*. He was joined at home by his dizzy and smothering mother, by sex-hungry frump sister Olive, and her layabout husband Arthur. At work there was his crumpet-chasing mate Jack, and his terrible boss Blakey, with his catch-phrase 'I'll get you Butler' – a line so ubiquitous that Michael Grade will still do his impersonation of it.

ITV sitcoms were built around characters like these. Charlie Drake's little man in *The Worker*, frustrating Henry McGee's Mr Pugh at the Labour Exchange. Bernard Bresslaw the simpleton ('I only arsked!'), Bill

Stan's toothy crumpet-chasing mate Jack Carter, as played in *On The Buses* by Bob Grant. Grant also co-wrote 11 scripts for the series with his fellow cast member Stephen Lewis.

Granada's *The Dustbinmen*
featured Trevor Bannister
(left), Bryan Pringle (centre)
and John Barrett (right) as
three members of a team of
refuse collectors.

Below: Richard Beckinsale
and Paula Wilcox starred as
Geoffrey and Beryl in
Granada's *The Lovers*.
Like *The Dustbinmen*, the
series was created by Jack
Rosenthal.

Fraser the bullying Sergeant Major, Alfie 'Excused Boots' Bass the luckless target of his hostility in Granada's *The Army Game*. Hylda Baker as the celibate, teetotal termagant Nellie in *Nearest and Dearest* and *Not on Your Nellie*. Peggy Mount as the formidable fire-breather in *The Larkins* and *George and the Dragon* – in the latter opposite Sid James, who also played another face of Everyman in *Bless This House*. Yootha Joyce, a woman of a certain age raging with unfulfilled desire in *Man About the House* and its spin-off *George and Mildred*; Brian Murphy as her limp spouse. Dora Bryan in *Happily Ever After* as a tiresome British clone of dizzy Lucille Ball, the star of ITV's first sitcom, the American import *I Love Lucy*. Her equally daffy successors, Wendy Craig in *And Mother Makes Three*, and Sally Thomsett in *Man About the House*. *Please, Sir* led by John Alderton's diffident schoolteacher Bernard Hedges, with a population of types in the classroom (wheeler-dealer, boaster, village idiot, sexpot, jack-the-lad), caretaker's office (officious jobsworth) and staffroom (shrew, ditherer, and Welshman). Among the laddish medicos of *Doctor in the House* and its successors was the formidable bully boss Professor Loftus. One episode, scripted by John Cleese, also included a terrible hotel in Torquay, and the ancestor of Basil Fawlty.

Some ITV characters and series transcended their stock origins. Jack Rosenthal's *The Dustbinmen*, with the foul-mouthed Cheese and Egg, self-styled lothario Heavy Breathing, no-description-necessary Smellie, dim-wit Eric and rabid Man City fan Winston, riding their dustcart Thunderbird Three, and battling authority in the guise of Corporation boss Bloody Delilah, brought an unusual element of grit to peak-time comedy (and topped the ratings with every episode in its first series of six). Rosenthal's next series was *The Lovers* with Richard Beckinsale as Geoffrey and Paula Wilcox as Beryl, she never letting her 'Geoffrey Bubbles Bon Bon' get as near to 'Percy Filth' on the sofa as he reckoned the permissive society allowed. Hywel Bennett as the musing idler *Shelley*, by Peter Tilbury. *Rising Damp* with Leonard Rossiter's incomparable embodiment of writer Eric Chappell's character Rigsby, interfering, petty, randy and bigoted, and so vividly realised that you could feel the stickiness of the furnishings in his rented house. Elaine Stritch and Donald Sinden as abrasive American mistress and suave English butler, as good a double-act as television sitcom ever had, in *Two's Company*. Pauline Collins and John Alderton as odd-couple dizzy deb and orphan actor in *No – Honestly*. And the trembling *A Fine Romance* of real-life couple Judi Dench and Michael Williams.

Above: (Left to right) Alan Moore (Richard Beckinsale), Rupert Rigsby (Leonard Rossiter) and Philip Smith (Don Warrington) were the residents of a run-down boarding house in Yorkshire's *Rising Damp*.

All those belong in the roll-call of British television's best comedies.

Others were positively dire. Jimmy Edwards as cowardly knight *Sir Yellow*. Dora Bryan stuffing sausages in *Both Ends Meet*. Robin Askwith bringing his obnoxious persona from the *Confessions* movies to *Bottle Boys*. Arthur Mullard and Queenie Watts in Wolfe and Chesney's lumpen *Yus My Dear*. *On the Buses* spin-off *Don't Drink the Water*, in which Blakey and his sister move to Spain to exploit the full hilarity of foreign plumbing – which still makes Michael Grade's toes curl.

Many ITV sitcoms had no pretensions to greatness, but got on with the job of pulling viewers. *In Loving Memory*, *Bless This House*, *My Good Woman*, *Father Dear Father*, *Oh No – It's Selwyn Froggitt*, and *Robin's Nest* were among the high-rating comedies. Along with other, lesser creations, they peppered the schedules. It was hard to imagine anyone laughing out loud at some of the plodders. They made you wonder if Light Entertainment should be renamed Slight Entertainment, their ambition apparently limited to being inoffensive enough to avoid viewers making the effort (in the days before remote controls) of getting off the sofa to change channels. They passed the time. It would have passed anyway.

Below: John Alderton and Pauline Collins starred as Charles and Clara Danby, recalling the earlier years of their relationship in LWT's *No – Honestly*.

Television comedy was almost entirely created, written, produced and commissioned by middle-aged white men. Many of them knew what to get laughs out of; anyone not like them.

It is sometimes hard to remember the extent to which misogyny, homophobia and racism were staples of mainstream comedy in the Seventies and Eighties. Women were funny – when they wanted sex, when they didn't want sex, when they tried to drive, when they forgot things, when they put too much starch on their husband's shirts (come in *Happily Ever After*). The mere fact that they possessed breasts was considered cause for hilarity. Gay men were funny – dressing in lavender, mincing around, camp as Christmas but never ever involved in Percy Filth. The mere hint that they possessed penises was enough to frighten the horses and the straight population. Foreigners were funny – talked funny, dressed funny, ate funny. And what rib-tickling nick-names we had for them in all their ethnic variety.

Entertainment threw up some ghastly sights, performers turning tricks to please their audiences. Charlie Williams, black comedian, telling jokes about blacks to white audiences. Michael Barrymore (perhaps the most gifted of all television performers when it came to meeting the public and coaxing confidence out of them) hung up in the closet tossing off gags about homosexuality.

On the whole, the sitcom dealt with a sanitised version of life. When it tried to rub up against more challenging subjects, it often looked a very dubious proposition. Especially when it tackled race.

Johnny Speight famously proceeded from writing his Arthur Haynes scripts to creating the BBC's *Till Death Us Do Part*. Less famously, Speight also wrote the ITV series *Curry & Chips*, in which Spike Milligan spent some of his least fine hours as Kevin O'Grady the Irish Pakistani (try not to fall off your chairs), coming up against racial prejudice from white and black alike. It was intended to mock discrimination, diminish it by making it look stupid. The problem was that whatever the intention, Milligan's artificially tinted turn, straight out of a Bangalore Army concert party, was jaw-droppingly ill-judged.

More controversial still, if only because there were weeks when it was the most-watched programme on television, was Thames Television's *Love Thy Neighbour*. Written by Vince Powell and Harry Driver, the story began when a black couple moved in next door to white couple – the white husband hilariously worries his wife will be raped (she responds even more amusingly, 'Promises, promises') and decides they must move. The series was and is still defended by people who say that the way both

Opposite page: Comedian Michael Barrymore broke into television on the ITV shows *New Faces, Who Do You Do?* and *Russ Abbott's Madhouse*. He went on to appear in comedy and variety shows throughout the Eighties and Nineties, ultimately becoming one of ITV's most popular performers as the host of quiz and game shows such as *Strike It Lucky, Strike It Rich* and *My Kind Of People*.

Barry Evans (standing, left) played English teacher Jeremy Brown in LWT's *Mind Your Language*. Intended to illustrate that bigotry and prejudice were not simply limited to black and white, the resulting series often resorted to racial stereotyping for easy laughs. Despite becoming one of LWT's most popular comedies, the series was cancelled in 1979 after its third season. It returned for 13 new independently-produced episodes in 1986 with Evans teaching a mostly new class of students, but the programme was shown in only four of the ITV regions.

black and white male characters traded insults ('nig nog' and 'honky' were the favourites) balanced the show. The ITA's research found black viewers who hated it, and others who thought it the funniest thing on TV. But the humour rarely rose above name-calling. In a climate in which the National Front was recruiting, and bigotry was openly expressed by millions of the majority white population, it raises huge doubts. However idiotic the male characters were made to appear, it never even tried to match Speight's intentions. The bluntness of the ITV sitcom style just didn't seem up to the job.

Mind Your Language, which originally ran from 1977 to 1979, was another series in which good intentions went awry. The series was set in a school teaching English to speakers of other languages. Michael Grade conceived and commissioned it for LWT.

> *You had all the races and all the religions mixed up in a room from all four corners of the globe. Classrooms are always funny, for some reason, and adults behaving like children is one of the sure-fire formulae for successful comedy. The idea was that you would show, through comedy, that prejudice and bigotry wasn't just black against white, or white against black but everybody's bigoted; the Chinese, the Japanese, the Asians. Everybody's got*

prejudices and it's a part of the human state.

That was the premise and Vince Powell, who was a very successful television writer, took up the idea and thought he could do something with it. He came up with Mind Your Language. *We cast Barry Evans, who'd been in the* Doctor *series* Doctor in the House *and* Doctor at Large. *He was very popular. He was the teacher, trying to hold the ring between these warring factions. We did two series. It was enormously successful but I got very, very uncomfortable about it because I felt that, rather than enlightening people, it was actually reinforcing stereotypes. Vince was writing shorthand. When you're writing 24 minutes for a half hour slot in commercial television, you haven't got a lot of time to develop character. They were all a bit stereotypical, the humour was just a bit too glib and it didn't really get us beyond the prejudice. He was writing gags. In the famous words of Bridget Plowden, Chair of the Independent Broadcasting Authority, when she was asked what was wrong with* Crossroads, *'Well the Authority find it distressingly popular.' And I think that was true of* Mind Your Language. *The public enjoyed it but I was uncomfortable about it, politically.*

Up to 18 million members of the public tuned in to each episode. But

(Clockwise from top right) Lenny Henry, Lawrie Mark, Isabelle Lucas, Sharon Rosita and Norman Beaton were British television's first black sitcom family in LWT's *The Fosters*, adapted from scripts of the American sitcom *Good Times*.

after it was roasted by members of the industry at the Edinburgh Television Festival, Grade acted on his discomfort. He axed one of LWT's most popular programmes.

I made the decision myself but there was a big debate and I was concerned. I'd never knowingly transmitted anything in my career which I didn't feel I could defend publicly, and after that debate at Edinburgh where the show was criticised by a lot of my peers in the business, I had a long, long think about it. And in the end, I came to the conclusion that I could mount a defence of the show, but I didn't really believe the case and therefore, if I couldn't defend it, it had to go.

Grade and LWT were more politically correct when they made British television's first black sitcom, *The Fosters*, in 1976.

In America I saw a show called Good Times, *which was a huge hit on American television. It was basically an all-black, blue-collar, working-class family. They happened to be black, but all the problems were about parents not understanding the kids, kids not understanding the parents, they won't go to work, they won't get up in the morning, all the traditional family sitcom plots. The thing I loved about* Good Times *was that it didn't make a thing about them being black; they just happened to be black, that was the joy of the show. And I saw this and I thought, 'We could do this in the UK.' And then I talked to everyone and they all said, 'Well you'll never*

Eric Morecambe (top) and Ernie Wise broke into television on the BBC in the 1950s, but it was on LWT's *The Morecambe and Wise Show* (1961-67) that they redefined their act and became firmly established as Britain's best comedy double act.

be able to cast it, there aren't any black actors, they won't be able to do it'. I got a very good producer, Stuart Allen, and we talked about it and we looked at the original scripts and we said, 'We could rewrite these scripts and make them anglicised', So we had 50, 60 scripts to pick from for the first series. And Stuart did a brilliant job casting. We picked Lenny Henry to play the youngster, which was the star part, and Norman Beaton played the father. Isabelle Lucas, another wonderful actress, played the mother. And we launched The Fosters, *the first black sitcom — shock horror, the world's holding its breath, you know. And the reviews were very kind of, 'We can't see what all the fuss is about, this could just be a white family.' Ah, that's the whole point. The press just completely missed it. It wasn't a massive hit but it did very well for us and it broke through. And of course it was a fantastic launch pad for all those performers.*

As well as situation comedies, ITV continued to present sketch shows. It had some of Britain's favourite comedians. Morecambe and Wise struggled at the BBC in the Fifties; for the rest of his career, Eric Morecambe carried round a review of one of their first shows, which included the line 'Definition of the week: TV set — the box in which they buried Morecambe and Wise.' It was at ITV that they hit their stride in the early Sixties, and the legendary 'short fat hairy legs' entered the act, along with a lot more of their trademark material. The BBC lured them back with the promise of colour in 1968. Thames poached them in turn ten years later, but their longstanding writer Eddie Braben was still contracted to Auntie, and they never matched their highest standards again.

Tommy Cooper had also begun his television work at the BBC, in 1952, but ITV gave him his own show in 1957, and carried on doing so until 1980. Guest appearances continued after that — indeed he died during a broadcast of LWT's *Live at Her Majesty's* in 1984. He was one of television's most brilliant clowns, with conjuring skills behind his bungled magic tricks.

Les Dawson made over 70 shows for Yorkshire Television between 1969 and 1977, revisiting the spirit of veteran comic Norman Evans's drag act in his over the garden wall conversations with Roy Barraclough, indulging in rococo flights of verbal fancy before plummeting to a bathetic punch-line, maligning his wife and mother-in-law, and murdering favourites at the piano with a wrong-note routine every bit as practised and dextrous as Cooper's magic.

But ITV's biggest comedian was the man who became the most

Yorkshire Television's *Sez Les* established Les Dawson as one of Britain's best-loved comedians and ran to 68 editions from 1969 to 1976. Throughout this period, Dawson also starred in a number of comedy specials and the sitcom series *The Loner* and *Dawson's Weekly*, all for Yorkshire Television.

Les Dawson as Cissie, a character usually seen gossiping with neighbour Ada (Roy Barraclough) in *Sez Les*.

popular and most-recognised comic performer in the world – Benny Hill. He worked for the BBC and ATV in the Fifties and early Sixties, but it is the 58 hour-long programmes that he made for Thames between 1969 and 1989 for which he is mainly remembered.

Hill came out of the theatrical variety circuit. For a while he played straight man to Reg Varney. He was not a great success, lacking the presence to project to the back of large venues. But he turned that to an asset on television, where he was one of the first comedians to tailor his act to the close up-camera, whether in the size of expressions on his naughty-cherub face, or the way he used the frame of the screen for visual gags. He guarded against over-exposure and, unusually for a comedian, wrote all his own material as a guarantee that he wouldn't have to perform what he considered to be substandard scripts. He developed broad but often sharp parodies of other television programmes, and created a range of comic characters. He is now chiefly remembered for the scantily-clad girls, from the Cuddlesome Cuties of his first ATV shows, to the Hill's Angels of some of his last for Thames, who adorned his sketches and pursued him in the set-piece speeded-up chases that ended his shows. They were a staple of the variety world that he grew up in. His humour was the seaside postcard made flesh, never politically correct. And as tastes changed in the Eighties, the combination led Thames to write him off.

In 1989, he was invited to a meeting with Thames's Head of Light Entertainment, John Howard Davies. His audiences had been declining for five years, but Hill evidently expected to discuss the details of his next project. Instead, he was thanked for 20 years of programmes, and told he was no longer wanted on the channel. Time and taste, Thames felt, had passed him by.

Nicholas Parsons appeared regularly on Hill's programmes:

There was an innocence about Benny's attitude because he adored women, and when he took them out I know he made a great fuss of them. When Thames Television decided to drop him, as he understood on the basis that he was anti-feminine, he was deeply upset. In fact he was so upset he went into a decline. He always had an eating problem which I knew very well because I became very friendly with him, and he just gave up then and started eating, and he ballooned in size. And drinking as well I think. And he just got very ill and died. He was heartbroken. Because of the success of his show in America he'd had many offers to go and work in the States. He didn't want to; he loved working over here, he was British, loved the British audiences and enjoyed presenting British humour to them. So he never understood why the British employers didn't still want him. And it's very interesting to note that Benny has achieved more international success and fame than any comic, other than perhaps Charlie Chaplin. Benny's programmes are still being shown on American television and in lots of other countries all round the world. I get minuscule cheques coming in from Namibia and Angola and all kinds of places. What they make of some of the very British humour there I don't know, but there must be a very international flavour to Benny's work because he's deeply enjoyed and appreciated around the world. But his programmes are not repeated very much in this country.

This page: Three faces of Benny Hill from ATV's *The Benny Hill Show* (1957-60).

Comedy was changing. The Eighties had brought a new wave of comic performers and writers with a new approach to their craft. ITV had always managed to unearth new talent. Its problem was often finding ways to keep it.

In the Sixties, Terry Jones, Michael Palin, Eric Idle and Terry Gilliam (along with David Jason, Denise Coffey and the Bonzo Dog Doo-Dah Band) created *Do Not Adjust Your Set* (1967-69), which began as a children's show but was soon given an early evening repeat. (Palin and Jones also went on to write and star in *The Complete and Utter History of Britain* [1969] for LWT).

John Cleese, Graham Chapman, Tim Brooke-Taylor and Marty Feldman (an experienced writer appearing on camera for the first time) wrote and starred alongside 'the lovely Aimi Macdonald' in *At Last the 1948 Show* (1967). It was here that the Four Yorkshiremen sketch was

Above: The short-lived 1983 Granada sketch show *Alfresco* introduced viewers to the considerable talents of (clockwise from top left) Robbie Coltrane, Hugh Laurie, Emma Thompson, Ben Elton, Stephen Fry and Siobhan Redmond.

Below: Central's *Tiswas* spin-off *O.T.T.* showcased risk-taking 'Albanian' comedian Alexei Sayle.

first performed, not on *Monty Python's Flying Circus* (1969-74).

The BBC's *Python*, with Cleese, Chapman, Idle, Jones, Palin and Gilliam, can properly be described as the offspring of *Do Not Adjust Your Set* and *At Last the 1948 Show*, but eclipsed both of them. Brooke-Taylor went off to be in *The Goodies* (1970-82), also at the BBC. Feldman soon had his own award-winning series *It's Marty* – BBC again (1968), though he returned to ATV for a much less successful series aimed at the American market in 1971.

ITV's *New Faces* put Victoria Wood on screen in 1974, but it was the BBC's *That's Life* that gave her a regular slot (1976). Granada paired her with Julie Walters in one series of *Wood and Walters* (1981), but it was at the BBC that she triumphed in the sketch show and sitcom.

Granada signed up Cambridge Footlights talents Emma Thompson, Stephen Fry, Hugh Laurie and Paul Shearer, brought in Ben Elton, Siobhan Redmond and Robbie Coltrane, and let them spread their wings in the series *Alfresco* (1983-4). It was patchy, but they all developed through it. None went on to give ITV an original comedy hit.

Alexei Sayle blew into *O.T.T.* (1982), Central's attempt to recreate the magic of *Tiswas* for the post-pub audience. He was an original, aggressive and risk-taking comedian, but seeing him storm through the Albanian National Anthem in front of the bemused figures of fellow performers Chris Tarrant and Lenny Henry was like watching a fish riding the wrong bicycle.

Witzend Productions gave Central Tracey Ullman, Dawn French, Jennifer Saunders and Ruby Wax as a set of abrasive flat-mates in *Girls on Top* (1985-86). This attempt to bring a female perspective to television comedy (Saunders, French and Wax were also the writers) lost some kudos when, with a keen sense of irony somewhere in the scheduling department, the second series skipped a week to allow ITV to show Miss World 1986.

One area where ITV was able to score some

successes was in late-night slots on Sunday. Away from the strictures of family viewing, there was room for new comic styles.

Anna Raeburn and Len Richmond marked the territory as early as 1979, with *Agony*. Maureen Lipman played Jane Lucas, the magazine advice columnist who was too busy dealing with other people's problems to sort her own life out. The series scored a TV first by depicting her gay neighbours as sympathetic and fully-rounded characters.

Hale and Pace spent almost a decade pushing at the boundaries of good taste in their LWT sketch show (1988-97). The response of the studio audience when they pulled a frizzled cat out of a microwave, and the game of cricket played with frogs instead of a ball (every bit as messy as it sounds) live in the memory. So do their moronic heavies 'The Management', and kids' TV presenters Billy and Johnny, who no sensible parent would want anywhere near their little ones. Their work hugely enlivened the post bag and the in-house duty log of viewers' phone calls. Hale and Pace did question what sense of morality prompted a hundred complaints about the frog cricket, but only one about a sketch in the same programme about a boy dying in a motorbike accident.

'Based on an original lunch by Martin Lambie-Nairn' was the lead credit at the end of *Spitting Image* (1984-96). Lambie-Nairn was a graphic designer at LWT who hit on an idea to send up the politicians who populated the shows he worked on. He contacted caricature model-makers Peter Fluck and Roger Law, and their brilliant designs provided the puppets for what is probably the most deadly satire show ever on television (champions of the BBC's *That Was the Week That Was* might go back and watch a few episodes rather than relying on gilded memory). Like all the best cartoons, the exaggerated likenesses seemed more real than the people they lampooned; their portrayal of David Steel as a schoolboy is sometimes

Above: Tracey Ullman (second from right) starred in the first series of Central's *Girls on Top* alongside co-stars (and writers) Ruby Wax (left), Jennifer Saunders (second from left) and Dawn French (right).

Below: Maureen Lipman was *Person* magazine agony aunt Jane Lucas in the popular and ground-breaking LWT sitcom *Agony*.

blamed for destroying his credibility as a political leader. It laid into the worlds of showbusiness and television as much as politics, and though it ran out of steam before it ran out of time, it was the sharpest sketch show of the Eighties.

The sitcom counterpart was Yorkshire's *The New Statesman* (1987-92), in which writers Laurence Marks and Maurice Gran created Tory MP Alan B'stard, brought to the screen in all his devious, bullying, amoral, greedy, hypocritical, lecherous, vain, swivelling glory by Rik Mayall. Many MPs hated it. Many viewers though they probably recognised too much reality in its wild excesses.

In *The New Statesman*, ITV had a sitcom that defined its political times as well as any Alan Clark diary or *Private Eye* exposé. They almost had the sitcom that defined the state of Nineties coupling as well as any New Lads mag photospread or *Cosmo* poll. Simon Nye's *Men Behaving Badly* played for two series on ITV, saw original cast member Harry Enfield replaced by Neil Morrissey, and was then terminated. Thames took it to the BBC instead, and ITV looked on enviously as it hit its stride in successive runs.

Men Behaving Badly exemplifies one of the ways in which mainstream sitcoms have become a problem for ITV. They take time to bed in, for the characters and cast to work comfortably together, for audiences to be provoked to laughter in anticipation as well as in reaction. Even series as revered as *Dad's Army* were baggy in their first outings. But today's competitive commercial market demands instant success. And while the BBC has traditionally had a second channel where it can feather-bed its fledgling comedies before deciding expose them to BBC1, ITV has had nowhere else for them to grow up.

The content of sitcoms is also more difficult. In their prime years, they were family viewing, playing in slots around seven or eight o'clock. That's not the place to show reflections of many aspects of modern family life. *Robin's Nest* broke new ground in 1977, with an unmarried leading

Opposite page: Central's *Spitting Image* was one of British television's longest-running puppet series – 141 editions between 1984 and 1996. The show's grey portrayal of Prime Minister John Major was said to have greatly influenced the public's perception of him.

Rik Mayall starred as Alan Beresford B'Stard, the unscrupulous Conservative MP for Haltemprice and holder of the Commons' largest majority in Yorkshire Television's *The New Statesman*.

(Left to right) Neil Stacy, Joanna Van Gyseghem, Carlos Douglas, Gwen Taylor and Keith Barron starred in the adulterous Yorkshire Television comedy *Duty Free*, the last ITV sitcom to top the ratings.

couple living together. But they had to go to the IBA to get special permission to tackle such racy matters. More typical was a programme like *Keep It In the Family* (1980-83) a well-watched Thames series in which parents lived upstairs, two nubile daughters had the basement flat, and Dad kept a watchful eye on the procession of boyfriends. It was the sort of show in which a man might stay over, but we all knew he had slept on the couch, and all of father's outrage would be specious. Like the teenage children in *Bless This House* before them, the more they were supposed to look like the face of thrill-seeking contemporary youth, the more it was apparent that they were twittering ninnies.

The last ITV sitcom to top the ratings was *Duty Free*, the not quite adulterous adventures of two couples on holiday, in 1984. The will, the time, the material, the money, and the opportunity to generate another peak-time success seem to have ebbed away. Frank Skinner was a fan of many of the old comedies, but when he set out to write *Shane* it was aimed at a later adult audience.

I had grown up with On the Buses, Rising Damp, Nearest and Dearest *and stuff like that. And I think if you watch* Shane *you can see there's an old fashioned feel to it. People said to me, you shouldn't really be making a sitcom now with a studio audience, that's a bit passé, it should be like* The Office *– single camera, not about comedy lines but about performance and stuff like that. And I basically like lots of one-liners and big audience laughs, so I went for it.*

A sitcom is more expensive than a game show, generally speaking, and a game show generally speaking gets more viewers. So if you're a boss at ITV there's no decision to make really. I can spend six months sweating blood over a sitcom, really caring about it, wanting to get it as perfect as I can and get brilliant actors and a brilliant director and all that and get it right, but at the end of the day if it's on the other side from When Pets Get Agitated *people will probably watch that. And I think if that's the case then the public have to be given what the public want.*

But though the prime-time sitcom has become an endangered species, there is still plenty of comedy on ITV. A lot of the talent has turned towards the comedy drama, which can offer more depth of character and more chance to develop plot and themes than the half-hour sitcom ever could. At its worst, it's a form that can end up neither comic nor dramatic. At its best, it can be *Cold Feet*.

Comedy has increasingly been woven into the chat show. And it has been fused with another classic television form, the talent show. Now it is not just the pick of the aspiring stars who are exposed to the viewers. Series like *Pop Idol* and *The X Factor* have recorded the whole range of talentless wannabees as they audition, and the resulting footage is edited together with laughter in mind. As Simon Cowell put it,

Granada's comedy drama *Cold Feet* starred (left to right) Robert Bathurst, Hermione Norris, James Nesbitt, Helen Baxendale, John Thomson and Fay Ripley as three middle-class thirtysomething Manchester couples. The series initially performed poorly with viewers but eventually became one of ITV's major successes of the late 1990s.

I think a lot of people like me like seeing people make a complete fool out of themselves. I love it.

The stock character types who populated the sitcoms of old have not disappeared from ITV's prime-time viewing. They have just taken on the faces of real people. Look at the reality shows that now occupy so many slots once devoted to sitcom, at the cast of celebrities on their tropical island waiting for the viewers to get them out of there, and you find a very familiar line-up: the good-time girl (often as not with her comedy breasts); the lecherous jack the lad; the slightly slow-witted one; the member of the upper classes, rubbing up against the hoi polloi; the joker; the dragon; the inept weakling; the dizzy dame.

They are cast for type. Often, they perform accordingly. Sometimes they confound expectation, like Christine Hamilton, expected to behave like a dragon, but turning out to be sympathetic and supportive.

Some of the situations the shows put them into are genuinely challenging. Often they are comic, and the petty rivalries, jealousies, misunderstandings and fits of anger which ensue were the stuff of many a vintage sitcom plot. But there's a huge difference. In the old comedies, we were expected to side with particular pre-determined characters, and laugh at the others. Now we can choose whose side we are on, even getting to vote for who stays and who goes, and laugh accordingly. The old middle-aged, middle-class, white male point of view, which used to dominate comedy, no longer holds sway.

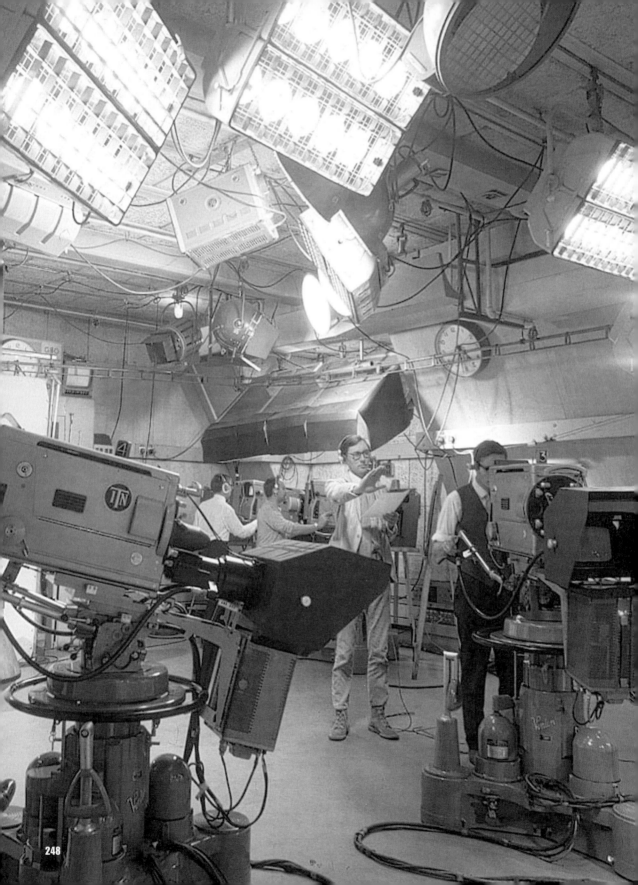

16
TONIGHT'S HEADLINES

We don't intend, on any night, to tell you everything that's happening in the world on that day. What we do is we do select the stories we think are of interest to people and we tell it in an interesting and fascinating way.

Trevor McDonald

NEWS COVERAGE ON ITV is and always was required by law. When ITV was founded, the ITA and the first companies decided to set up a separate, jointly-funded company to produce the national news bulletins for them. It made sense economically to share the costs; and it made sense politically to keep editorial decisions at arm's length from their mostly Tory-dominated boardrooms. ITN – Independent Television News – was created. It soon set about putting a rocket up existing news coverage.

BBC television news was dull. They knew it was – and the official line was that it was fine for the news to be dull. It was there to inform, not to entertain. The last thing they wanted was a scoop. Stories were to be verified from at least two other sources – 'Always third with the news' might have been their slogan. Anything the Royal Family did was given top priority, however insignificant. The tone was as racy as a civil service memorandum. The pictures were still, the words read off-screen by announcers chosen to fit the brief of stating the news 'soberly and impersonally'. They only put their newsreaders in vision when they found that was what ITN had planned.

But ITN were still ahead of the BBC's game when they opened for broadcasting. Auntie's newsreaders were meant to be aloof; ITN's were picked for personality. Chris Chataway, popular with the public since his days as an athlete, was chosen for the late-evening bulletin; a young barrister called Robin Day for the early evening; and for the lunchtime

Opposite page: The newsreader's view – an early autocue system is employed in the ITN studio for a late afternoon bulletin in 1969.

The original 1955 on-screen caption for ITV's *ITN News* bulletin.

broadcasts the groundbreaking choice of a woman, Barbara Mandell.

They had far more to do than sit at their desks; they went out to report on stories and interview people; they were involved in writing their own words for the studio. It was all part of ITN's aim to be friendly where the BBC kept its distance, to be the *Daily Mirror* to its *Times*. ITN wasn't suspicious of scoops, it was hungry for them. It used 16mm film instead of the usual 35mm as it was easier to get to the scene of the story and quicker to get on air. ITN recorded sound on location, another first for the news. Suddenly, events made a noise.

And ITN didn't just relay the official line on stories. It blew away the deferential attitude with which the BBC treated politicians and senior figures as wiser and better than the rest of us. BBC interviewers would routinely thank their subjects for making their valuable time available, before inviting them to address the nation on their own terms. ITN set Robin Day on them. He was no respecter of rank, however high.

He is still in the archives from 1956, asking Harry Truman whether he regrets dropping the atom bomb on Japan. 'Certainly not,' smiles Truman, 'if you read my memoirs it will tell you all about it.' Back comes Day. 'Of course, this programme is designed for people who may not be able to afford your memoirs at thirty shillings a copy, Mr Truman.' Former Presidents of the most powerful nation on earth weren't accustomed to being spoken to like that.

Nor were visiting Japanese ministers. In one of Day's most memorable encounters in 1957, he presented the Japanese Foreign Minister and his compatriot interpreter with evidence of the way the Japanese were deviously tapping in to international markets by passing off goods. 'This is a British packet of ball-bearings, and this is an almost identical packet of ball-bearings made in Japan. What do you have to say about that?'

'I think this is out of order,' responds the interpreter, not even putting the question to the minister.

'What does the Foreign Minister have to say about it? That was my question to the Foreign Minister.'

'Yes, the Foreign Minister needs time to answer this kind of question. If you had this in mind you should have given him advance knowledge.'

'He didn't ask for advance knowledge of any questions whatever.'

'Of course we don't, because we didn't expect you were so treacherous.'

It was one thing to put foreign politicians on the spot, quite another to put one's own leaders under such pressure. In 1958, ITN's Sunday programme *Tell the People* secured the first long interview ever with a sitting Prime Minister. Harold Macmillan was asked bluntly by Day how he felt about widespread criticism of Foreign Secretary Selwyn Lloyd. It is quite likely that Macmillan was planning to dismiss him. But when faced with such an unprecedented question on camera, the PM was forced to defend him. The next day, the papers were full of it. The *Daily Mirror*'s Cassandra column summed up the controversy:

> *The Queen's First Minister was put on the spot. What else could he say about his colleague? How could he suddenly reject him? How could Mr Macmillan be anything but complimentary to his colleague? Mr Day, by his skill as an examiner, has been responsible for prolonging in office a man who probably doesn't want the job and is demonstrably incapable of doing it. The Idiot's Lantern is getting too big for its ugly gleam.*

But ITN also knew when to make the news by just listening. They interviewed Nasser in Cairo in 1957, his first contact with Britain since the Suez crisis. And in 1961, ITN's Brian Widlake was taken to a secret hideout in South Africa to conduct the first ever television interview with Nelson Mandela, to find out at first hand the aims of the black freedom movement. Twenty-nine years later, it was ITN's Trevor McDonald who was the first to interview Mandela on camera after his long imprisonment.

More than anything, at home and abroad, ITN changed television news by making people and their stories the prime focus. They didn't just ask questions of society's leaders, they went and found out what the rank and file, their viewers, thought too. They got their opinions on the potato shortage or the latest union dispute. This was television news, exploiting the possibilities of the medium, not just the spoken version of a newspaper that Auntie offered. And the papers recognised it. 'ITN with deft flashbacks and live interviews with bystanders, established their usual lead over the BBC's News

In November 1990, just prior to the Gulf War, Trevor McDonald was granted an exclusive interview for ITN with Saddam Hussein in Baghdad. It remains the only British television interview with the Iraqi president.

International correspondents use the latest technology to file their reports: here, CNN correspondent Brent Sadler uses a satellite dish transmitter to broadcast a report from the Gulf War in 1991.

Department,' was the *Observer*'s verdict of the rival coverage of a story in 1957.

Watch ITN's news coverage today and you'll see evidence of the same priority; to look at stories from the angle of the people involved in them, to turn statistics and figures into lived experience. Trevor McDonald:

> *I never forget a story which, I think, illustrates the point. It was in the height of the Bosnia war and there were incidents happening all over the place, mayhem in that conflict as there usually was. In one of these instances of mayhem, one of my colleagues chose one story about one young boy who was playing football in the garden and lost both his eyes. This story was part of a rather larger picture in which there was chaos, there was confusion everywhere, people were being killed in cemeteries even. We chose one incident to demonstrate, poignantly I thought, just what a tragedy this thing was. And that encapsulates what ITN tries to do.*

Alastair Stewart:

I think the story that I was involved in that had the greatest single impact upon me was the Berlin Wall coming down in 1989. It was capturing the faces of those young East German soldiers, the students who suddenly realised that they couldn't only look over the wall, but they could climb over the wall.

Michael Nicholson:

It was no use talking about hundreds of thousands of people starving and showing a wide shot of a refugee camp. What you had to do was sit down with a starving person, sit down among the dying. I remember during the Indo-Pakistan War when all the Bengali refugees were flooding into India, coming across a camp where children were dying of malnutrition. I actually held a baby, a dying baby, in my arms and said, 'The child that has managed to survive the war, has survived weeks of trudging through the monsoon, is now going to die in safety.' Now, people were saying, 'Oh, the melodrama, why does he do it?' but I tell you, that had impact. You don't look at hundreds of thousands, numbers are meaningless to the viewer, but you hold a dying child in your arms and say, 'By the time I finish my commentary, this child is dead,' and that has impact. Call it melodrama, criticise it if you like, but it gets to the heart of the viewer and that's what you're after.

But ITN could also get to viewers with a lightness of touch and tone, particularly with its 'and finally' items – a line in humorous sign-off stories about waterskiing squirrels, beer-drinking mice, and schools for Santas.

ITN broke new ground again in 1967 by extending their main evening programme with the launch of *News at Ten*, gambling that it could hold a mainstream audience for half an hour. That length allowed them to be more flexible when a major story broke, and made room for more depth of coverage. It soon paid off. On the third night of *News at Ten*, 5 July 1967, an 11-minute story from Aden kept the audiences glued to their sets – a single item that was almost as long as the whole of the old 15-minute bulletins.

Another early success was their coverage of the climax to the Palestinian aircraft hijacking at Dawsons Field in Jordan in 1970. *News at Ten* got the only close up pictures of three planes being blown up, and flashed them round the world.

News at Ten's 1970 exclusive – Palestinian guerrillas destroy hijacked jets at Dawsons Field in Jordan.

Michael Nicholson:

The guy who shot that called me out to go back to the desert and I said, 'Forget it, we've already got plenty of shots.' He said, 'You must come back,' because he couldn't go without me, I had the press pass. When afterwards I said to him, 'How did you know they were going to blow up those planes?' he said, 'I'm a PLO guerilla.' He was our freelance cameraman, but it turned out that he was actually a PLO guerrilla, and they'd told him to get out there because they were going to blow them up. That's how we got our story.

Getting the story on film was always the challenge, particularly on the front line. Michael Nicholson:

Newspaper reporters can sit at a bar stool all day and overhear conversations, pump other journalists, look at the copy that's going out, and they can file a perfectly good story without even moving out of the hotel. Now we can't do that. The thing about being a TV reporter is you're next to the TV cameraman and he has to be right up front, and if he's not, you don't get the story. I remember during the Belfast days we used to stay at the Belfast Europa, which was a high rise hotel overlooking a great deal of Belfast. I remember one cameraman, one of the old Movietone newsreel guys who joined ITN. He said, 'If we could actually get a really long lens, we don't have to go up the Falls Road, we can get it from here.' Well, that's great isn't it. A long lens may be able to get the picture, but a reporter can't report from the roof of the Belfast Europa. You've always got to be up there, which is why it can sometimes be dangerous, but then that's the name of the game. I know this is going to sound very macho but I don't think I've ever been frightened under fire. I think there's so much happening under fire and if I have to be honest, I quite enjoyed it. I've been to what, 18 war zones over the last 40 years. People say, 'Why do you do it?' and you can come up with all kinds of silly answers, but if I was honest, I would say it was because I enjoyed it – which is an awful thing to admit, isn't it? That you enjoy war.

Like other ITN front-line reporters, Nicholson had an appetite for being first to the story that put ITN viewers in the thick of the action. But one of his most memorable reports came out of what appeared to be

a failure to be ahead of the pack. The occasion was the surprise Turkish invasion of Cyprus in 1974.

At about three o'clock in the morning the phone rings and I'm drunk. I'm lying on bed having had a great night out with the lads, and the phone rings and it's Peter Snow. He was our diplomatic correspondent then, and he's a great cloak and dagger man. He said, 'Nick, I can't tell you too much but they – repeat they – are coming in at dawn from the north.' I said, 'Oh thanks, Peter,' and put the phone down, fell back to sleep. And I suddenly woke up and thought, Giddy Aunt, they must be the Turks, they must be invading. So I managed to get myself up, tiptoed down the corridor with shoes off, because the BBC were in the same corridor, woke up Alan Downs and Bob Hammond, my crew, and said, 'I think it's happening, we've got to get to the north.' We tiptoed down and we pushed the car out of the car park so we wouldn't wake anyone up and off we

Reginald Bosanquet reads the *News at Ten* on ITN's late evening bulleting in 1973.

went. Well about three miles, four miles outside of Nicosia, the car stopped, we'd run out of petrol. Twenty minutes later, there's a car coming along. It's the BBC, so we thumb and they give us the v-sign. The second car comes along, second BBC car, we thumb and they give us the same sign. We're devastated, we've lost. We start to walk back and suddenly Alan and I heard it together, we heard a familiar sound; there's a drone and we knew what it was because we'd heard it time and time again in Vietnam. A great big mass of planes came in. We started to film and then overhead it was pop, pop, pop, pop, out came the parachutes, and there we were, it was like falling snow in the midst of a Turkish paradrop. We were still some distance away from the actual landing zone. We tried to steal a car and got hit over the head for doing so.

And then suddenly somebody opened a window and a little man in his pyjamas shouted, 'Hey, News at Ten!', because we had the ITN sticker on our film magazine. And he said, 'You want to go there?' and we said, 'Please.' He came rushing down in his pyjamas, jumped into the Volkswagen and off we went. We were made. But we weren't because we came to a Turkish checkpoint and they said, 'No, no, no, no' and they pointed their guns at us and said, 'You follow us' and they got into their jeep and we followed them.

And then I remembered, and believe this if you will or believe it not, but I remembered an Alan Ladd movie where exactly the same thing happened to him in Nazi Germany, and as he went through a village he told his driver, 'Slow down when they're out of sight and we'll jump out and you'll carry on,' which is what we did. And we rushed through the village and we got our pictures of the landing Turks. It was a world scoop and probably the best I'd ever had.

Trevor McDonald had just joined ITN at the time, and remembers watching the story:

If I had been in that position, where I saw parachutists coming from the air into a field, I would make sure that the cameraman got into the right position and I would stand ten paces behind to make sure I was not involved in anything coming from the air with guns. Michael Nicholson walked into *the field and greeted the parachutists coming down and said, 'My name is Michael Nicholson, welcome to Turkey.' Sensational. Live a thousand years, I would never do that. I still think it's one of the greatest moments for me in journalistic television.*

That was brilliant skill, but Nicholson acknowledges that fortune played a large part in getting them to the right place at the right time.

Whenever I give little lectures to media study groups and aspiring journalists, I always say, 'Take check of yourself and see how much luck is on your side, or has been on your side. Because if you haven't got it, go and drive a bus.'

Shooting the story was only part of the job. Getting it home could take just as much luck. The Cyprus film had to be smuggled to an RAF base on the island. That subterfuge was unusual, but foreign reporters routinely faced a challenge when it came to getting their footage flown back.

Michael Nicholson:

You had to find a flight that was going anywhere near civilisation and then you had to find somebody who would take it for you. We'd call them pigeons. You'd go to an airport and find the departure queue, and you'd look for a friendly face, hopefully a Brit, and you'd hold the ITN bag up in your hand. It was a transparent bag with 'ITN News Film – Urgent', and there

Reginald Bosanquet (in dark suit) and Andrew Gardner (far left) anchored ITN's *News at Ten* throughout the Seventies.

was the film can in there so they could see what it was. And you'd say, 'Could you take this back to London for me? It's going to be on the news tomorrow night.' And sometimes they'd be thrilled to bits. Sometimes you had to make sure he did carry it because quite often they'd leave it in the departure lounge when they had second thoughts. But that was how you got your film back. Sometimes you'd leave London on a Monday to cover, say, the floods in Bangladesh in 1974, and that film wouldn't be back in London until maybe the following Thursday, but it would still be treated as news. Nowadays if it's five minutes late, your editors consider it history.

Sir Trevor McDonald, OBE, joined ITN as a reporter in 1973, becoming its sports correspondent in 1978 and diplomatic correspondent in 1980. He currently presents ITV's flagship bulletin, *ITV News* at 10.30pm, and has presented Granada's current affairs programme *Tonight with Trevor McDonald* since April 1999.

The pace of newsgathering has changed immensely in recent years. The first transatlantic satellite link happened only in ITV's infancy in 1962. But in ITN's master control room today, banks of screens show news stories beaming in almost instantaneously from all round the world, bounced back from space. ITN can airlift its own transmitters to hot news spots, as it did when Sandy Gall sent fuzzed images back from the Mujaheddin in Afghanistan in the early Eighties, or when rather sharper pictures were sent from the Queen's visit to the Great Wall of China in 1986. Cameras are lighter, easier to take anywhere. Some stories are even recorded and relayed on video phones. This change of pace has brought new challenges to the reporters. Trevor McDonald:

When I joined ITN you used to shoot your stuff on film and get a friendly pilot to take it to London. What innocent days they were. And then you had a long time to cogitate about what the commentary was, and what the finer points of these issues should be as you should present them in your story. You have to make instant judgments now. One of my colleagues memorably said to me, 'If you turn on to number 69, you can see people looting live in Haiti.' I had no intention to see people looting live in Haiti but you can do that. And I think that speed has made the job much, much, much more difficult. It's all instant, you watch wars start, wars end, presidential press conferences, people reacting to them, all instantaneously. It emphasises the need for more reasoned comment, for more deliberate judgements about things, not falling into the trap of being too pre-emptive in what we think.

Technology has changed the face of news. It has also, as we'll see, revolutionised the market in which ITV operates.

17

AFFAIRS AND ARGUMENTS

There were people in ITV who said, 'Oh God, Roger, do you have to do this?' and in the end I thought, 'Yeah, we do have to do it.'

Roger Bolton, Editor of *This Week* on *Death on the Rock*

I N AN AGE when politics often seems to be ruled by spin and media opportunities, it is hard to imagine that this was not always the way. But when ITV was young, television avoided current political issues. Until the end of 1956, it was bound by law not to broadcast controversial material about any subject that was due to be discussed in Parliament in the next fortnight. Elections, too, were closed to its cameras. The 1949 Representation of the People Act was interpreted as forbidding broadcasters from possibly influencing the result. Better no coverage, they thought, than being accused of interfering with parliamentary democracy.

When a by-election was called in Rochdale in 1958, the BBC announced that they would follow their usual stance: 'We do not intend to depart from our usual practice in by-elections that we do not influence voters, nor report the campaigns in the news bulletins.'

Granada, whose licence covered Rochdale, thought this was absurd, took legal advice, and put the candidates on air in a discussion in which two of the three froze with nerves. They were also present at the counting of the votes at the Town Hall – which took longer than expected and left presenter Brian Inglis floundering to keep going on such topics as the life of Gracie Fields, and the civic coat of arms.

It was not the most polished programming ever, but it pushed open the doors. A year later, both ITV and BBC covered the General Election. Granada decided to offer airtime to every candidate in the more than 80

Above: Leonardo Da Vinci's *Vitruvian Man* formed a distinctive part of the title sequence for Granada's *World in Action.*

constituencies it covered. They called it *The Marathon*. It was stupefyingly dull, but it was a huge statement of serious intent.

Granada continued to extend their political coverage, first to the annual conference of the TUC, then to those of the main parliamentary parties. In 1963, they stayed on air late in the day at the Tory gathering, and got live coverage of Alec Douglas-Home's announcement that Macmillan was resigning. It was a huge scoop – though not immediately appreciated outside the Granada region, where the companies had switched to the scheduled broadcast of *Criss Cross Quiz*. For better or worse, modern political television coverage had been born.

It was at Granada, too, that the current affairs programme was turned into a truly televisual form. Tim Hewat, the sharp Northern Editor of the *Daily Express*, was wooed to bring punch to the screen. With *World in Action*, which began in 1963, he and his team developed a style which told stories with arresting and memorable images; the report on bronchitis with a line of coffins being carried down a terrace street, like an outtake from Murnau's *Nosferatu*; the examination of the arms race with actors playing Kennedy and Khrushchev facing off through a bristle of missiles. Denis Forman:

> *We wanted to have a hard-hitting tabloid programme that would look at authority and identify failures in authority, whether it was the city or whether it was big firms or the government or local government and go for them absolutely tooth and nail.*

With an ethos that defined a good story as something that somebody wanted to keep hidden, *World in Action* was bound to get into trouble sooner or later. It managed sooner. Its second edition, about overspending and waste by the Ministry of Defence ran into problems with the ITA. They didn't argue with the facts, but they decided it wasn't impartial, as the Television Act required. They banned it.

Granada found an interesting way to break the ban. They gave the film to their rival *Panorama* at the BBC – who weren't subject to the same legal restrictions. *Panorama's* editor Paul Fox happily screened about half of it, under the banner of 'the programme they don't want you to see' (always good for ratings and headlines the next day). Denis Forman:

> *This upset the Independent Television Authority as they had never been upset before – a shabby public relations trick by the BBC, they called it. We were very pleased, we thought it was lovely.*

It was the beginning of a bumpy working relationship with the authority. There were plenty of lighter editions of *World in Action* (a look at life on the Paris fashion catwalk, anyone?), but it is the exposés that are remembered now.

In 1964 they found that the British Olympic team were being underfunded. The ITA banned the programme, saying it was opinion, not fact. Granada did not concur. They recut it and broadcast it. The ITA said it still broke the law.

In 1965 the programme accused the drug industry of overcharging the NHS. The drug companies were outraged. Again, the argument at the ITA was that the programme was not impartial. Sidney Bernstein responded that it was the facts that weren't impartial – it wasn't Granada's fault that the drug companies came out of it badly. Counsel was instructed by both sides; did the legal term 'due impartiality' mean that every programme had to be absolutely impartial, or did it make allowances when there seemed to be a matter of right and wrong involved? The ITA was advised that it was the only arbiter of impartiality; Granada were warned they were in breach of contract and could be taken

Mick Jaggar (right) – seen here with John Birt – was newly released from jail on appeal for drug possession when he met several establishment figures for a 1967 *World in Action* programme.

off the air.

The 1971 programme about Idi Amin, *The Man Who Stole a Million*, caused further controversy. At the time, Amin was seen by the Foreign Office as a valuable bulwark against Communism. The brigade of old-school-ties was mobilised to outrage. Within a year, he had blood on his hands and few defenders.

In 1973 the series included a programme exposing the business affairs of bankrupt architect John Poulson. The Authority couldn't believe how many establishment figures were allegedly implicated in bribery and corruption – all the way to high-ranking Tory MP Reginald Maudling. They banned the programme, and achieved the dubious distinction of uniting the *Sunday Times* and the *Socialist Worker* in a protest about political censorship. The press began to uncover connections between members of the Authority and people involved in Poulson's tawdry empire, raising questions about the ITA's authority and competence to regulate the programme. It took three months of recuts for it to reach the screen.

An international row was caused by journalist John Pilger's first television film, the 1970 *World in Action* programme *The Quiet Mutiny*. Pilger went to Vietnam to talk to the ordinary conscripted foot soldiers, the 'Grunts', and found the US army's command structure unravelling.

Award-winning Australian journalist John Pilger has produced uncompromising investigative documentaries since his early days on *World in Action*. His films have exposed atrocities in Cambodia and East Timor, the treatment of Vietnam war veterans in the USA, and the power of the World Bank and giant multinationals.

I picked up, as other journalists had, the first signs of the cracking of the American army. The American army was then receiving what was known as the Chicago generation; the demonstrators who'd brought the democratic convention to a standstill in 1968 in Chicago. So it was very much a rebellious army, split between lifers, the officer class, and the Grunts, conscripted soldiers. It was an enormous army, it was the biggest army in history at that point in one place, and you could see the cracks appearing. Things started to happen that were not reported, such as ordinary soldiers shooting their officers, disobeying orders, refusing to go out on patrol.

Vanessa Redgrave (centre) and Tariq Ali (on left with moustache) were seen in a 1968 *World in Action* programme on resistance to the Vietnam War.

Now, interestingly, none of this was reported in the United States, and I suggested to World in Action *that this was a story that we might break best on television, if only I could get some of these soldiers to talk. So I spent quite a lot of time in Vietnam speaking to soldiers, and because I didn't want to incriminate them and naturally they didn't want to incriminate themselves, we agreed on a formula that they would speak in the third person — that they knew somebody — but in fact it was them.*

Pilger's film elegantly captured the routine of the Grunt's life, while the interviews dropped their quietly-stated third-person bombshells.

— Mostly, unpopular officers, from what I heard, if they mess with the Grunts too much, they get shot at.
— A friend of mine, a captain, kind of got shot in the back.

The US Ambassador in London lodged an official complaint with the

ITA. John Pilger:

> *They took aim at Granada and said this was a disgrace, suggesting that the American army was falling apart, it was anti-American. In fact, far from being anti-American, I'd never made a film that was so embraced by ordinary GIs, it became almost a cult film among them in the United States later. But what was interesting for me to watch, and rather thrilling actually, was how Sidney Bernstein personally defended the film and Granada's right to show any kind of dissenting, revealing enquiring documentary.*

Bernstein stood squarely behind his programme makers when outside forces attacked. The only *World in Action* he ever appears to have pulled was one which investigated the Masons, and then it was under family pressure from his brother Cecil, himself a Lodge Master, who told him he would have to resign from Granada if Sidney let the programme go out.

At one meeting in 1967, with Granada's licence shortly up for renewal, the ITA took Sidney Bernstein to task. They showed him a stack of files containing the complaints they had received about the programmes made by all the other companies. It was dwarfed by a single file of complaints about Granada programmes, with *World in Action* the chief culprit. 'We consider that a compliment,' was Bernstein's unruffled reply.

This willingness, some would say eagerness, to get up the noses of the Establishment, led to accusations that Granada was a hot-bed of left-wing propagandists. Working in an industry in which Associated-Rediffusion's Tom Brownrigg could tell his staff he required them to make 'balanced documentaries of the right', Granada thought the accusation a bit rich. Denis Forman:

> *I would certainly say that there were not many conservatives on the benches in* World in Action. *Tim Hewat himself was a conservative, he was not left wing, but he recognised the power of left wing politics in television because every other company was so right wing you couldn't believe it. But the people who worked on it were mainly mainstream Labour people. And people would say, 'Granada's left wing,' and we said, 'No, the other companies are right wing and so is the BBC – we're central,' and there was some truth in that.*

Leslie Woodhead was a producer and director on *World in Action* from 1965 to 1967, then edited it until 1969:

> *Of course, this was a label that was stuck on* World in Action *throughout*

its history. You're a bunch of Trotskyites and Marxists who are bent on the overthrow of the state. You only have to think of some of the people who worked on the show. I don't think people would claim that Jack Straw or Margaret Beckett, both of whom were researchers on it, were exactly determined to overthrow the state. I think the mistake that was always made was that that kind of extremely aggressive journalism does indeed discomfort the comfortable, and might look to those who are sitting in government offices as though it's driven by politics. While it was certainly a liberal agenda you would have struggled to find anybody who was a card-carrying member of the Communist Party in its ranks.

World in Action's films weren't the only type of current affairs programmes to make waves. David Frost brought politics and news events into the arena of the talk show, first at Rediffusion, and later at LWT. The roll call of his guests is a list of almost everyone who shaped the times, from Enoch Powell, Bernadette Devlin and Moshe Dayan to John and Yoko. In one famous encounter in 1970 Jerry Rubin, of the radical American Youth International Party (or Yippies), packed the LWT studio with sympathisers. On his signal, they took over the studio floor, elbowed Frost aside, swore into the microphone, and passed round a joint. Frost retreated

David Frost interviewed Harold Wilson on a 1970 edition of LWT's *Frost on Sunday*.

Above and below:
David Frost (left) interviews
John Lennon and Yoko Ono
in front of a studio audience
in August 1968.

to an adjacent studio to conduct the second part of the programme, an interview with the author of a book called *The Territorial Imperative*.

Frost's most famous encounter came in 1967, when he interviewed Emil Savundra, the boss of a collapsed insurance firm. Savundra had signed the firm away to his managing director before it went down, leaving thousands of claims unpaid. Savundra had contacted the programme himself, after they ran a sketch based on the story, to ask for a copy. He clearly wasn't short of confidence. They invited him into the studio. David Frost:

> He called back within five minutes and said 'You polish your rapier and I'll polish mine'. And so that was that.

It remains one of the most highly-charged encounters in television history. Savundra, the suave and slippery businessman, exuding self-satisfaction where others might have felt shame. David Frost:

We'd told him that there were 10 or 12 victims in the audience, people who failed to get their insurances paid when they'd lost their husband in a car crash or whatever. And one of them called out at some point. And, he said 'I didn't come here to talk to these peasants, I came here to joust with England's premier swordsman.' The thing mounted from there.

It reaches full force when Savundra declares: 'My selling out was the wisest thing I ever did. By selling out I have no legal responsibility, and no moral responsibility.'

Frost is indignant. 'How do you sign a bit of paper that gets rid of past moral responsibility? Tell me that?' David Frost:

Whenever I see it I'm amazed by the electricity and level of anger. And at the end of the programme, you know the old thing in programmes, the lights go down and in the half light, the silhouette, the two people carry on talking civilly together. And I wasn't feeling civil. I was still angry and I was damned if I was going to stay there pretending to be civil when I was angry. So I ended the programme and I just walked off and left him as the sole person in silhouette. And on the Monday following the programme the Director of Public Prosecutions, who had done nothing about him, said, 'We've got to take action against this man before the end of the week or else we're going to look ridiculous.' And they did charge him. And then a year or so later there was a huge fuss with Lord Justice Salmon, who attacked the idea of trial by television in this programme and said, 'They must have known that action was about to be taken.' Now the point was we specifically knew that until our programme action was not going to be taken. So we were not in contempt.

Savundra had been exposed in the newspapers for six months but it was his appearance on ITV that forced the action. It was television now rather than newspapers that were making the running. Politicians discovered that a studio audience could be an accurate barometer of public opinion. And programme makers wanted to use their ability to gain public attention. As the Sixties gave way to the Seventies they harnessed the power of images to bring home the tragedies and injustices of the world.

In 1973, Jonathan Dimbleby reported on the famine in Ethiopia for Thames TV's *This Week*. The parched landscape, the dead cattle and, above all, the suffering people had immense impact. Jonathan Dimbleby:

It was devastating film for lots of people because they hadn't actually ever seen these kind of images ever before on television. It raised in today's money in the order of $150 million. It was the most important programme that I think I have ever done in my life.

Few programmes can measure their impact so tangibly. Most programme makers have less quantifiable hopes – to inform, to educate, to influence opinion. They have adopted many different approaches.

John Birt and Peter Jay invented the 'mission to inform' that lay behind LWT's uncompromisingly text-driven *Weekend World*.

(Left to right) Martin Bashir, Jonathan Maitland, Vanessa Collingridge, Trevor McDonald, Fiona Foster and Michael Nicholson are the presenters of Granada's current affairs magazine programme *Tonight with Trevor McDonald*.

World in Action developed the drama-documentary, recreating events where the originals could not be shown – particularly behind the Iron Curtain, with the incarceration of a dissident Soviet general in a lunatic asylum, or a Red Guard trial during China's Cultural Revolution. Scrupulous journalistic standards were the key. There is a line of descent to more recent dramatised treatments of events such as the Hillsborough disaster and the murder of Stephen Lawrence.

Tonight with Trevor McDonald has inherited from *World in Action* a catholic range of subjects and a tabloid style. John Pilger had continued to expose corruption and tragedy around the world, from the killing fields of Pol Pot's Cambodia to the expulsion of the people of the Chagos Islands to make way for an American military base. And the art of the political interview has been honed by Brian Walden and Jonathan Dimbleby.

Cumulatively, the impact of these programmes has been immense. They have changed people's view of the world. But with that power comes a responsibility to get things right. When accuracy is disputed, justifiably or not, there can be trouble on the grandest scale.

One ITV programme caused a major international incident. A Foreign Office source described it as the most difficult row since the Suez crisis.

In 1977, a Saudi Arabian princess and her lover were publicly executed for adultery. Filmmaker Anthony Thomas looked into the case, and found questions about the standards of justice involved, and interest in the lavish

lifestyles of the participants. He made a drama documentary for ATV, *Death of a Princess*, in which he and the people he spoke to during his investigations were played by actors, and some scenes were re-enacted, including one in which bored princesses cruised the desert highways for pick-ups.

The Saudi royal family tried to prevent its broadcast in 1980, lobbying ATV and the British government. Allegations were made that the re-enactments blurred the line between fact and fiction, and that some scenes were based on hearsay. But the IBA, which had approved the programme, was never approached with any formal complaint, and never asked to consider forcing changes to the programme or even banning it.

The government told the Saudis they had no power to impose a direct ban – in fact, by law the Home Secretary could black out any programme he wished. But it would be a brave or foolish politician who would risk the backlash that would follow, particularly if it was done only to avoid offence to a foreign regime.

The programme was screened, to the fury of the Saudis. But the Saudis

ATV's *Death of a Princess* was a controversial drama documentary about the execution of an Arab princess who had contravened strict adherence to Islamic religion by committing adultery. Saudi Arabia was so offended by the programme's criticism of Islamic culture that diplomatic relations were cut.

had ways to retaliate. They threatened to pull out of contracts between the two countries worth hundreds of millions of pounds, to stop oil deliveries and break off diplomatic relations. Foreign Secretary Carrington was forced to send a private letter of apology to an incensed King Khaled. The Foreign Office, with that filigree nicety of diplomatic language, later stated it was not an apology but an expression of regret that offence had been given. Lord Carrington:

> I was the person who had to soothe the ruffled feelings of the [Saudi] royal family, which was extremely disagreeable. I mean, to go and have to apologise for something which you're not even remotely responsible for, and which I felt at the time, and still feel now, was pretty irresponsible, was a very distasteful thing to do. And I had to go and see the King and tell him that it wasn't the Government and so on. Almost everybody you talk to outside Europeans and North Americans actually think that the Government controls what goes on in the broadcasting media and in the newspaper media. And so they blamed the Government. And they didn't really understand that it's nothing whatever to do with the Government of the day.

In the case of *Death of a Princess* the British Government had ended up apologising for an ITV current affairs programme. Eight years later, it entered into a bitter conflict of its own.

In March 1988, Roger Bolton, the editor of Thames Television's *This Week* series, had his radio tuned to Radio 4's *Today* programme. Three members of the IRA had been shot dead while apparently planting a bomb on Gibraltar. Roger Bolton:

> I remember waking up in the morning and hearing about the shooting in Gibraltar and I thought, 'Not much in that. The IRA admitted that they had a team out there. Bombs had been found. There had been two sides shooting, people got killed. Well, that happens. It happened in Northern Ireland. Is it proof of "shoot to kill"? Not really. Ah, nothing much for us to do.' Next morning, of course, Geoffrey Howe stands up in front of the House of Commons and says, 'Ah, there wasn't a bomb. Ah, the shooting was entirely one way since the IRA members were unarmed.' And you thought, 'Whoops.'
>
> And knowing a little bit about Northern Ireland, having produced and reported there for about ten years, it wasn't difficult to foresee that the young woman who was killed would soon have her portrait on this gable end of a house in Belfast and she would be seen as the Virgin Mary. So you could see how this would just be taken into the propaganda war on either side. I thought,

'Well, it's a job for us to go and try and find out and see what happened'.

Bolton sent a team to Gibraltar to investigate the circumstances of the shootings. What they found there from interviewing eye witnesses raised questions about the official account of events.

The uncomfortable evidence for the British government kept on coming forward. I knew it was going to be a lot of trouble, I did not expect it to be as much trouble as it was and I'm still rather surprised that it caused that amount of trouble. Because in the end, we didn't say there's a 'shoot to kill'

policy, in the end we didn't say the SAS murdered or shot dead without warning the IRA members. What we said was there was a large amount of evidence that one of them was shot in the back, a large amount of evidence that they were filled with a very large number of holes, the soldiers themselves don't even know whether they gave a warning, and no witnesses who watched it thought there was a warning, and a lot of people said, 'Well actually they could have been arrested quietly at a number of different locations on Gibraltar.' So I knew it was going to cause trouble. But in the end how could we not do it? That was one of our jobs. There were people in ITV who said, 'Oh God, Roger, do you have to do this?' and in the end I

The *This Week* programme *Death on the Rock* investigated the circumstances surrounding the fatal shooting of three unarmed IRA members – Daniel McCann, Sean Savage and Mairead Farrell – by the SAS outside this petrol station in Gibraltar on 6 March 1988.

thought, 'Yeah, we do have to do it'.

We weren't in a position to decide what had happened. We were in a position to say that all this evidence raises all of these questions and the British Government's view doesn't seem to square with much of it.

Requests for co-operation with official sources, and offers to share information gathered by the programme were turned down. The Government clearly did not like this project. Foreign Secretary Geoffrey Howe argued that broadcasting the programme in Britain would prejudice the inquest that was planned to take place in Gibraltar, even though it would not be seen there. Intense pressure was applied, but the IBA withstood it and backed the programme makers. Roger Bolton:

We knew that there were various people, ministers and so on, suggesting to people in ITV it wasn't a good thing. But on the whole Thames and the IBA kept us apart from that. They said basically the job for me was to get it right, consult the IBA properly, answer their questions. And we just went down and did our job. Then the programme went out. And then the sky fell in.

Mrs Thatcher went on television to address the nation about the dangers of trial by television:

If you ever get trial by television, or guilt by accusation, that day freedom dies.

Her allies in the press, red white and blue in tooth and claw, set about doing all they could to discredit the programme's eyewitnesses and the production team.

The *Sunday Times* accused the programme of leaning on witnesses and misrepresenting the facts. Some tabloids mounted campaigns of character assassination. It was the programme-makers it seemed who were in the dock. And if found guilty they'd be hung out to dry. The IBA stuck to its position. Thames, whilst standing by the programme, commissioned a judicial review by Lord Windlesham and Richard Rampton, QC, to try to defuse the crisis.

The resulting report, two minor reservations apart, eventually exonerated the programme. The government announced that they rejected the report. Roger Bolton:

Sir Geoffrey Howe said it was a report about television, by television, for television. I'm not sure if he read it properly. As a result, his friend, Lord Windlesham, who had chaired the independent inquiry, was so disgusted that he refused to accept a fee for conducting the inquiry over several months. No, the government had made up its mind in the propaganda war.

I mean, to be fair to Geoffrey Howe, I learned later that he'd been the subject of an IRA assassination attempt in Northern Ireland. I tried to say to my producers and researchers when we were dealing with this, 'Hold on, imagine you're Mrs Thatcher or a member of the government, the IRA have blown her up once in Brighton, killed some of her friends, she's living in a fortified camp, her children are targets, presumably. What must it be like having to live in those circumstances and then watching television programmes interviewing these people looking calm and rational, Sinn Fein, and other people, when they're out to kill her?

So I mean one had to understand a politician's position, but that was their position. It wasn't and shouldn't be the job of the journalist. So we had to stand steady, not do anything that was biased, I hope not biased, but simply saying, 'This is the evidence. Now these questions are raised, what are the answers?'

Death on the Rock won awards from the Broadcasting Press Guild and the British Academy of Film and Television Arts.

Some *Sunday Times* journalists complained that their paper had used their copy misleadingly. And eyewitness Carmen Proetta successfully sued the *Sun* for libel.

Lord Thomson, IBA Chairman, concluded in an article in the *Daily Telegraph*,

Sir Geoffrey Howe did his duty and I did mine, and if you do not like that sort of conflict of duty between government and broadcaster, you should not be chairman of an independent broadcasting authority.

There are plenty of people in television who will tell you that it was *Death on the Rock* that cost Thames its franchise in the round of licence applications that followed the Thatcher government's 1990 Broadcasting Act. But there is no evidence that the members of the ITC who judged the applications acted with anything but professional objectivity.

The ITC was only sitting in judgement because the same act abolished the IBA. There are plenty more in television who will tell you that was because the IBA paid the price for showing so much backbone in defending the programme.

18

A WINDOW ON THE WORLD

Above and opposite page:
Melvyn Bragg has been the
presenter of LWT's arts
programme *The South Bank
Show* since its inception in
1978.

*Before I left the BBC for LWT in 1977, the
then Director General of the BBC, Alasdair
Milne, asked for a meeting, and he more or less
told me I was going to a place of
unreconstructed savagery. That they were
philistines and they were money mad… It did
feel like a major change of culture, but after
about a day it wasn't, because I was doing the
same thing – I was making arts programmes.*

Melvyn Bragg

O VER 40 YEARS AGO, *World in Action* trained
its cameras on a group of seven-year-old
children, to discover how they saw the world,
and the extent of their expectations and
dreams for the future. *7 Up!* was intended to
dissect the way in which the inequalities of the
British class system bounded their lives. It was conceived as a single film,
but it has become a series which has revisited its subjects at seven-year
intervals. Director Michael Apted, now a major figure in Hollywood, has
followed the whole course of their lives; the public schoolboy who
became a teacher in the East End; the schoolgirl friends who are now at
the heart of families of their own; the cab driver who once dreamt of
being a jockey. It has long transcended its original schematic class-based
approach, to chart fluctuating fortunes and hopes, personal and
professional, the landmarks of life. It has become one of the most
remarkably revealing and vivid social documents of the past 50 years. It

Above: The *World in Action*
documentary *7 Up!*
focussed on a group of
seven-year-olds who have
subsequently been revisited
by film-maker Michael Apted
for follow-up programmes at
seven year intervals – the
latest in 2005.

In Paul Morley's 1979 film *Kitty – Return to Auschwitz*, Kitty Hart, one of the few survivors of the Nazi prison camp, revisited Auschwitz and recalled her internment there with her mother in 1943.

could only have been achieved on television. It was (allowing for the defection of *42 Up* to the BBC) only achieved on ITV. 2005 sees the latest instalment, *49 Up*.

News programmes tell us what happens. Current affairs programmes try to tell us why. Beyond these is the documentary, which aims to record the substance of life, often what John Pilger has called 'the ordinariness that isn't ordinary'.

Pilger was talking about another *World In Action* film that he made, the 1971 *Conversations with a Working Man*:

> *Jack Walker was a dye worker in Keighley in Yorkshire. When I met him, I was struck by just how eloquent he was in describing this dreadful, mundane working life; he stood in dye and slush up to his shins every day and his job was simply to watch this great vat of dye. Jack and his family had a very rich life outside this terrible job he did; his wife, Audrey, worked as well and his daughter went to the local school. He talked about what he thought about during work; he talked about cricket and he talked about politics, he talked about the better life he wanted for his daughter, Beverley. It took away the stereotype of a union convenor, saying something aggressive and inevitably 'balanced' by a silk-voiced boss or a Tory politician. I think it held up a mirror to a lot of people in this country of the kind of lives that they led and they could identify themselves with it. So often with television, the subject of work is almost never addressed, other than as clever drama, like* The Office. *Fly-on-the-wall films and reality shows are mostly zoos; and people seldom see true lives, their own lives. Following* Conversations with a Working Man, *I found huge appreciation among so-called ordinary people that their extraordinariness had been revealed.*

To show the extraordinariness of ordinary people would become one of the distinctive aims of ITV's documentary-makers. In some of the most memorable programmes, LWT took us on a raucous day out in *Derby Day* (1971) or to the nuptial celebrations in a village on the west coast of Scotland in *Wedding Day* (1978). Director Frank Cvitanovich conveyed the devotion of a farmer to his shire horses in *Beauty, Bonny, Daisy, Violet, Grace and Geoffrey Morton* (Thames, 1974).

Others showed people in extremis. *Creggan* (Thames, 1980), laid bare the agony of a community in Northern Ireland torn apart by the Troubles. *Kitty – Return to Auschwitz* (Yorkshire TV, 1979) revisited one of the most terrible of all human experiences. Paul Fox was Yorkshire's Managing Director:

Peter Morley found a woman called Kitty, who was one of the survivors of Auschwitz. He persuaded her to go back to Auschwitz, so it was inevitably a very emotional, and a deeply moving programme. Because this woman had her dignity. She came back to Auschwitz where she had suffered so much. Where she had seen so many of her fellow inmates die. It was a remarkable programme that was shown all over the world, thanks to the woman herself. Her dignity, her style, the way she dealt with this, and the way Peter Morley filmed this.

Hill farmer Hannah Hauxwell was the memorable subject of the 1973 Yorkshire Television documentary *Too Long a Winter*.

Yorkshire had a strong line in documentaries. Barry Cockroft depicted a tight-knit fishing family in *The Linehams of Fosdyke* (1973), and the line of succession on a farm in *Sunley's Daughter* (1974). And he discovered the indomitable hill farmer Hannah Hauxwell, holding on in her moorland farm in *Too Long a Winter* (1973). It made her an unlikely star, and Yorkshire later took her to make programmes on a Grand Tour of Europe and in America.

But she wasn't Yorkshire's most seasoned traveller. They also had the urbane and uniquely imitable Alan Whicker. Paul Fox:

Alan Whicker was one of the original founders of Yorkshire Television. And, of course, he was a shareholder. And so he made a certain number of programmes. Now one of the great things about Alan is you can't hurry him along. He doesn't do sort of 15 or 20 programmes a year, he will do six or maybe nine programmes a year. But each programme is remarkable. It's an audience grabber, because Alan is a star. He's a

Alan Whicker, Britain's most travelled TV reporter, met the Sultan of Brunei in the 1992 *Whicker's World* programme *The Absolute Monarch*. Originally a BBC series from 1959, *Whicker's World* transferred to Yorkshire Television in 1968.

great television star and always has been, and he was a wonderful attraction. A wonderful catch for Yorkshire really, right from the beginning. The trouble with Alan is that you always had to send him abroad. He didn't like filming in this country. He did very little filming in this country. And Alan was happiest when he was filming in California. But some wonderful programmes came out of that. Whicker's World *was a name that attracted an audience, and attracted contributors, and it was television at its best.*

As Whicker stalked the super-rich you could never be sure whether he was disdainful or envious of his subjects' lives in all their eccentric excess. It often appeared he was both, and that combination made him a compelling guide.

However exotic Whicker's interviewees might be they were nothing to the truly extraordinary ordinary people who were sought out by the team from Granada's *Disappearing World*. It was a series that went to places where life had not yet been altered by contact with the rest of the world, in Africa, South America, Eastern Europe, Papua New Guinea. Here were fiercely individualistic Sherpas in Nepal, herding yak and fighting any neighbour who tried to build his house too close. Here were the feudal

Kirghiz of Afghanistan, demonstrating skills in horsemanship that were traced back to the Mongol horde of Genghis Khan. Here were the Wodaabe of the Sahara, the men beautifying themselves with make-up.

One of the series' important innovations was the use of subtitles, sometimes four or five hundred in an hour. This was unprecedented in peak-time evening slots and there were arguments about their use. But avoiding simplified voice-overs or précis of what the people in the films were saying was a key decision. When, for example, we heard a group of wives discussing the shortcomings of their shared husband, we realised we were listening to sophisticated and often witty minds. The series was the brainchild of Denis Forman:

It gave them dignity and status; that was one of the great achievements of Disappearing World. It changed some viewers' ideas of what natives are. Do you remember the scene showing the Masai parliamentary meeting? As they made their speeches they walked up and down shaking a spear. They were going to war with another tribe. My God, it was a better debate than the Falklands, and a better debate than Iraq, and what's more everyone had their say.

The 1975 *Disappearing World* programme *The Shilluk of Southern Sudan* analysed the kingship of the Shilluk people and followed a procession of priests on a journey of spiritual renewal.

One of the regular directors of the series was Leslie Woodhead:

Somebody else had been asked to go and make a film in Africa. He didn't want to do it because he didn't want to go without a unit doctor. I was young enough and daft enough to go and do it. And it turned into the most extraordinary experience of my entire working life. Still is. That was in 1974. We walked 200 miles. We were in the middle of a tribal war. We all got malaria. But it was an extraordinary overwhelming experience. And I went back to that same tribe in Southern Ethiopia. I've made six films with them now over the intervening years. It's like a sort of Bush 7 Up.

The tribe was the Mursi. Within the span of Woodhead's visits, their lives have changed immensely.

By 1990, when I made the last film, they were regularly in contact with modern Ethiopia. They were inside a cash economy. The last film was about how some of the young men had run off with their newly acquired Kalashnikovs and slaughtered a bunch of a neighbouring group and were required to submit themselves to the law. Which is not an idea that they even understood, still less felt much moved to respond to. So really the films are about an extraordinary movement in the lives of people who'd previously run their own lives in the way they thought fit. Usually that involved a lot of rushing around and murdering their neighbours. But it was a very self-sustaining,

The *Disappearing World* film *The Quechua* explored the secular life of a family living in the village of Camahuara in the Southern Peruvian Andes.

very hard-pressed, very self-confident and proud culture, which we're now seeing under great pressure.

He showed some of the films to the Mursi in the mid-Eighties. The moment is caught on camera. They ask what use the films are. You can't eat them. You can't tie up your bull with them. One man thinks they might help his children to understand how they used to live.

Over the years, ITV has committed substantial resources to other ambitious series. Two of the most memorable brought images of the past to vivid life. In *The World at War* (Thames, 1973) Laurence Olivier told the story of the Second World War over archive footage in 26 episodes. And in *Hollywood* (Thames, 1980), Kevin Brownlow and David Gill captured great stars and their fellow workers from the silent age of cinema.

As well as looking out to the world, and to the past, ITV has made programmes about the inner life – religion and spirituality. Their styles have been legion; acts of worship; studio debates, sometimes dry, sometimes raucous; homilies to camera from a studio fireside. Many have tried to add entertainment to their appeal – comic sketch shows, guitar-strumming youth groups, hymn request shows. None has ever been more popular than the only religious programme ever to feature in ITV's top

20 ratings – *Stars on Sunday*, created for Yorkshire Television in 1969 by organist and producer Jess Yates.

Some of the *Stars on Sunday* who appeared in the Yorkshire Television series – (left to right) Gene Pitney, Gracie Fields and Ken Dodd.

Its format was simple. Stars – greater and lesser – performed religious or otherwise suitably inspiring music. Actors and senior figures in the church read passages from the Bible. It was booked as a six-week summer schedule makeweight. The first run was extended by nine more weeks. It was soon back for 45 more. Paul Fox:

> Stars on Sunday *attracted Bing Crosby, Grace Kelly, Gracie Fields. They all turned out for Jess and they were paid four pence halfpenny because Jess told them this was a religious programme and very important. Quite frankly the Authority thought it was dreadful.*

They were not the only ones. A modern-day Dante might invent an extra circle of hell in which producers of shoddy television are forced to endure endless reruns of the few surviving excerpts. The programme defined light-entertainment naffness; a ghastly country house studio set, with grotto, fake lake and gliding swan, and choreographed fountains playing in coloured lights. Yates exuding sanctimoniousness like snail-trail, often as not surrounded at the piano by a family of buck-toothed moppets. Clive James once admitted it to his *Observer* television review, noting that in the BBC's *I, Claudius* Caligula ate Drusilla's baby, but for those of a stronger stomach, Noele Gordon was on Yates's show.

Stars on Sunday ran for ten years. It survived the departure of Yates after his newsprint defrocking in 1974, when the more popular Sundays broke the story that he was having an affair with a showgirl. At its peak in 1972, it was attracting 15 million viewers every week.

The Authority, and their board of religious advisers, despised its sugary sentiment, its absence of the pain of life or the pain of the Passion. There were complaints that far from being a religious programme, it traduced the central message of Christianity so much that it was effectively blasphemous. The most the Authority could do was require Yorkshire – many of whose senior management liked the programme little more than they did – to limit the number of episodes they bestowed upon the viewing public.

Christianity was not always treated so glibly. In particular, ITV has presented not one but two major histories of the faith, in Bamber Gascoigne's *The Christians* (Granada, 1977) and Melvyn Bragg's *Two Thousand Years* (LWT, 1999).

Bragg is most usually associated with the television world's longest-running arts programme, *The South Bank Show*, which began in 1978, and is still robustly alive. It marked its territory very quickly. Melvyn Bragg:

I wanted to talk about the arts in terms of quality of achievement across a broad spectrum, treating popular music as seriously as classical music, television drama as seriously as drama in the West End of London, and

Melvyn Bragg spoke to Paul McCartney about his hit single 'Mull of Kintyre' on the first edition of LWT's *The South Bank Show*, broadcast on 14 January 1978.

photography as seriously as painting, and we did that. We did it quite aggressively. At the beginning I had a film with Paul McCartney on his song 'Mull of Kintyre', which wasn't a great song but was the biggest seller of all time in this country. And he hadn't been interviewed much at all in those days. And then I had the Berlin Philharmonic and Von Karajan conducting, and I decided to put McCartney in the first programme. Later we had something coming up from Stratford upon Avon, one of the Henrys with Alan Howard in it, and we had Dennis Potter, Pennies from Heaven. And I led with the Potter, the television play.

ITV's big arts series had always been eclectic. The first, *Tempo* (1961-67), was established by Brian Tesler at ABC. Tesler was looking for an editor who would appreciate a broad range of the arts; he chose the intellectual drama critic and writer Kenneth Tynan after seeing him applauding wildly at a London Palladium concert by American pop singer Johnny Ray. *Tempo* certainly had range; from avant-garde French novelist Alain Robbe-Grillet telling us why he doesn't care if people don't read his books, to French film clown Jacques Tati; from the art made by inmates of the Broadmoor high-security hospital, to Yehudi Menuhin rehearsing a Mozart string quartet; from Indian erotic sculpture – rather daring for its Sunday afternoon slot – to the famously terrible Scottish poet William McGonagall.

The South Bank Show's eclectic range of subjects has included Tom Jones, interviewed by Melvyn Bragg for a programme shown on Christmas Eve 2000.

The South Bank Show's precursor at LWT, *Aquarius* (1970-77), also had a wide gaze. Russell Harty dropping in on Salvador Dali; the music of Erik Satie with an inventive and surreal animation by Pat Gavin (who would create the title sequences for *The South Bank Show*); apocalyptic Victorian artist John Martin; Twyla Tharp's dance tribute to Jelly Roll Morton; a debate about pornography and censorship; and a programme about two railway enthusiasts who ran their model trains to the 1938 St Pancras timetable.

The South Bank Show had a shaky start, assailed by critics as it tried both to be a topical magazine programme and present films about artists. The magazine elements were soon dropped, and it hit its stride with

Derek Bailey's ambitious programme on Kenneth Macmillan's ballet *Mayerling*, which won ITV's first Prix Italia.

Its eclectic approach has produced impressive and memorable programmes. Leiber and Stoller explaining (and singing) just how Elvis ruined their song 'Hound Dog'; Dustin Hoffman and Peter Hall in the rehearsal room for a day as the film star prepared to play Shylock on stage; Olivier Messiaen describing how the colours of stained-glass became the sounds of his music; Barbara Cartland rattling her way through what seemed to be a hundred vitamin tablets before breakfast.

One of the most memorable encounters of all took place over a restaurant lunch as Bragg pressed Francis Bacon to distil the essence of his art. They were both very, very, drunk. Melvyn Bragg:

Francis Bacon was wonderful. The big decision in the cutting room was whether we were going to let this footage out where both of us were completely smashed. We had started drinking champagne in his studio at nine o'clock in the morning. And we had a lunch while we shot the restaurant full of people having lunch. And then at three o'clock we set up for an interview and we had another lunch – well, we didn't eat, we just drank. Hell. But I thought it was both funny and very revealing of Francis. And Francis was drunk a lot of the time. And so I thought, well, let's go with it.

What I find is that when I see it again, it's actually even more painful now. You'd think it would fade. Couple of old farts getting drunk. I showed it at a festival recently when the place was packed. And the audience was in hysterics. I stopped it half way through and said, 'We started a bit late, so we'll talk about Bacon now. What happens in the second half is it just gets worse'.

The eclecticism is still a hallmark of the series. The latest run has included programmes about North African Rai music, Charles Jencks's extraordinary Garden of Cosmic Speculation, television dramatist Paul Abbott and a film about the evacuation of the National Gallery's art collection during the Second World War, alongside an argument about the marketing of classical music and an interview with author Ian McEwan.

LWT and ITV have supported the programme far more consistently than the BBC did their now defunct equivalent, *Omnibus*. But in spite of that, *The South Bank Show* is sometimes cited as 'fig-leaf programming' in its late-night slot. Melvyn Bragg:

The accusation that we are tokenistic or fig-leaf is absurd. If you want a fig leaf you don't commission 22 hours a year on a big arts programme, set up

In March 1981, *The South Bank Show* focussed on movie icon Elizabeth Taylor whose most recent film, the Agatha Christie adaptation *The Mirror Crack'd*, had just been released.

a substantial department, and encourage that department to do more arts programmes. ITV is not mandated to do arts programmes. I pretended it was for quite a long time when it suited my purpose but it isn't. It's good if it does, but it's mandated to do religion, it's mandated to do children's programmes, it has to do regional programmes.

I think it's deeply bedded in now, the idea of an arts programme on ITV. It just comes with the weather.

Off-peak scheduling and accusations of tokenism are older than *The South Bank Show*. They go back to the very first weeks of ITV's life, when a cash crisis prompted changes to the programming. ITV has always presented a high proportion of 'Public Service Broadcasts' – news, current affairs, regional programmes, children's, arts, religion. Some were required by successive Broadcasting Acts and Authority licenses, but many more were not. Their strength has made ITV unique among the world's commercial broadcasters. But the climate of broadcasting has changed immensely in recent years. And there are those who wonder whether ITV can afford to stay unique.

19

A LEVEL PLAYING FIELD?

Above: Teatime wrestling was one of the main attractions of ITV's *World of Sport* throughout the Seventies.

It's up for grabs now!
    Brian Moore, live ITV commentary to Liverpool v Arsenal First Division Championship decider, 1989

Above: Formula 1 racing is one of the main attractions of ITV's current sporting schedules. Jim Rosenthal is the anchor of the *ITV-F1* presentation team.

FOURTEEN MILLION VIEWERS tuned in to ITV's coverage of the penalty shoot-out that was the climax of Liverpool's unlikely triumph in the 2005 Champions' League final. Together with Formula 1 racing and the quadrennial treat of the Rugby World Cup, major football matches are big sporting attractions in the current ITV schedules.

It was not ever thus. In its early days, ITV lagged behind the BBC in its sporting coverage. The BBC had existing links with many of the country's favourite sports, and when it saw its new commercial opposition coming over the hill it took the unusually enterprising step of signing them up on long-term contracts; athletics, cricket, rugby union and swimming among them. Association Football was not yet a serious contender; *Match of the Day*'s highlights programme was only launched in 1964 on BBC2, so much a minority channel then that only twenty thousand viewers saw Liverpool play Arsenal.

The first ITV companies looked for sports which might appeal to both sexes. Tennis and ice-skating were considered. They tried a magazine

programme, *Cavalcade of Sport*. In November 1955 they brought rugby in its northern League code to the south, transporting the players of Wigan and Huddersfield to Woolwich to play for the Television Trophy, with Eddie Waring at the commentator's microphone. But there was as little enthusiasm for the match as there was conviction in ITV's approach to sport in general.

One problem for ITV was that Lew Grade at ATV, one of its major players at one of its major companies, had no feel for television sport. According to one of those stories that you hope are true, Grade was once heard ticking off an employee who had been negotiating with the Amateur Boxing Association and the Amateur Athletics Association, two of the most important bodies in British sporting life. Grade was apparently appalled – he only wanted professionals on his television station, not amateurs.

But ITV began to make inroads. In 1964, ABC set up the Saturday afternoon programme *World of Sport*, with ATV on board. It began to take off two years later, when the companies formed a central Sports Unit, making it easier to plan strategy and negotiate deals.

The sports on offer were often a rough and ready line-up. Rallycross, in which cars raced on courses of grass and gravel, was invented for the programme, and took its place alongside other motorised sports such as speedway and stock-car racing. Angling, table tennis and schoolboy football internationals were called into service. One of the programme's greatest assets was presenter Dickie Davies, who could twinkle at the viewers and promise them a great afternoon's sporting entertainment even when he knew he had been dealt a hand consisting of cliff-diving from Acapulco, the all-Canadian log-rolling championships, and the biggest trotting meeting in Kentucky's social calendar.

World of Sport was built on two planks. The bulk of the afternoon was given to horse-racing, with two meetings offering a gambling opportunity every 15 minutes. The big audience-pleaser was the tea-time wrestling. ITV cameras toured the town halls and civic centres of Britain, anywhere that men in trunks practised the noble art of grunt and grapple. Did it hurt? Undoubtedly. Was it rehearsed? Can a thousand ladies leaping from their ringside seats to lash miscreant fighters with handbags and umbrellas be wrong? Its driving force was not the normal notion of sporting competition, two opponents trying their skill and strength. It was a test of justice; good against bad. We cheered when the virtuous took victory, and felt indignant when the sly fist or choke-hold perpetrated by known villains won the day. There were hard men – Jackie

Opposite page: Big Daddy (left) was arguably the most popular wrestler in British wrestling history and was regularly seen in feuds with Mick McManus and Giant Haystacks on ITV's *World of Sport* programme. Born Shirley Crabtree (named after his father, oddly enough), he was 6' 6" tall and weighed in at 350 lbs.

Above: 'Have a good week – until next week!' Kent Walton was ITV's foremost wrestling commentator from the sport's earliest appearances on screen in 1955 until its removal by Greg Dyke in 1988. Best known for his wrestling commentary on *World of Sport*, he was also a disc jockey on Radio Luxembourg.

Pallo and Mick McManus. There were immovable objects – Big Daddy and Giant Haystacks. Actor Brian Glover moonlighted as Leon Arras. Pat 'Bomber' Roach wrestled before starring in *Auf Wiedersehen, Pet*. There were character performers – Crybaby Jim Breaks who would bend the rules as far as he could go and throw a toddler tantrum when his opponent retaliated; the prancing pomaded glam-wrestler Adrian Street and masked combatant Kendo Nagasaki. And there was a great clown, who combined granite toughness with mickey-taking. He is remembered fondly by Frank Skinner:

My single biggest comedy influence, the guy who I laughed at most when I was a kid, was an ITV regular that most people won't have heard of. He was a wrestler called Les Kellett, and he was on most Saturday afternoons on World of Sport. *Now you might want to call that sport but in fact that was light entertainment, and that's why people watched it. It was reality TV to some extent, it was sitcom to some extent, it was a morality play to some extent – the good guy versus the bad guy. Les Kellett was a fantastic physical comedian, I mean I would put him up there with Benny Hill, Rowan Atkinson, any of those guys, he was amazing. And that was genuine working class entertainment.*

Richard 'Dickie' Davies became the main presenter of *World of Sport* in 1968, replacing the show's previous host Eamonn Andrews. Davies remained with the series until its cancellation in 1985, although he later shared his chair with Fred Dinenage.

Some other sports regarded ITV's devotion to wrestling with suspicion. Did they want to be associated with the channel that put this stuff out?

Nevertheless, ITV managed to extend its sporting coverage. It wasn't always a marriage made in heaven. In 1968, LWT struck a deal with the MCC for the rights to the one-day cricket competition, the Gillette Cup. With a breathless hush in the close one night, one over to play and a match to win, the broadcast cut away to go to an advertising break – and never came back. The MCC were furious, tore up the contract and took cricket back to the BBC. LWT took them to court – an interesting case in which Aidan Crawley, the chairman of LWT, sued the President of the MCC, Aidan Crawley.

A more successful ITV innovation was the football panel. There was a time when football coverage meant introduction, match, and sign-off

from the presenter at the ground (sheepskin coat optional). But LWT tried introducing a few pundits into its local highlights programmes, former pros who could give us their experienced insights (command of English permitting) into the game of two halves. ITV brought the idea to its coverage of the 1970 World Cup in Mexico, and were generally considered to leave the BBC as sick as the proverbial parrot. The panel was pioneered by LWT's Head of Sport John Bromley, who housed Malcolm Allison, Paddy Crerand, Derek Dougan and Bob McNab in an outer London hotel for the duration of the tournament. Their fees were modest, but their expenses were not. Allison in particular was not a cheap booking, with his liking for Cuban cigars and the finest that room service could provide. After a week, the hotel manager warned Bromley about the size of the tab the four were running. Bromley told him to give them champagne every morning – he realised that he was getting full value for money, trouncing the BBC in the audience figures while rewriting the rulebook of sports broadcasting.

By the early Seventies, *World of Sport* was regularly outstripping its rival *Grandstand* on the BBC. By the Eighties, ITV was carrying the fight to the BBC. Granada tried and failed to make croquet (green background,

Pioneering sports presentation – a panel consisting of former pros (left to right) Bob McNab, Paddy Crerand, Derek Douglas and Malcolm Allison offered their insights during the *World of Sport* coverage of the 1970 World Cup in Mexico. The programme's production team are seen standing behind.

coloured balls) the new snooker. But ITV began to outbid the BBC for some of the most popular sporting attractions. Boxing delivered big audiences. The Amateur Athletics Association moved across to ITV in 1984. And in 1988 (the year ITV's Head of Sport Greg Dyke dropped the wrestling from Saturday afternoons), ITV bagged the big one, an exclusive four-year contract for the rights to live football league matches. It cost them an unprecedented £11 million a year.

But ITV got a shock when Greg Dyke tried to hold on to his prize. In 1992, Rupert Murdoch's satellite channel Sky Sports offered the newly-formed Premier League £38 million pounds a year, and blew ITV out of the water.

There was bad blood over the deal. Dyke felt that Sky had inside information, which meant they knew what they had to do to top the rival bid, and that ITV were given no chance to come back at them. He is more philosophical today:

> *In retrospect it was inevitable. It wasn't inevitable at that time, but it was inevitable. There was so much more money in pay television and it was worth so much more to them compared to what it was worth in advertising revenue to ITV. They won because Rupert Murdoch wanted to win and was prepared to pay any price for winning. The football clubs could always get more money from pay television than they could from advertiser funded television, assuming that the government didn't step in. Now in lots of countries across Europe, the government did step in. Here we had the Thatcher government which was very close to Rupert Murdoch.*

Murdoch called the football a 'battering ram' to break into the market. His huge investment attracted new subscribers, and took his BSkyB company out of debt and into profit for the first time. Satellite broadcasting had become a serious player.

ITV was going to have to learn how to operate in a new broadcasting world. The days of the advertising monopoly, or the time when leftfield Channel 4 was its only commercial rival, were gone. Murdoch had the financial muscle to go after attractive and marketable programming. And around him were a growing crowd of smaller satellite and cable channels, nibbling at the advertising market.

ITV found itself in a fight – a fight that would change the shape of British broadcasting, and ITV with it.

Things had to change. In an international media market the regional companies that made up ITV were small and commercially vulnerable.

The law was reformed on 1 January 1994 to allow takeovers within the ITV system (with limits on any one group of 15 per cent of the audience or 25 per cent of the advertising revenue). Carlton's Michael Green was first out of the blocks, buying into Central. Granada pushed through a hostile bid for LWT. Lord Hollick's Meridian Group took over Anglia Television and United Newspapers. These were the three main players who manoeuvred round each other in the market as the limits on ownership were progressively slackened.

In 2000, a planned merger between Carlton and United was hijacked by Granada, who snapped up Anglia and Meridian and, finding its total holdings over the legal limit, passed HTV across to its rivals over the Thames.

In October 2003, the Department of Trade and Industry approved the merger of the last two big players, with Granada's Charles Allen and Carlton's Michael Green set to form what many thought would be an uneasy working relationship at the head of the new company. Within days a group of Carlton shareholders forced Green's resignation. He had first tried to take over Thames in 1985, but had been blocked by the IBA because the nature of the company would have changed from the one they had licensed. He had vociferously lobbied Margaret Thatcher to be allowed to buy into the ITV club, and had muscled Thames out of its franchise when the 1990 Broadcasting Act opened up the market. But after 18 years of dealing he now found himself ousted as chairman designate of the consolidated network.

It was Granada's Charles Allen, instead, who came out on top of a decade of negotiation as ITV's Chief Executive. Only UTV (formerly Ulster), Channel and the Scottish Media Group's coupling of Scottish and Grampian are outside the new heavyweight single ITV company.

Granada's Charles Allen became Chief Executive of the single ITV company following the merger of Granada and Carlton in 2004.

Many in the City reckoned that when Green was ousted he was paying the price for an expensive previous misadventure by Carlton and Granada. In the Nineties ITV recognised the commercial need to move away from relying on a single network. The future was multi-channel,

broadcasting high-quality digital signals. In November 1998 Carlton and Granada launched their new subscription service OnDigital. It seemed a good idea at the time, a cheaper alternative to Sky for people who wanted a bundle of new channels, a digital signal that came through their normal aerial into a decoder box, with MTV, Film Four, Granada Men and Motors and Carlton Food among the extra channels on offer.

Carlton and Granada had originally set up the venture in partnership with Murdoch's BSkyB. But broadcasting and trade regulators judged that Murdoch would be too powerful, dominating the satellite market and holding a significant stake in this new terrestrial digital service. They ruled against his involvement in the new project. Suddenly, OnDigital had Murdoch as a rival. It wasn't the only problem they faced.

Charles Allen:

There was a real demand from people who wanted more than four or five channels but didn't want to spend £400 a year on multi-channel, so there was definitely a market. Unfortunately the regulator wouldn't allow Sky to be a partner, and effectively put us on a collision course with Sky commercially. Secondly the regulator thought we would be able to get 80 per cent coverage in the country and when we started operating it only half the people in the country could receive the signal. That was a big issue for us. And because Sky were no longer inside, they became an aggressive competitor and they started giving away boxes. And that became much more difficult.

Opposite page and above: A crude knitted monkey puppet, named Monkey, was recruited alongside comedian Johnny Vegas to promote ITV Digital in an intensive advertising campaign in 2001. Despite the popularity of Monkey, the campaign failed to prevent the collapse of the service.

Murdoch dealt with the fledgling as he had dealt with other commercial rivals. He dug into his deep pockets and entered a pricing war. He gave away satellite dishes for BSkyB, and set-top boxes for his own new service Sky Digital, forcing OnDigital to follow suit or die.

At first, the take-up of OnDigital was ahead of target. But there were more problems. Decoder boxes were at first in short supply, potential customers forced to wait. Picture quality was erratic. The decoder cards were easy to forge. Too many customers failed to renew their subscriptions. OnDigital was spruced up, offering more quality channels. But the sums were not working.

OnDigital needed a battering ram of its own. Like BSkyB, it looked

Some of ITV's brightest stars – including Ant and Dec and Scooby Doo – helped to relaunch ITV Digital in April 2001, to no avail.

to football, and in June 2000 signed a contract to pay £315 million for three years of rights to the Nationwide League, the division below the Premiership. At that time, the terrestrial ITV contract for four years of Champions League football, the elite European competition, had only cost £250 million for four years. OnDigital had paid far too much for the wrong type of football. Sky and the Premiership had Manchester United, Arsenal and Liverpool. OnDigital had Huddersfield, Watford and Gillingham. Fans of other clubs had little interest in their games. Some of the televised matches had fewer viewers than there were spectators in the ground – even when the ground was Burnley's Turf Moor, with a cold wind whipping sleet down from the Pennines.

In April 2001, OnDigital was relaunched as ITV Digital, harnessing the marketing power of the best-known brand in commercial broadcasting. Johnny Vegas and a woolly monkey became the faces of its advertising. The woolly monkey became a star. New subscribers were given an exclusive knitted replica – at one point they were changing hands on internet auction site eBay for £200.

But OnDigital failed to pull out of its downward spin. City pundits reckoned losses ran to a million pounds a day. It was put into administration in March 2002. The plan had been that it would need about £300 million of seed funding. When it went down it took a thousand million pounds with it. What had been intended to be a bold entry into the brave new world of multi-channel television had become an object lesson in how hard it was to get it right, and how costly it could be to get it wrong.

ITV has now re-entered the multi-channel arena, with a new and far more successful game plan. Instead of subscription, it is back on the familiar turf of providing free-to-view services funded by advertising. It is using the Freeview system, available through a one-off payment for a set-top box. ITV2, aimed primarily at 16 to 34 year olds, is the most popular digital channel on Freeview, and is rapidly catching Sky One's viewing figures. ITV3, launched in November 2004, is targeted at the wealthier than average 35 and over audience, and now has 15 million potential viewers, and an average share of over one per cent of the most affluent population. With its rolling news channel as well, ITV now has a small family which is growing in popularity. ITV finally has the potential to air complementary programmes across different schedules – an idea that is as old as the channel itself.

ITV1 still aims to offer something for all viewers. ITV2 and 3 can be used to try to hold different audience groups when the main channel switches programmes. Charles Allen:

When we change the content on ITV1 from a young person's programme to say drama, then where do those young people go? Now they can go off and watch their type of programme on ITV2. If we take a Saturday night show like The X Factor, *you get 70 per cent of young audiences watching us. They are then very keen to see what happens behind the scenes on ITV2, and then they come back later on for the final vote back into ITV1. So I see people being streamed into the other channels and then coming back. We are able to constantly cross promote and remind you what you are missing on other ITV channels.*

Nigel Pickard, ITV Director of Programmes:

We will start to develop programmes specifically for ITV2 in particular, that are unique to ITV2. We will then have an opportunity to roll them out on

ITV1. What you have to remember about ITV2 is it's for a 16 to 34 female skewing audience. So there are certain slots that will work on ITV1. I don't think you can use it as a generalised nursery slope. We have to be quite careful about it. To launch a show on multi-channel, without any help from ITV1, that is quite tough. But as ITV2's audience grows, I see opportunities for us to use it as a testing ground. That's the beauty of multi-channel.

ITV's channels have multiplied, but successive mergers and corporate consolidations have slimmed the company down to a single decision-making centre. Charles Allen:

When I came into ITV you sat around a table with 15 colleagues and tried to make decisions. That was a very frustrating process when you could see competitors like Sky and even the BBC being able to make decisions more quickly than we could. I saw the opportunity to create a single ITV and have stuck with it for 14 years.

Simon Shaps, Chief Executive, Granada:

The consolidation of ITV has brought enormous and pretty straightforward benefits. We can think as one organisation, we can make decisions fast, we can put our priorities in the right place and we can spend money effectively and efficiently. And we can take an enormous amount of cost out of the business which frankly has been a drag on our ability to invest in programmes.

Duplication of buildings, equipment and systems has been cleared away. There have been redundancies, and the casualisation of parts of the work-force. All this has achieved massive savings in ITV's operations, gearing it to an increasingly competitive broadcasting market. Charles Allen:

It's definitely more challenging. Our creative colleagues have to work even harder than they would have done a dozen years ago, because there's more competition. But what I am particularly proud of is that we have put more money on the screen. You know when I came into television roughly 25 per cent of the advertising money ended up on the screen, now over 50 per cent of the advertising money ends up on the screen. We invest nearly a billion pounds in programming and none of our competitors do that, so I think we have got a better chance of actually creating programmes that the viewers want to watch.

Greg Dyke:

ITV still spends twice as much on original television as any other commercial channel in Europe and that's what ITV is about. It's about indigenous original production that reflects our culture and our society. BBC1 and ITV have competed to do that, which is why we have a television system in this country that reflects our culture and our society, not an American culture and an American society.

The changes that ITV has experienced in recent years are not over. The company has been lobbying its current regulator, Ofcom, to change the rules under which it operates – rules which do not apply to its multiplying commercial competitors. The aim is to produce a level playing field on which to compete. The need will become even more acute in 2008, when the government plans to begin to switch off the old analogue transmitters on which the ITV network was built. Then there will be no shelter from the multi-channel digital broadcasting world.

ITV's first target was a substantial cut in the licence fees it pays for the right to broadcast. In June 2005, Ofcom slashed it from £215 million to £85 million – a substantial fiftieth birthday present. Its second target was to reduce the number of public service programmes which are required by law. Changes have already been agreed; religious programme hours cut by half; regional feature programmes reduced from three hours to one-and-a-half hours a week, and cut further to half an hour a week by 2008. ITV's argument is that though any one of these feature programmes is relatively inexpensive, making one for each region adds up to a production cost that is not justified by the number of viewers. Regional news programmes, however, are safe, and large amounts have been invested in kitting out news operations around the country. Charles Allen:

What we have got to really work on is: what is our strategy, what is the funding model that allows us to be able to compete with, say, the BBC? And I passionately believe it should not only be the BBC that provides public service broadcasting. We in ITV have unique talent, skills and infrastructure to provide public service broadcasting going forward, but we need to sit down with the government and the regulator and find a funding model that works for ITV.

In providing public service broadcasting the things that we do best I believe are our news and current affairs, particularly our regional news. We now have invested nearly £50 million in state-of-the- art digital technology, so I think we are well placed to provide that. We are equally well placed to provide a billion pounds of programming that the viewers want to watch. To me those are the two key areas of public service broadcasting for ITV going forward.

ITV Chief Executive Charles Allen presides over the development of the three digital channels that have joined the original service, now renamed ITV1.

Public service broadcasting has been a hallmark of ITV from the outset. Traditionally, it has meant programmes in specific genres – children's, religion, current affairs and arts – in specific slots. The definition is now being revised. One future approach may be to break down the genre boundaries – for example, to make drama with a religious theme, integrating the public service element into the mainstream. Simon Shaps:

Opposite and page 302: Just some of the biggest and most enduring programmes seen on ITV over the last 50 years – (top to bottom, p301) *Footballers' Wives*, *Cracker*, *Rising Damp*, *A Touch of Frost*, *Space:1999*, (top to bottom, p302) *The Prisoner*, *The Sweeney*, *Cold Feet* and *Coronation Street*.

I think public service broadcasting is going to mean something slightly different in the next five to ten years than it has meant in the previous 50 years. We will no longer be ticking particular boxes to do particular types of programmes in particular ways, but we will be thinking about public service broadcasting in a much broader sense. I think incidentally we will continue to be the only major terrestrial broadcaster who runs current affairs in peak time, and we will maintain a strong commitment to arts programmes on ITV because I think arts programmes are something that we do uniquely well. However, in terms of the other more marginal bits of public service

broadcasting I think the definition of what we mean by public service broadcasting is going to change. It will include the very high levels of original programming that ITV schedules, and it will include a clear commitment to making 50 per cent of the programmes that we currently broadcast outside of the London area. Those are new components to what we mean by public service broadcasting compared to what we meant ten or 15 years ago.

Nigel Pickard:

I think our public service is also about our commitment to drama. A lot of people don't realise that ITV commissions and transmits more drama than any other single channel in the UK. And that is public service as well. I won't ignore the questions of what do we do about kids and what do we do about arts? They form a very important element of the whole breadth of what we transmit. I think, however, there is an issue in that while the obligations we have in public service haven't changed for 50 years the market has. And in many areas the market has better provided for some of these genres. For example, there are 21 children's channels now. It seems to be rather commercially suicidal but you keep pressing away there. On the other hand, for us to ignore children would be silly, not the right strategy at all for the future. If we do not engage children in ITV at a young age, they'll never be engaged. It's very tough to ever get them back. So children's programmes, or news, current affairs, arts, they're all important for separate groups, which make up the whole of the ITV audience. So there's no way that we should ever move away entirely from them. What we've striven to do is get a better balance. Religion has been a big issue, and I have got myself into more trouble with more bishops than I ever thought I'd do. For ITV to continue with an act of worship which is an obligation no other broadcaster – including the BBC – has, just seemed to be very out of touch and very out of time. I think there is a balance that you've got to strive for between those two issues, the commercial and the PSB. And sometimes we do have to tiptoe through it; it's quite difficult. But I think we do that quite effectively. I don't think we should alienate any part of our audience by not providing some of those shows.

A fiftieth anniversary is a landmark, an invitation to look back and take stock. But it is not a full stop. ITV has always changed. It has always had to be ahead of the game. Its ratings have depended on it. That flexibility has defined its character through its life. It still does. Simon Shaps:

I think there are many things about ITV 50 years on from the start that are

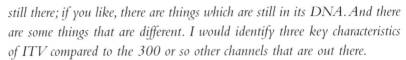

still there; if you like, there are things which are still in its DNA. And there are some things that are different. I would identify three key characteristics of ITV compared to the 300 or so other channels that are out there.

First, ITV is still the home of some of the biggest, longest running, most watched brands in British television, principally in drama and principally in soap, but in some other areas as well.

Second, it still is a channel that is interested in the world, that wants to say sometimes difficult things about life in Britain in the 21st century. It is still a channel that takes its public service remit, not literally, but translates that public service remit into other types of programming, so that it's not purely an entertainment channel.

And the third thing is that it has become the channel, more than any other channel on British television that takes big risks with its entertainment, factual and reality programming, everything from I'm a Celebrity, Get Me Out of Here! *to* Hell's Kitchen, *to* The X Factor, *and those are big, bold, expensive shows. In thinking about inventing new programmes there really is only one criterion, which is that fortune favours*

the brave. If you look at the history of the great shows on British television it's almost impossible to find one that is an enduring classic that didn't at the time that it was invented seem foolhardy and insanely ambitious. There's a direct continuity between Coronation Street *and other crazy ideas 30 or 40 years later. And an infallible criterion for having a hit show is at least half the people you talk to will say that you should never make it. There will always be people who say it's going to fail and it won't work.*

The programme mix is shifting. The proliferation of channels is just the start of a new wave of technology. Broadband and mobile phones will be increasingly popular platforms, and will demand new programme content. Interactivity has taken its first steps – used already for audience votes, quizzes, and to access extra content on other ITV channels or websites, it may radically change the way programmes are conceived and watched. ITV appears to be entering one of the most dynamic periods in its history. Charles Allen:

Yes, the competition is tougher but I'm extremely confident that whatever the future holds ITV will continue to thrive because its roots are deep. It will remain what it always has been – The People's Channel.

BIBLIOGRAPHY

General Reference and History of Television

Sendall, Bernard,
Independent Television In Britain Vol. 1 :
Origin and Foundation, 1946-62, Macmillan, 1982

Sendall, Bernard,
Independent Television In Britain Vol. 2 :
Expansion and Change, 1958-68, Macmillan,1983

Potter, Jeremy,
Independent Television In Britain Vol. 3 :
Politics and Control, 1968-80, Macmillan, 1989

Potter, Jeremy,
Independent Television In Britain Vol. 4 :
Companies and Programmes, 1968-80, Macmillan, 1990

Bonner, Paul with Aston, Lesley,
Independent Television In Britain Vol. 5 :
ITV and IBA, 1981-92, Macmillan, 1998

This series is an authoritative and reliable (though sometimes
rather dry) record of the history ITV, particularly strong on the
politics and business of the industry, but generally less
informative on details of particular programmes.

Black, Peter,
The Mirror In The Corner, Hutchinson, 1972

Buscombe, Edward (ed.),
British Television, A Reader,
Oxford University Press, 2000

Corner, John (ed.),
Popular Television In Britain, BFI, 1991

Davidson, Andrew,
Under The Hammer, the inside story of the
1991 ITV franchise battle, Heinemann, 1992

Docherty, David,
Running The Show, 21 Years of London Weekend Television,
Boxtree, 1990

Finch, John (ed.),
Granada Television, The First Generation,
Manchester University Press, 2003

Franklin, Bob (ed.),
British Television Policy: A Reader, Routledge, 2001

Gable, Jo,
The Tuppenny Punch and Judy Show,
25 Years of TV Commercials, Michael Joseph, 1980

Goodwin, Peter,
Television Under The Tories, BFI, 1998

Jones, Ian,
Morning Glory, A History of British Breakfast Television,
Kelly Publications, 2004

Kingsley, Hilary and Tibballs, Geoff,
Box Of Delights, Macmillan, 1989

Norden, Denis, Harper, Sybil and Gilbert, Norma,
Coming To You Live, Behind The Screen Memories of Forties and Fifties Television, Methuen, 1985

Rotha, Paul (ed.),
Television In the Making, Focal Press, 1956

Vahimagi, Tise,
British Television, An Illustrated Guide (Second Edition),
Oxford University Press / BFI, 1996

GENERAL SOCIAL HISTORY

Hopkins, Harry,
The New Look, A Social History of the Forties and Fifties,
Secker & Warburg, 1963

INDIVIDUAL MEMOIRS

Day, Robin, *Grand Inquisitor*,
Weidenfeld & Nicolson, 1989

Dyke, Greg, *Inside Story*, Harper Collins, 2004

Forman, Denis, *Persona Granada*, Andre Deutsch, 1997

Forsyth, Bruce, *The Autobiography*,
Sidgwick & Jackson, 2001

Frost, David, *An Autobiography, Part One –
From Congregations To Audiences*, Harper Collins, 1993

Grade, Michael, *It Seemed Like A Good Idea At The Time*,
Macmillan, 1999

Graham Scott, Peter, *British Television, an Insider's History*,
McFarland & Co., 2000

McDonald, Trevor, *Fortunate Circumstances*,
Weidenfeld & Nicolson, 1993

Nicholson, Michael, *A Measure Of Danger*,
Harper Collins, 1991

DRAMA

Bignell, Jonathon, Lacey, Stephen
and Macmurraugh-Kavanagh, Madeleine (eds),
British Television Drama Past, Present and Future,
Palgrave, 2000

Brandt, George W. (ed.),
British Television Drama in the 1980s,
Cambridge University Press, 1993

Caughie, John,
Television Drama; Realism, Modernism and British Culture,
Oxford University Press, 2000

Chapman, James, *Saints & Avengers,
British Adventure Series of the 1960s*, I B Tauris, 2002

Cooke, Lez, *British Television Drama, A History*, BFI, 2003

Nelson, Robin, *TV Drama In Transition*, Macmillan, 1997

COMEDY AND ENTERTAINMENT

Lewisohn, Mark,
Radio Times Guide To TV Comedy, BBC, 1998

NEWS, CURRENT AFFAIRS & DOCUMENTARIES

Apted, Michael, *7 Up*, Heinemann, 1999

Bolton, Roger, *Death On The Rock*, W H Allen, 1990

Davis, Anthony, *Here Is The News*, Severn House, 1976

The Windlesham / Rampton Report, Faber and Faber, 1989

SPORT

Holt, Richard and Mason, Tony,
Sport In Britain 1945-2000, Blackwell, 2000

Websites

The following websites are also of interest:

ITV's home site – *www.itv.com/*

405 Alive: general information about vintage British TV
www.bvws.org.uk/405alive/info/index.html

Avengerland: a guide to filming locations used in many classic British TV series – *avengerland.theavengers.tv/*

The Avengers Forever: guide to the cult series
theavengers.tv/forever/

BFI: useful information about television as well as film
www.bfi.org.uk/index.html

The Continuity Booth: dedicated to presenters and announcers, national and regional
www.continuity-booth.co.uk/index.html

Coronation Street unofficial fan site – *www.corrie.net/*

Crossroads Appreciation Society
www.crossroadsappreciationsociety.co.uk/cas_site_002.htm

Cult TV: guides to many cult series – *www.cultv.co.uk/*

Fanderson: The Official Gerry Anderson Appreciation Society - *www.fanderson.org.uk*

ITN's own site – *www.itn.co.uk*

Kaleidoscope: vintage TV – *www.kaleidoscope.org.uk/*

Mark One Productions:
guides to *The Professionals* and *The New Avengers*
www.personal.u-net.com/~carnfort/home.htm

The Morning After: The Official *The Persuaders!*/ITC Appreciation Society – *www.itc-classics.com*

Nostalgia Central
includes pages on TV decade by decade
www.nostalgiacentral.com/index.htm

Ofcom: site of ITV's statutory regulator
www.ofcom.org.uk/

Off The Telly: good articles, including 'The Glory Game', Steve Williams and Jack Kibble-White's excellent history of Saturday night television
www.offthetelly.co.uk/

On The Buses fan club
members.lycos.co.uk/busesfanclub/

Sixties City includes a television section
www.sixtiescity.com/Television/60STelly.htm

Television Heaven: a comprehensive site
www.televisionheaven.co.uk

Terra Media contains a section on UK Media Laws
www.terramedia.co.uk/law/UK_media_law/list_of_statutes.htm

Transdiffusion: various TV memorabilia online
www.transdiffusion.org/pmc/index.htm

TV Cream: collation of television fan material
tv.cream.org/

The TV Room: more than most people want to know about presentation and onscreen idents
thetvroom.com/

UK Gameshows:
a guide to game shows past and present
www.ukgameshows.com/index.php/Good_Game_Guide

Upstairs Downstairs site – *www.updown.org.uk/*

Whirligig: 1950s television
www.whirligig-tv.co.uk/index.htm

INDEX